"MICHEL GUÉRARD STARTED IT ALL."

—Julia Child, *Boston Globe*

"It's here. And one look at Guérard's long-awaited opus will convince doubters that what he has to say has been worth the wait. Guérard's revolution—elegant cookery sans butter, cream, flour—is an entirely new cuisine. Built on classic principles without the classic calories, his 'cuisine of slimness' (*cuisine minceur*) is a marvel of ingenuity and imagination. The slimming dishes here are as spectacular as they are delectable. The book is a gem: handsome, fascinating, practical and unique... Hail this as a landmark in culinary publishing."

—*Publishers Weekly*

MICHEL GUÉRARD'S CUISINE MINCEUR

*Winner of Three Tastemaker Awards—
Including "Best Cookbook of the Year"*

"MICHEL GUÉRARD IS THE CIVILIZED WORLD'S HOTTEST KITCHEN PROPERTY. GUÉRARD IS THE CREATOR OF *LA CUISINE MINCEUR*—CELESTIAL DIET COOKING...JOYFUL PENITENCE FOR THE OVERINDULGER."

—Gael Greene, *New York* Magazine

MICHEL GUÉRARD'S CUISINE MINCEUR

BY MICHEL GUÉRARD

Translated by
Narcisse Chamberlain
with FANNY BRENNAN

MICHEL GUÉRARD'S CUISINE MINCEUR
*A Bantam Book / published by arrangement with
William Morrow and Company, Inc.*

PRINTING HISTORY
Originally published in France under the title
La Grande Cuisine Minceur

Morrow edition published December 1976
1st printing . . . November 1976
2nd printing . . . December 1976
*A selection of the Book-Of-The Month Club, January 1977 and
the Cooking and Crafts Book Club, July 1977*
Excerpts appeared in HOUSE & GARDEN MAGAZINE, *September 1976
and* MCCALLS, *February 1977*
Bantam edition / November 1977

Prologue

For forty-two years, I have been a dreamer—as much in the daytime, for that matter, as at night. On this particular morning, I awoke from a leaden, adipose sleep. All night long I had tried to fly away, to escape—alas, in vain. My poor body, long crammed with rich and luxurious food, had become so rotund that it seemed about to nail me eternally to the ground... where dreams must lose their footing. How many centimeters had encircled my waist since the picture taken long ago at my first communion—me, knock-kneed, skinny-faced, ears sticking out! Look what my profession had done to me.

I must tell you that, as others are gardeners who relish the landscapes they make, I am a chef *gourmand*—a chef who simply loves to eat. I come by this through my profession and by temperament, not at all from father to son, and I have never really known which one gets ahead of the other, the chef or the *gourmand*.

The evening before, the beautiful and mysterious Christine, who perhaps had (already?) decided to marry me some months later, had sweetly murmured in my ear, "*Vous savez*, Michel, if you would lose some weight, you'd look GREAT."

What a shock! I realized that I had to get rid of this disgraceful fat, shed this *embonpoint* to win Christine's heart. I did not know then that she was sowing the seeds of this book or that she would take a large part in writing it. I did know that my tendency joyously to stuff myself was going to receive a body blow in the taste buds. I began the Long March through fields of grated carrots and other such appealing delicacies that make you sorry you ever saw the light of day and sadistically drive you to despair. The ritual of broiled meat and boiled beans quickly took my speech away. No longer was I allowed to know the marvelous, profound resonance that is produced when the eye, the nose, and the palate join together in a symphonic wave to savor a finely crafted dish. I felt suddenly alone, isolated, quarantined, as if I were contagious; a feeling of claustrophobic frustration overwhelmed me.

The punishment was too severe to be borne, some evasive action had to be taken. After all, even before the reign of Louis XIV books of *cuisine* had concerned themselves with nutrition for living a long and healthy life; this was not a new problem. But I had to·solve it in a way that first of all pleased me, and this would entail modifying many of the entrenched practices of our *gourmand* heritage.

That is what I did for several long weeks, with more or less satisfaction and even sometimes with some pleasure. And then, after a while, I began to be at ease with this emerging technique which I gradually tamed to comply with my needs. I finally managed once again to formulate new recipes, a little as a painter remixes his colors to achieve a different nuance.

After I had unloaded a substantial number of pounds, at last I emerged from the tunnel, another man: the one I had been before. The battle had been won, the goal had been reached! But reached for me—not for others.

Just as someone who doesn't know how to swim may drown, someone who doesn't know how to cook may founder in a measuring cup. Therefore, the first part of this book is a brief orientation in the principles of cooking which will give you an understanding of the physical and chemical phenomena that are involved. Go over this section several times and soon you will find that cooking no longer harbors major mysteries, and you will also see how the basic principles extend to *cuisine minceur*.

The second part is really my favorite. There I reveal, for you to emulate, my secret harvest of the past three years: the techniques themselves, presented in detailed recipes, of *cuisine minceur*. And I did not want to do a book of isolated recipes, each a stranger to the others. On the contrary, I wanted to write a cheerful roundelay of festive meals with which to lose weight—encompassing salads as fresh as the laughter of children, gleaming fish redolent with the aroma of the sea, fragrant fowl reminiscent of the picnics of my childhood, a collection devised for the planning of your own *minceur* feasts. So, read how this book should be used, on page xvii.

I intend to prepare, very soon, a second book of original recipes, some of which may indeed be rather fattening. But also I cherish an old dream that one day in the future I may combine *cuisine gourmande* with *cuisine minceur* to create a new art of living for the deserving *gourmands* of today and tomorrow.

MICHEL GUÉRARD

Acknowledgments

The publishers of this book and its translators are grateful first of all for the help of the gracious, busy, astute, and ever-humorous Michel Guérard . . .

. . . and, in approximately chronological order, to: the publishing house of Robert Laffont, Paris; Claude Jolly, Paris; the incomparable, hospitable young *doyenne* of Les Prés d'Eugénie, Christine Barthélémy Guérard; the talented and resourceful photographer, Didier Blanchat, Paris; all of the Guérard staff who gave of their time and skill during days of photography while they were also preparing for the opening of the restaurant and the hotel at Eugénie . . .

. . . to Fanny Brennan, without whom the job could never have been done—who marketed for, weighed, measured, cooked, counseled upon, and knowledgeably tasted everything that the French manuscript and the conflicting peculiarities of American ingredients required; and to Hank Brennan, who also tasted everything and who made the drawings.

N.C.

Contents

NOTE: All the recipes are numbered. When a recipe is referred to in text or in a list of ingredients, its name and number are printed in **boldface** type.

How to Use This Book

It is important not to use this book as one usually uses a collection of recipes: **Do not make the recipes in isolation, one at a time.** Instead, decide that for seven days in succession you will have a completely *minceur* week. Whether you do this once, twice, or ten times a year depends on your own concern about *embonpoint*.

Then make out your menus in advance, and, on the weekend before, get ready the basic elements (the stocks in particular) that you will need during the course of the week. (*This advice is crucially important in all cooking; some of the simplest, most practical dishes become great productions if, on the same day, you must also make the prepared ingredients instead of having them on hand in the refrigerator or freezer. Plan your menus so that the supply of these ingredients can be used in a number of recipes during the week. Any experienced cook knows how practical this is; it will be a revelation to the less experienced how functional these advance preparations turn out to be. Ed.*)

Examples of menus such as I prepare at Eugénie begin on page xxi; on page xxvii begin fourteen simpler menus devised for home kitchens. And preceding each group are some views on choosing menus for daily or special circumstances.

For this *minceur* week to be fully effective, it is important that you drink neither wine nor alcohol; at the most, one glass of light wine at each meal.

The herb tea *minceur* that we serve at Eugénie-les-Bains (*tisane minceur d'Eugénie*) is flavored entirely with plants from our garden and meadows. Here is the recipe for it:

INGREDIENTS: Dried heather flowers, corn silk, horsetail (shave grass), bearberry, and cherry stems. These herbs can be found in your health-food stores. PROPORTIONS: 1 level tablespoon of this mixture (use equal parts of each herb) to each cup of boiling water.

Proceed as for any herb tea. While it is steeping, add also slices of lemon and sprigs of fresh mint. Strain the tea into a pitcher, sweeten with artificial sweetener, and add lemon juice to taste. To serve, pour the tea into tall glasses with ice cubes and decorate with colorful fruits that are in season (strawberries, cherries, grapes, slivers of apple) and a few leaves of fresh mint.

BREAKFAST:

While you are dieting, this meal assumes particular importance. It is advisable not to leave it out but rather to adapt it to *minceur* needs. Here are three combinations among which you can alternate:

1. Tea with lemon and a baked egg steamed in water—Oeufs au plat à l'eau (50).
2. Black coffee, and fromage blanc (173) served with fresh berries.
3. Hot herb tea Eugénie, and a boiled egg (*oeuf à la coque*) with fresh green asparagus tips, or canned white asparagus tips, to dip in the egg instead of toast.

Finally, if you have the courage (and you are not working that day), have an all-bouillon day; see the recipe for Bouillon de légumes d'Eugénie (21).

And then, if you feel like it, and I hope you do,

forget everything you have just read about a *minceur* week just for yourself. Don't hesitate to cook for your friends, at any time, a *grand dîner minceur*. Its subtlety and lightness will astonish them. Like every meal, a *minceur* meal can and should be festive. That is the aim of this book.

A Week of Menus at Eugénie-les-Bains

These menus are an example of one week of *minceur* luncheons and dinners that would be served to the guests who come to *faire la cure* at our spa at Eugénie. Since they are prepared by myself and the staff of Les Prés d'Eugénie, as the restaurant-dining room and the hotel are both called, they are more elaborate than *minceur* meals you would cook at home every day. But you can rely on any one of them for entertaining your own guests at a luncheon or dinner party.

Lundi		**MONDAY**
Déjeuner	Tourte aux oignons doux	**LUNCHEON**

Onion Tart (60)

Gigot de poulette cuit à la vapeur
Stuffed Chicken Drumsticks with Marjoram (119)

Fruits frais à la gelée d'amandes
Fresh Fruit with Almond Jelly (154)

Dîner	Soufflé aux tomates fraîches	**DINNER**

Individual Fresh-tomato Soufflés (62)

Sabayon de saint-pierre en infusion de poivre
Baked Porgy with Pepper Sauce (94)

Purée mousse d'artichauts
Artichoke Purée (145)

Banane en papillote
Bananas Baked in Foil (158)

❊

Mardi   TUESDAY
Déjeuner   LUNCHEON
Mousseline de grenouilles au cresson de fontaine
Baked Mousse of Frogs' Legs with Water Cress (65)

Gigot d'agneau cuit dans le foin
Leg of Milk-fed Baby Lamb Baked in Hay (114)

Confit bayaldi
Baked Zucchini, Eggplant and Tomatoes (132)

Blancs à la neige au coulis de cassis
Floating Island with Black-currant Purée Sauce (167)

Dîner   Soupe à la grive de vigne   DINNER
                    Song-thrush Soup (25)

Truite en papillotes à l'aneth et au citron
Baked Trout with Dill and Lemon (88)

Purée mousse de champignons
Mushroom Purée (136)

Sorbet fraise ou framboise
Strawberry or Raspberry Sherbet (161)

❊

Mercredi   WEDNESDAY
Déjeuner   Salade des Prés à la ciboulette   LUNCHEON
          Fruit, Mushroom and Chive Salad (69)

Poulet en soupière aux écrevisses
Poached Chicken in Tureens with Crayfish (117)

Orange aux zestes
Oranges with Candied Rinds (152)

Dîner   Bouillon de légumes d'Eugénie   DINNER
              Vegetable Bouillon (21)

Turbotin clouté d'anchois à la vapeur de safran
Turbot or Red Snapper Steamed with
Anchovies and Saffron (96)

Oignons Tante Louise
Baked Stuffed Onions (128)

Soufflé aux fraises des bois
Individual Wild-strawberry Soufflés (169)

❋

Jeudi   **THURSDAY**
Déjeuner   LUNCHEON
Terrine de poissons au herbes fraîches
Fish Pâté with Herbs and Greens (64)

Aiguillettes de caneton au poivre vert
Breast of Duckling with Green Peppercorns (121)

Petit pot de crème au café
Coffee Custards (166)

Dîner   Gâteau d'herbage à l'ancienne   DINNER
Cabbage Leaves Stuffed with Garden Greens (57)

Bar aux algues, sauce vierge
Baked Bass in Seaweed (95)

Purée mousse de cresson
Water-cress Purée (139)

Pomme à la neige
Snow Apples (156)

❋

Vendredi   **FRIDAY**
Déjeuner   Salade de moules au safran et   LUNCHEON
aux cœurs de laitues
Mussel Salad with Saffron and Hearts of Lettuce (73)

Rognons de veau "en habit vert"
Veal Kidney Braised in Spinach and Lettuce Leaves (110)

Ananas glacé aux fraises des bois
Pineapple Stuffed with Pineapple Ice and
Wild Strawberries (164)

A Week of Menus at Eugénie-les-Bains / xxiii

Dîner Crème d'oseille mousseuse
Cream of Sorrel Soup (23)

Le grand pot-au-feu de la mer et ses légumes
Seafood Platter with Vegetables (98)

Tarte fine aux pommes chaude
Hot Apple Tarts (157)

❀

Samedi SATURDAY
Déjeuner Caviar d'aubergine LUNCHEON
Eggplant Caviar (56)

Ragoût fin d'Eugénie
Sweetbread Ragoût Eugénie (113)

Mousse d'épinards aux poires
Spinach Purée with Pears (140)

Fruits au vin de graves rouge
Fresh Fruit in Red Wine (151)

Dîner Gâteau de carottes fondantes au cerfeuil DINNER
Carrot Cake with Chervil (58)

Homard à la tomate fraîche et au pistou
Lobster with Tomato and Basil Sauce (84)

Granité de chocolat amer
Bitter-chocolate Sherbet (163)

❀

Dimanche SUNDAY
Déjeuner Salade de crabe au pamplemousse LUNCHEON
Crab Meat and Grapefruit Salad (75)

Grillade de boeuf "aux appétits"
Grilled Fillet of Beef with Shallot and Garlic (99)

Purées mousses de haricots verts et de céleri au persil
Green-bean Purée (141) and
Celery-root Purée with Parsley (143)

Paris-Brest au café
Cream Puffs with Coffee Whipped Cream (168)

Oeufs poule au caviar
Scrambled Eggs with Caviar (54)

Foie de veau à la vapeur aux blancs de poireaux
en aigre-doux
Steamed Calf's Liver with Sweet-and-sour Leeks (111)

Soufflé aux poires
Individual Pear Soufflés (170)

Menus for Home Kitchens

These menus are not composed as a one-week, two-meals-a-day, festive regimen as are the preceding fourteen menus from Les Prés d'Eugénie. They are intended as a guide to using this book to compose home, rather than restaurant, menus and they are not paired off into daily luncheons and dinners—this being left up to the reader, who we suspect is not about to cook two three-course meals a day except on cooking-spree weekends.

We have concentrated on the simplest recipes in the main—not to suggest that more complicated ones should be viewed with alarm, but to point out with specific examples that all is not chef-level intricacy in cuisine minceur. On the contrary.

Our personal view of menu-building at home is that the main course is the point, perfectionism with other, simpler courses rounds out the perfect meal; that to cook a great dish is one thing, but to emulate an entire professional menu for anything but a special occasion is a mistake. We had no difficulty in putting together these more modest menus—which is to say that Michel Guérard's spectacular meals for entertaining do not give you an inkling of the intelligent minceur home menus that can be made with many other recipes in this book. Ed.

1

Salade des Prés à la ciboulette
Fruit, Mushroom and Chive Salad (69)

Homard à la nage
Lobster in Court-bouillon (82)

Fraises à la Chantilly
Strawberries with Whipped Cream (153)

2

Tarte de tomates fraîches au thym
Fresh Tomato and Spinach Tarts with Thyme (61)

Truite en papillote à l'aneth et au citron
Baked Trout with Dill and Lemon (88)

Petit pot de crème à l'orange
Orange Custards (165)

3

Artichaut Mélanie
Artichoke and Carrot Salad (68)

Escalope de saumon à l'oseille
Salmon Scallops with Sorrel Sauce (89)

Pomme en surprise
Apples Stuffed with Fresh Fruit (149)

4

Carrelet au cidre
Fish Baked in Cider (91)

Salade verte, sauce vinaigrette minceur II
Tossed Green Salad, French Dressing with Herbs (30)

Banane en papillote
Bananas Baked in Foil (158)

5

Huîtres au champagne
Baked Oysters with Champagne (80)

Grillade de boeuf, sauce Créosat
Grilled Fillet of Beef with Cold Vegetable Sauce (34)

Purée mousse de haricots verts
Green-bean Purée (141)

Fruits au vin de graves rouge
Fresh Fruit in Red Wine (151)

6

Palourdes, citron
Cherrystone Clams on the Halfshell with Lemon

Grillade de boeuf "aux appétits"
Grilled Fillet of Beef with Shallot and Garlic (99)

Purée mousse de céleri au persil
Celery-root Purée with Parsley (143)

Compote de pommes à l'abricot
Apple and Apricot Compote (155)

7

Soupe de tomates fraîches au pistou
Fresh Tomato Soup with Basil (22)

Grillade de boeuf, sauce béarnaise Eugénie
Grilled Fillet of Beef with Low-calorie
Béarnaise Sauce (38) (39)

Haricots verts
Green Beans, page 26

Blancs à la neige au coulis de framboises
Floating Island with Raspberry Purée Sauce (167) (147)

8

Gâteau de carottes fondantes au cerfeuil
Carrot Cake with Chervil (58)

Langue de boeuf à la fondue d'oignons
Baby Beef Tongue Braised with Onions (104)

Salade verte, sauce vinaigrette minceur I
Tossed Green Salad, French Dressing (29)

Petit pot de crème au café
Coffee Custards (166)

9

Soufflé aux tomates fraîches
Individual Fresh-tomato Soufflés (62)

Côte de veau "grillée en salade"
Grilled Veal Chops in Lettuce Leaves (105)

Orange aux zestes
Oranges with Candied Rinds (152)

10

Crème d'oseille mousseuse
Cream of Sorrel Soup (23)

Blanquette de veau
Veal Fricassee (107) (108)

Sorbet fraise
Strawberry Ice (161)

11

Salade verte, sauce vinaigrette minceur I
Tossed Green Salad, French Dressing (29)

Volaille "truffée" au persil
Roast Chicken or Game Bird with Parsley (115)

Purée mousse de carottes
Carrot Purée (137)

Fruits frais à la gelée d'amandes
Fresh Fruit with Almond Jelly (154)

12

Bouillon de légumes d'Eugénie
Vegetable Bouillon (21)

Poulet au tilleul en vessie
Chicken Steamed with Onions
and Linden Blossoms (116)

Haricots verts
Green Beans, page 26

Sorbet au thé
Iced-tea Sherbet (162)

13

Poulet cuit au gros sel
Chicken Baked in Coarse Salt, page 46

Gâteau d'herbage à l'ancienne
Cabbage Leaves Stuffed with Garden Greens (57)

Pomme à la neige
Snow Apples (156)

14

Soupe de tomates fraîches au pistou
Fresh Tomato Soup with Basil (22)

Cresson à l'oeuf poché
Water-cress Purée with Poached Eggs (53)

Sorbet framboise
Raspberry Ice (161)

In the
beginning
there was the earth

the man,
who
discovered
fire,

and then he began
to
cook . . .

MICHEL GUÉRARD'S CUISINE MINCEUR

Part One

Les cuissons

THE METHODS OF COOKING

Whatever method is used, a traditional method—such as in a fireplace or on an outdoor grill, roasting, in an oven or on a spit, sautéing, frying, steaming, "encased" cooking, in a crust, braising, stewing, poaching—or some method not yet discovered, cooking is the process by which a food passes from the raw to the cooked state, a phenomenon that changes its outward appearance, its color, its texture, its flavor, thus also bringing into being a cluster of aromas that awaken the appetite. Heat, the agent that causes the transformation, comes from many sources: wood, coal, gas, electricity, microwaves. . . .

The Two Main Principles

Cooking by "sealing": *Saisissement*
With browning: This method is designed to retain all the juices and nutritive elements of foods while browning and carmelizing their exterior surfaces over heat, sometimes with the addition of fat. This is the principle of broiling (or grilling), roasting, sautéing, frying.

Without browning: The same result can also be achieved without browning by cooking the food in boiling liquid, steaming it, or using a nonstick pan. This is the method employed in poaching eggs, fish, poultry, meat, and vegetables, and for pastas.

Cooking by "interchange": *Echange*

With browning: This is the method used for pot-roasting (*poêler*) or braising (*braiser*) meat, poultry, game, and variety meats. They are sautéed quickly in hot fat to retain their juices and nutritive elements. Then liquid is added halfway up (wine, stock made from veal, poultry, game, or fish, or some other flavored bouillon). In fact, the preparation of light-brown stocks (*fonds blonds*) is based on this principle. The juices within the food are gradually released and mix with the cooking liquid, and the food is enriched in turn by the various elements in this liquid, hence the term "interchange."

Without browning: The procedure is the same as above except that the food may be sautéed in fat but is not browned. That is, it is gently steamed in butter (which is the principle of fricasseeing). It may first be soaked in fresh water to remove any trace of blood (*dégorgé;* this is done for veal, sweetbreads, and brains) and blanched for a few minutes, if necessary (this is also done for sweetbreads, brains, *blanquette de veau,* tripe, *poule au blanc,* etc.). Then the sautéing may be done in a nonstick pan. When the moisturizing element is added, it will become the basis of the sauce, again through the phenomenon of "interchange."

Contrary to the procedure in braising meats, the braising of fish does not begin with sautéing but simply with placing the fish on a baking dish (buttered or not) with cold fish stock (*fumet*) or white or red wine added halfway up. The fish is then placed in the oven, sometimes covered with silicone or parchment paper, or aluminum foil, to keep it from burning. This is actually a very good example of cooking by "interchange without browning," as the fish rapidly renders up its juices and aromas to the stock, which becomes richer and in turn makes possible a tender and juicy final dish.

In this same class of techniques are the preparation of white stocks from poultry or fish (*fonds blancs*) and consommés and the poaching of fish starting in a cold seasoned liquid (*court-bouillon*), the temperature of which is progressively raised.

Cooking in a Fireplace or on an Outdoor Grill

Men began to cook over a wood fire, and that certainly remains the best school from which to gain an understanding of the use of heat in the art of cooking. I direct this chapter specifically and affectionately to those whose cooking may be conducted exclusively on a hearth and to all outdoor cooks and Sunday cooks. I want to tell them that with a little ingenuity, they can make use of the entire range of cooking methods with this equipment.

COOKING ON A GRILL: This is an outdoor version of cooking by "sealing with browning."

The heat is provided by burning prunings from grapevines, wood from fruit trees or other nonresinous wood, or charcoal, over which the grill is placed. There are, of course, several models of grills that cook with gas or electricity or infrared heat. There is the ridged or corrugated cast-iron griddle, slightly slanted, that is placed directly on the fire. (*There is also the invaluable "indoor" ridged cast-iron skillet; see page 290. Ed.*) But no one could devise anything better than the savory tang woodsmoke imparts to food cooked on an open grill!

HOW TO GRILL RED MEAT: The grill must be clean and very hot; the meat should be at room temperature and very sparingly coated with peanut or olive oil.

To grill meat very rare *(bleu):*
When the meat is placed on the grill, it is first seared and then shifted by 90 degrees (without being turned over) to make a crusty crisscross of brown marks on the surface of the meat (*quadrillage*). Then the meat is turned over and the same thing is done on the second side.

After the meat has been on the grill for a very short time, you will find very little resistance when you press your finger on the crust, and the meat is still soft: It is now very rare (*bleu*). At this stage the heat may not have penetrated the inside of the meat. Therefore, slide it to one side, away from the hot center of the fire, and keep it over only warm heat for a little while longer.

To grill meat rare (*saignant*):
If you keep the meat over the center of the fire, a few drops of pinkish blood will soon appear on the upper surface. When you press the meat now, you will feel a little resistance, although the meat is still soft: It is rare (*saignant*).

To grill meat medium rare (*à point*):
If you continue the cooking somewhat longer, you must do it more slowly; therefore, keep the meat considerably farther from the main source of heat. There will now appear more drops of blood on the upper surface. When you press the meat, you will find it more solid and firmer than before: It is now medium rare (*à point*).

To grill meat well-done (*bien cuit*):
If you continue to cook the meat in this way even longer, the drops of blood begin to form pinkish-brown trickles on the surface of the meat. You will find noticeable resistance when you press the meat: It is now well-done (*bien cuit*).

How to grill white meats, poultry & feathered game, brochettes: The fire should not be so hot as for red meats, but the grill must be hot before the food is placed on it. In no event must the food be allowed to stay on the grill too long, or it will dry out; be careful to stop the cooking in time to preserve tenderness and juiciness. A chicken, for example, must retain some blood; it should be pale pink along the entire breastbone. This indicates that it is well cooked, while its tenderness remains intact. When you prick the breast (*filet*) with a fine skewer, it should sink in easily and release a trickle of almost colorless juice. The same test can be applied to lamb.

If you are cooking skewers of small pieces of meat (*brochettes*) that include such complementary garnishes as mushrooms, green or red sweet peppers, and bacon, it is sometimes desirable, first, to parboil them briefly in water (omit salt from the water if you are using bacon). The main elements (meat, poultry, variety meats, fish) are generally marinated in advance (in oil, thyme, bay leaf, parsley, slices of lemon, freshly ground pepper, etc.; the "short" marinade also used for fish, page 29.

How to grill fish: Fat and moderately fat fish (sardines, mackerel, herring, salmon) are extremely tasty when grilled, since this process drains off some of their fattiness. After marinating the fish (page 29), paint it very lightly with oil. The grill must also be oiled so that the skin will not tear when you turn the fish. Adjust the temperature of the fire as follows:

Very hot for small pieces.

Very hot for very large pieces, which—unlike other forms of fish—are usually given a searing in a square pattern (*quadrillage*) on both sides and then placed in the oven to finish cooking.

Hot for large pieces that are cooked entirely on the grill.

Flatfish—American lemon or grey sole, turbot, skate, Dover sole, dab—are placed on the grill white-skin side down.

Fat, fleshy fish (herring, mackerel, red mullet, bass, sardine) are turned over on the grill backbone side, not slit side, down so as not to lose the juices inside.

Some large fish are crosscut for grilling into "steaks" (*darnes;* the old word, *dalle*—roughly, "slab"—seems more logical to me). This is especially suitable for salmon and halibut. However, rather than cutting a small salmon into steaks, you can have it filleted and cut the fillets into strips 2 inches wide. It is essential to retain the skin on these pieces. Score the skin (that is, with a small knife, slash it in a crisscross pattern), and place the pieces skin side down on the grill. Cook it in this position, without turning it. The grilled skin imparts an irresistible odor of smoke to the fish and keeps its flesh moist and incomparably tender.

Oysters, sea or bay scallops (*coquilles Saint-Jacques*), and hardshell clams (*palourdes*) are placed in their shells directly on the grill and will open by themselves. They may be eaten as is, or you may add a little freshly ground pepper and whatever *fines herbes* you wish.

TIPS:

Salt tends to extract juices and blood from meat, which prevents it from browning. Therefore, it is always preferable **to salt small pieces of red meat halfway through the cooking.** And, if you are cooking a **big piece of meat,** which may be cut into slices afterward, or a fish from which you will lift the fillets, it is desirable if not **essential also to salt it a second time** after you have carved it. (You can then also add a little freshly ground pepper.) In fact, the salt would never be able to reach the center of the meat or fish the first time. This applies to all large cuts, such as a leg of lamb (*gigot*), beef or veal rib roasts, saddle of lamb, etc.

When turning the meat during the cooking, be careful not to pierce it with a fork, which would allow juices and blood to escape.

Large cuts must be cooked more slowly than smaller ones so that the heat will penetrate to the center; do not subject them to very high heat. You can facilitate their cooking by scoring the skin in several places (especially for leg of lamb and fish).

If the cut is one that becomes thinner at one end, you can cook it evenly by putting the small end farther away from the center of the fire than the large end.

If you are not afraid of excess calories, you can paint the meat or fish after it has been grilled with a little oil or melted butter (use a pastry brush). This will make it glisten and beautiful to look upon.

Grilled meat is usually served with the side cooked first uppermost.

After you have used the grill, while it is still hot, scrape it with a metal-bristle brush to loosen the residue that has stuck to it. Otherwise, the next time you use the grill, these particles will burn and give off a bitter taste.

COOKING IN A COVERED PAN IN A FIREPLACE OR ON AN OUTDOOR GRILL: Here the equivalent of cooking in a covered pan (*à l'étouffée*) is obtained by wrapping food in silicone or parchment paper, or aluminum foil, and sliding it under the hot ashes.

"Dry" cooking:
For potatoes, mushrooms, asparagus. For small game birds, squab (*pigeon*), young rabbit—seasoned with *fines herbes,* thyme, bay leaf. For apples, bananas—together with vanilla beans (and sometimes with a small amount of a fruit sauce).

"Moist" cooking: For poultry and fish.
With silicone or parchment paper make a case (*papillote*), place the food to be cooked inside, and pour in enough white or red wine, fish stock, or seasoned bouillon to cover or submerge the food. Close the case and place it on the grill or bury it under the glowing coals. The liquid will be completely absorbed by the food, while at the same time it will prevent the paper from catching fire.

STEAMING FISH IN A FIREPLACE OR ON AN OUTDOOR GRILL: On the grill, spread fresh seaweed soaked in seawater or moist wild grasses from the meadows. Place the fish over this and cover it with more seaweed or grass. It will take no longer than 20 minutes to cook a 1½- to 2-pound sea bass.

COOKING "THE LAZY WAY" IN A FIREPLACE OR ON AN OUTDOOR GRILL: A large piece of meat such as a rib roast or a leg of lamb can actually be cooked in a fireplace or on a grill without a spit. All you have to do is to brown the meat well on all sides first and sear it in a crisscross pattern or *quadrillage* on the grill. Then put a piece of aluminum foil on the hot—but not red—coals, and place the meat directly on the foil.

From time to time, turn the leg of lamb or whatever you are cooking, and don't be afraid to leave it there, very close to the heat, for 2 to 3 hours, depending on its size. Cooking by this technique takes longer than any other form of grilling, because the temperature is roughly the same as that of a warming oven—225° F. or less. When you slice the meat, you will be amazed at its tenderness and even, rosy color.

Cooking in a Fireplace or on an Outdoor Grill in *Cuisine Minceur*

The different ways of cooking over an open fire that have been discussed are very well suited to *cuisine minceur* provided that you take certain precautions:

If the meat to be grilled is coated with oil in the classic way before cooking in order to facilitate browning, you can wipe it with absorbent paper before and after the cooking.

It is also possible to marinate the meat, poultry, etc., in a little water in which thyme and bay leaves have been steeped, instead of using the traditional oil marinades; see page 29.

You can also pan-fry red meat on a bed of coarse salt spread in a well-heated skillet; wait until the salt crackles, then put the meat in.

If you are grilling poultry or cooking it on a spit, prick the skin well before and during cooking to release the fat underneath.

In short, cooking in a fireplace or on an outdoor grill adds wings to the imagination of every lover of cooking, and in my opinion, every chef worthy of the name should at least once explore this field of culinary lore.

Roasting

Roasting means cooking with heat acting directly on the food, without moisture and with frequent turning. It is another version of cooking by "sealing with browning."

To achieve browning and caramelization in foods that are roasted, it is necessary to coat them—without overdoing it—with some kind of fat (such as part oil, part butter). Roasting is done in the oven, on a spit, or even, as a last resort, in a casserole or braising pan (*cocotte* or *braisière*) without the lid.

NOTE: *Throughout this discussion of roasting procedures, the American reader should be aware that a French cut of meat for roasting is usually severely trimmed of its own exterior fat and in the case of beef, it may not originally have had the heavy layer of exterior fat we expect on our own "best" cuts for roasting. Hence the care with which the surfaces of roasts are painted (or barded) with a thin coating of additional fat for browning. Reducing the amount of this protective fat in the serving of a* minceur *roast is discussed on page 14. Ed.*

IN THE OVEN: The oven must have an exhaust of some kind to let steam escape. It should be preheated. The temperature depends on the kind and the size of the piece to be roasted; it must be sufficiently high (450° to 500° F.) to seal the surface well to retain the juices inside.

Meat, poultry, game, or fish should all be very lightly coated with some kind of fat, but no salt should be used at first. Place the food in the oven either directly in a roasting pan (this is known as *façon ménagère,* "home style"), or in a pan with a rack (*lèche frite*) that will keep the food from resting in the drippings; or on a bed of bones that have first been cracked and lightly browned. For fish, you may use a bed of seaweed.

As soon as the browning and sealing have been completed, lower the oven temperature a little, and baste often with the juices in the bottom of the pan (except if you are using seaweed) until the cooking is finished. Then you can salt the meat, bird, or fish.

As for red meats, the surface of white meats, poultry, game, and fat fish must first be sealed at a fairly high temperature. But then their cooking is finished at a lower temperature or they will become tough.

ON A SPIT—WHETHER IN THE FIREPLACE OR IN AN ELEC-
TRIC ROTISSERIE: When food is roasted on a spit, either
outdoors or indoors, there is a free circulation of air
and little moisture accumulates. This, in combination
with the constant turning on the spit, provides a considerably more savory result than can be achieved
in an oven.

A light coating of fat and browning and sealing are
required as for roasting in the oven. It is still advisable
to baste the food frequently with the fat that collects
in the bottom of the drippings pan.

HOW TO SERVE A TENDER ROAST: Food roasted on a spit
or in the oven is cooked by "sealing with browning."
The high temperature and the fat on the outer surface
produce the browning, keeping the juices and blood
inside. Through its own circulatory system, the juices
and blood are sent to the center of the roast, and it
consequently cooks in its own juice without losing any
nutritive elements. If you carve a roast immediately
after it has cooked, along the cleft that the knife
makes, you find a very well-done outer layer, another
less well-done, and a third in the center that is very
rare (*bleu*) and contains all the blood—which then
runs out.

You must let meat rest before carving it! When you
remove the roast from the heat, keep it warm on a
platter or carving board covered with a roasting-pan
lid, a large bowl, or aluminum foil. Exterior heat will
no longer exert pressure toward the center of the
roast, and by reverse process the blood will now flow
toward the outer layers of the meat, giving them an
even color—rosy or red depending on how long it
was cooked. At the same time, the muscle fibers, which
have contracted because of the heat, expand and relax,
producing the desired tenderness.

**It is therefore best to finish cooking a leg of lamb,
for instance, 1 hour before it is to be served.**

TIPS:
Salt the meat halfway through the cooking; then salt
again on each slice as you carve, adding a twist of
freshly ground pepper.

Avoid pricking the roast with a fork during the cooking.

If the food you are roasting is particularly delicate or sensitive to heat and begins to burn, protect it with aluminum foil. (This includes fragile parts such as the ends of the bones in a crown roast, the tail of a fish, etc.)

SAUCES FOR ROASTS: The best sauces or *jus* (gravies) for roasts are made in home kitchens, where the family cook instinctively preserves a simple authenticity, while professional chefs often seek to produce an elaborate, even sophisticated, sauce—which, in my opinion, should never be done.

If you use a pan of the proper size for roasting (not overlarge), then the juices of meat, poultry, game, and even of fish will collect in the bottom and will serve well and simply for a correct sauce or *jus*.

THE TRICKS THAT MAKE A GOOD SAUCE:

When you paint the roast with fat, use a mixture of oil and butter—1 tablespoon of the mixture per pound. Unlike oil, butter tends to separate and scorches at high temperatures; the addition of oil helps to prevent this. You may use half oil, half butter, or two-thirds oil, one-third butter.

Add one or more cloves of garlic, to your taste, unpeeled, to the pan, and put the roast in the preheated oven.

As soon as the roast has browned well on one side, in about 10 minutes, baste it with the juices that will already have accumulated in the pan. Turn it over. Repeat this operation again. Then baste frequently for the remainder of the cooking time.

Take the pan out of the oven, remove the roast, and keep it warm and covered. The juices at the bottom of the pan should be sufficiently caramelized. (**Be absolutely vigilant to avoid burning them,** which would give the gravy an irremediably bitter taste.)

Degrease (*dégraisser*) the pan; the sauce in *cuisine gourmande* may be about one-quarter fat so that it will thicken when you boil it up.

Deglaze (*déglacer*) the pan—that is, add twice as much hot water as the total amount of sauce you want to have at the end, and with a spoon loosen all the caramelized juices sticking to the bottom of the pan so they will dissolve in the hot liquid.

Let the mixture boil and reduce by half (allow 2 generous tablespoons per serving). Pour it into a small saucepan and keep it warm.

If you want a slightly garlicky sauce, pour it through a fine-mesh strainer into the small saucepan, and crush the garlic in the strainer with the bottom of a spoon or a small ladle.

At the end, to obtain the mellowest sauce, you may also incorporate small pieces of cold butter, blending them in by rotating the saucepan. Or, you may add a few drops of a good red-wine vinegar, which is the most effective way to bring out the character of the *jus*.

To enrich the *jus* of a roast *during* the cooking, you can lightly brown in advance, in the roasting pan, cracked veal bones for a beef or veal roast, lamb bones for a leg or a saddle of lamb, cut-up poultry carcasses for a fowl, etc., and place the roast on these as suggested before.

And, when you deglaze the pan, you can enrich the sauce *after* the cooking by using, instead of hot water, a light stock or bouillon of veal, lamb, or poultry.

Roasting in *Cuisine Minceur*

If the two versions of roasting—in the oven or on a spit—are carried out with the proper precautions, they can be utilized in *cuisine minceur;* in fact, the small quantity of fat used serves simply to prevent the roast from burning after it has been browned.

As in broiling poultry in *cuisine minceur,* when poultry is roasted, it must be pricked all over with a fork to release the fat lying between the meat and the skin. Then, to make the gravy, you need only remove all the fat in the roasting pan (in oven cooking) or in the drippings pan (in spit cooking).

Once the pan has been thoroughly degreased, put the roast back in it to rest, covered, for 15 to 20 minutes before you serve it. The juices trickling out of the roast will be the base for an excellent lean sauce made as described on page 13. This *jus* is served, of course, without the addition of butter.

In *minceur* roasting, contrary to the advice of most butchers, cuts of beef or veal must be roasted with the meat exposed (*à vif*), not barded with fat.

Sautéing

Sautéing is a very quick way of preparing dishes in a savory sauce. This technique of fast cooking by "sealing" is similar to both grilling and roasting since it first involves quick browning. It is done in a shallow saucepan (*sauteuse* or *sautoir*); a standard skillet (*poêle*) can fill the bill equally well. The food is prepared in small pieces—meat, variety meats, poultry, game, or fish, and sometimes vegetables—which are cooked in half oil, half butter, allowing about 1 tablespoon per serving in all. Since they are in constant contact with the hot fat, they become caramelized and browned while retaining their juices inside.

It is in the finishing of the cooking that the technique of sautéing differs from broiling and roasting. To come out perfectly, dishes based on this method must be made virtually at the last moment.

GENERAL PROCEDURE FOR SAUTÉING: After the food has been sautéed to a light brown on both sides, salted, and cooked to your liking—very rare, rare, medium, well-done, as in grilling—take the pieces out of the pan and place them on a hot platter close to the heat. They must never cook in the elements of the sauce that are now added to the pan; that would transform them into a *ragoût*.

Degrease (*dégraisser*) the pan completely, pouring

off all the fat. Deglaze (*déglacer*), that is, pour into the pan the liquid required by the recipe—a white or red wine, vinegar, madeira, port, sherry, vermouth, armagnac, cognac—allowing 2 teaspoons of a brandy or 2 tablespoons of a wine per serving. Bring this liquid to the boil; it will dissolve the caramelized juices sticking to the bottom of the pan. Simmer it to reduce it by three-quarters of its original volume.

Then, depending on the sizes of the pieces you are dealing with and the number of servings, add 3 to 5 spoonfuls of veal, poultry, game, or fish stock. Reduce the sauce again by one half.

Off the heat or over very low heat, and while rotating the pan, incorporate bits of butter (2 tablespoons per serving) or crème fraîche (172) (3 tablespoons per serving). This is the final *liaison;* see page 47.

The object is not to drown the *sauté* in the sauce, but rather to achieve a condensed liquid that just covers and delicately surrounds it.

TIPS:
The size of the pan must be right for the amount of food to be sautéed. If the food does not completely cover the bottom of the pan, the fat will quickly burn in the empty spots and will give the sauce a bitter taste when you deglaze the pan.

Small cuts (*tournedos,* chops, scallopini) should be cooked quickly, uncovered throughout the cooking. Larger pieces (dark meat of poultry, pieces of rabbit) take a little longer to cook after browning and are therefore covered after browning and then cooked more slowly.

THE PROPER WAY TO COOK A FISH À LA MEUNIÈRE: The technique known as *à la meunière* (lightly floured; literally, "as the miller's wife does it") is reserved for fish (trout, pike, sole, whiting, etc.) or other foods with similar texture such as brains. It is a form of sautéing, but it stops before the deglazing stage. Let us take trout as an example:

In a skillet or an oval pan just of a size to hold the fish, put a mixture of half oil, half butter; the combination will keep the butter from browning too quickly. Use 1½ to 2 tablespoons in all. *Optional:* Add a clove of garlic, unpeeled; the aroma of the garlic thereby remains muted and imparts a subtle nuance to the dish as a whole. Put the pan on the heat.

Dry the fish with absorbent paper or a towel. Salt and pepper it, then very lightly dust both sides with flour. Tap it to remove the excess.

Put the fish in the hot fat. Let it cook without too much heat for about 4 minutes on each side, until it is a nice golden brown. If this is done properly, the small amount of fat that remains in the pan will remain a pale brown.

Raise the heat and add 3 tablespoons of fresh butter. When this begins to brown, it no longer "sings" because the water it contains has evaporated. When it becomes a light hazelnut color, it is known as *beurre noisette* and is ready to serve.

Sprinkle the juice of a lemon into the butter (this will make it foam), remove the garlic clove, and immediately pour the butter over the fish.

I most strongly advise and entreat you to use a minimum of fat in cooking fish. A fish must retain its flavor of the sea or freshwater stream intact and is not to become a "sponge for butter."

Sautéing in *Cuisine Minceur*

This is feasible thanks to the nonstick utensils that make it possible to avoid using fat. Nevertheless, although a kind of "sealing" (*saisissement*) is produced on the surface of the food, this is not, properly speaking, the caramelization that imparts such a pleasant flavor to the juices in the bottom of the pan. You can compensate satisfactorily for this by marinating the food for a short time; see page 28.

If you want to sauté in *minceur* cooking, retaining the classic method I have described, you must make the following adjustments:

After the food has been sautéed, put it on absorbent paper to rid it of every trace of fat. Degrease the pan completely so that only the juices are left in the bottom.

In deglazing, reduce the wine or brandy until it has almost completely evaporated; this will eliminate the alcohol content and leave only the aroma.

Obviously you will have to find some thickening agent for the *liaison* other than butter and cream! Use only those suggested later on in our *minceur* recipes, and see also pages 47–9.

Frying

Frying (*friture*) is a form of cooking by "sealing with browning." The food is plunged into a bath of hot fat (also called *friture*) which may be peanut, olive, or vegetable oil; lard; or the rendered kidney fat of beef or veal. The fat is heated to a maximum of 340° F. and the temperature is maintained until the cooking has been completed. Butter and margarine must not be used because they decompose at high temperatures.

For this process to succeed, the food should be well dried and is cut into pieces small enough so that the heat will quickly reach the centers. It is also necessary to fry only a small quantity at a time; otherwise, the temperature of the fat drops too rapidly when the food is immersed in it.

The applications of deep-fat frying belong almost exclusively to *cuisine gourmande*. Foods are fried without an outside coating (*sans enrobage*), such as potatoes, eggs, parsley or sorrel for garnishing, tiny game birds, and various forms of pastry (*pâte à chou, pâte brisée, pâte à brioche*). With a coating (*avec enrobage*) are fried fish dipped in milk and then flour and a variety of foods dipped in the "croquette" coating of flour, beaten egg, and fine bread crumbs (*chapelure*) or in fritter (*beignet*) batter. Virtually no *enrobage* has a place in *cuisine minceur*.

Furthermore, foods that are fried absorb part of the fat in which they are cooked. For instance, when you use oil, 1 tablespoon of peanut oil = 1 tablespoon of olive oil = 1 tablespoon of corn oil, etc. . . . That is, equals close to ¾ ounce of oil, which amounts inescapably to close to ¾ ounce of fat! In other words, there is no "miracle" oil for frying. And, fried foods are not the most digestible because of the fat that they absorb. Deep-fat frying, therefore, challenges one's ingenuity if it is to be adapted for *cuisine minceur!* However, for the diehards, here are the basic rules of deep-fat frying:

Frying oil cannot be used more than 4 or 5 times.

After each use, leave all the scraps and impurities at the bottom of the pan, and pour the oil carefully into another container through a fine-mesh strainer or a strainer lined with cheesecloth.

Always store the oil in a tightly covered container; air must be kept out.

If you make the rash effort to adapt deep-fat frying to *minceur* cooking, the oil or fat is not to be allowed to heat past 300° F.

Finally, potatoes can be replaced by celery root (celeriac), which has very few calories and which can be made into surprisingly delicious *"frites."*

How to make good french-fried potatoes: The technique is of interest because of its application to celery root.

Cut the potatoes (preferably a mealy variety) into small sticks of whatever thickness you prefer—from ⅜ inch for standard french-fried potatoes (*pommes pont neuf*) down to ⅛ inch for matchstick potatoes (*pommes allumettes*). Rinse them in cold water, and dry them in a towel. Put them in the frying basket.

Heat the oil to a temperature averaging 300° F. Test it by throwing in a potato stick; if it boils up quickly (in about 25 seconds), the oil is at the right temperature.

Plunge the potatoes into the oil and give them a preliminary cooking of about 7 or 8 minutes. If you pick up a potato stick that has been removed from the hot oil and allowed to cool and you can crush it easily, it is done for this stage of the cooking.

Lift out the frying basket, and turn the potatoes out onto a plate covered with a towel or with absorbent paper.

Now heat the oil to 340° F.—but be careful not to let it heat to smoking point. Return the potatoes to the oil, shaking the basket to keep them from sticking together. In 2 or 3 minutes, they will be golden brown and crisp.

Take the potatoes out of the oil again, and turn them out onto the plate covered with a fresh towel or fresh absorbent paper. Sprinkle them with salt or, better, with freshly ground coarse salt.

It is the second plunge into the hotter oil that seals and crisps the surface of the potatoes, which also puff up because of the evaporation of the water still inside. (This is the principle of the more difficult, thinly sliced *pommes soufflées*.) It is essential to control the temperature of the oil, which must not go above 340° F. If the oil gets hotter than this, it rapidly becomes toxic. An electric fryer with a thermostatic control or a deep-fat-frying thermometer are both helpful.

Covered Cooking: Steaming, "Encased" Cooking, Braising & Stewing

Covered cooking (*cuisson à l'étouffée;* literally, "smothered" cooking), can be a version of cooking by "sealing," or of cooking by "interchange," or sometimes by both principles.

STEAMING: This form of covered cooking, *cuisson à la vapeur,* relies on "sealing." The food draws only on the steam of a hot liquid, which may or may not be seasoned, and it imparts nothing to the liquid in return. You can use the simplest of bouillons—salted water. There are two methods of steaming:

Use a pot or pan with a closely fitting lid and of a size and shape just to hold the food to be cooked: a saucepan with a footed steaming rack (see page 288); a round or oval casserole (*cocotte*), or a covered roasting pan with its own perforated rack (which may be raised above the level of the rack with metal jar tops placed underneath); a two-part steamer or *couscoussière* (see page 288); or a fish poacher (see page 287). Fill the pan one-quarter of the way up with bouillon, seasoned or not, or with stock or *fumet*, depending on the circumstances. The rack should sit just above the level of the boiling liquid, permitting only the steam to reach the food placed on it.

Here is another, original method of steaming that uses the same principle: In a utensil of the appropriate size, with a tightly fitting lid, place saltwater fish on a bed of seaweed or freshwater fish on a bed of wild meadow grass. Then cover the fish with another layer of seaweed or grass moistened with a ladleful of water to start the cooking and the steam. See **Bar aux algues (95)**. The same method is used to cook a leg of lamb. See **Gigot d'agneau cuit dans le foin (114)**.

In the first method, when the steam is generated from a meat- or poultry-based stock, this stock can be the starting point for an accompanying sauce. This cannot be done when you use seaweed or hay.

"ENCASED" COOKING: There are many forms of this technique. It is a variation of "smothered" cooking, this time by "interchange."

Cuisson en vessie is a very old method in which food is cooked in a pig's bladder (*vessie*), and it is also a type of steaming. A modern example, a chicken encased in a plastic bag, is **Poulet au tilleul en vessie (116)**. The chicken cooks in its own juices, receiving flavor from the ingredients put in the bag with it, and also returning some of its own juices to these ingredients which will become the sauce. The sealed plastic bag is immersed in boiling water for cooking.

Cuisson en papillote requires that the food, with flavoring ingredients, be wrapped in silicone or parchment paper, or in aluminum foil. It is another form of cooking by "interchange," and the *papillote* is placed in the oven, or in the hot coals of a grill, for cooking. Examples are **Truite en papillote à l'aneth et au citron**

(88), **Banane en papillote** (158), and **Foie de veau à la vapeur** (111).

The process of "interchange" which takes place inside the sealed *vessie* or *papillote* also produces a remarkable concentration of aromas.

Cuisson en croûte, cooking in a crust, breaks down into two forms: edible and inedible crusts. The edible crusts do not apply in *cuisine minceur*. They include *pâte feuilletée, pâte à brioche, pâte brisée,* and *pâte à pâté,* which are used in a variety of ways for beef fillet, boned leg of lamb, poultry, game, and *pâtés.* The final cooking is done in the oven.

The inedible crust most frequently used is a paste of coarse salt dampened with water. The food is encased in this paste, sometimes further encased in aluminum foil, and is cooked in the oven. A rib roast of 5 or 6 ribs may be cooked *sous la sel.* After a preliminary browning, it is entirely encased in the salt paste and roasted slowly in a moderate oven, producing a tender, juicy, evenly cooked roast. This is also a good way to roast a chicken:

Line an oval ovenproof casserole with aluminum foil, and line the foil with a good quantity of the salt paste. (*Proportions, 4 tablespoons of water to each cup of coarse salt; we used 5 cups of salt and 1¼ cups of water. Ed.*) Put in a trussed 3- to 3½-pound chicken, and bury the chicken completely in more salt paste. Bake the chicken, uncovered, in a hot (475°–500° F.) oven for about 1 hour. When you break open the salt crust, you will find a chicken more tender than if it had been conventionally roasted, with all its juices retained inside.

BRAISING & STEWING: Braising is the example *par excellence* of cooking by "interchange." A piece of meat for braising may be larded and marinated in advance; see page 28. Then, all surfaces of meat or poultry—but not of fish—are first sealed by light browning. The meat or bird is removed, diced vegetables (*mirepoix*) are added to the pot and briefly cooked in the juices. The meat or bird is placed back in the pan on top of the *mirepoix*, and a flavorful liquid (bouillon, wine, veal or chicken stock) is added to reach halfway up the piece.

An appropriate utensil is a heavy-bottomed, cast-iron casserole (*cocotte*) with a tightly fitting lid. Even better is the deep, oblong braising pot called a *braisière* which has a lid that fits down closely over the sides of the pot.

In braising, the cooking must be gentle, long, and even. The cooking is done either in a slow oven or on top of the stove. (The latter requires an asbestos mat or other protection for the bottom of the pot.) As its fibers are tenderized, the meat or poultry exudes juices that heighten the savor of the braising liquid, which is thereby gradually transformed into a rich and fragrant sauce. At the end, this sauce is usually carefully strained.

An example of braising is **Jarret de veau aux oranges** (109); in this instance, the marinade is used as the braising liquid. Another example is the braising of sweetbreads, versions of which appear within the recipes for **Gigot de poulette cuit à la vapeur de marjolaine** (119) and **Gâteau de ris de veau aux morilles** (112).

The braising of fish is handled a little differently. The fish is not cooked in a pan covered with a lid, but rather placed in a buttered (or *minceur* unbuttered) baking dish. Seasonings are added, and the fish is sprinkled, most usually, with minced shallots. A mixture of half fish stock and half wine (white or red, as specified by the recipe) is added, and the dish is baked in the oven. The cooking time is much shorter than for meat or poultry. Instead of using a lid to shield the fish against the heat, a sheet of buttered silicone or parchment paper, or of aluminum foil, is placed over the baking dish. In some instances, even this protection is not necessary and may prevent the braising liquid from reducing sufficiently.

As a general rule (including the braising of fish particularly), to preserve the moisture in braised foods, the top part of which is not immersed in liquid, the piece should be basted often with the braising juices—

with a large spoon, a small ladle, or a bulb baster— throughout the entire cooking time.

Even when braised foods are cooked for a very long time, properly cooked they will always remain moist and tender. Meats can be allowed to cook virtually to shreds, to the point where they could be eaten with a spoon—hence the expression *à la cuiller* in the names of some braised dishes and *daubes*. This is why, toward the end of his life, the Duc de Richelieu, who had lost most of his teeth but who was an incurable *gourmand*, demanded that even squab be prepared for him by braising.

Stews (*ragoûts*) are cooked in the same way as braised dishes, starting with browning at the beginning. The signal difference is that the meat or fowl is cut into pieces (as in *boeuf bourguignon, navarin* of lamb, veal Marengo, *coq au vin*). After the pieces have been sealed and browned, they are sometimes *singés*, that is, sprinkled with flour (preferably browned flour; see page 46), which provides from the beginning the ingredient of *liaison* for the final sauce. A higher proportion of liquid eliminates the need for basting in *ragoûts*. An example of a *ragoût* is **Estouffade de boeuf aux petits légumes (102).**

Covered Cooking in *Cuisine Minceur*

Steaming offers real advantages in *minceur* cooking. It is a process filled with fragrances that also causes the fat to "sweat" out of food, while preserving the nutritive elements (minerals, vitamins) and the original, essential flavors.

"Encased" cooking in a plastic bag or *en papillote* confines the aromas of several elements together and in this way makes possible a natural and unembellished, yet highly flavorful form of cooking—without the use of any fat at all.

Cooking *en croûte* requires adaptation from the traditional pastry crust. We use instead a temporary coating of coarse salt.

Braising and stewing, contrary to what you may

think, can be included in *cuisine minceur* if you take the following measures:

Completely trim meat of all fat.

As soon as the meat or poultry has been browned, throw out whatever oil remains in the bottom of the pot, wipe the food with absorbent paper, and then put it back to cook with the required liquid.

If there is still a little fat in the sauce, chill the dish in its pot overnight in the refrigerator. The next day, with a spoon, you can easily remove the layer of fat that will have hardened on the surface.

Poaching

Poaching is cooking by immersing a food in a liquid (such as water, broth, meat or fish stock, *court-bouillon*, or a sweet syrup). The poaching liquid at the start may be cold, simmering slightly, or boiling vigorously.

STARTING WITH A COLD LIQUID: This is a form of cooking by "interchange with or without browning."

Beginning with a cold liquid prevents "sealing" and consequently makes it possible to release the flavors of the food to the enhancement of the broth in which it is cooked. This is the situation in a *pot-au-feu*, which is cooked to the enrichment of its broth but to the detriment of the savoriness of the meat. A similar richness is achieved in a veal stock (using bones that have first been browned in the oven) or in a fish stock (*without* browning the fish bones); see **Fond blond de veau I (1)** and **Fumet de poisson I (9)**.

If you want to obtain the opposite result and preserve the flavor and aroma of the food, you must enrich the bouillon by incorporating into it seasonings, vegetables, wine, juices of meat or fish, etc.— all of which will "pay back" flavor to the food that cooks with them. For example, poach fish in *court-bouillon* or fish stock; poach a stewing hen in chicken stock or bouillon; poach brains in a *court-bouillon* containing vinegar.

If the foods thus cooked are to be served cold, it is best to let them cool in their cooking liquid; if this is done, reduce the cooking time a little.

STARTING WITH A HOT LIQUID: This is a form of cooking by "sealing without browning." Beginning with a hot liquid makes it possible to preserve intact virtually all the flavor and nutritive elements.

Green vegetables should be cooked in a large quantity of salted water (from 2 to 4 teaspoons per quart), uncovered, and at a rapid boil.

In cooking fish *au bleu*, the live fish is given a sharp blow on the head, gutted, sprinkled with vinegar, and plunged into simmering, not boiling, *court-bouillon*.

Boiling eggs is also a form of poaching.

Fruits are cooked by poaching them in a syrup usually flavored with vanilla (pears, apples, peaches, apricots, raspberries, etc.).

HOW TO COOK GREEN BEANS:

Certain vegetables, among them green beans, contain organic acids which, when they come into contact with heat, produce a change in the color of the vegetable from its original fresh garden green to various shades of yellow or even brownish green.

These acids are also volatile, therefore they can be made to escape rapidly before the color of the bean is damaged. To do this, proceed as follows: In a large kettle or saucepan, enameled or otherwise stainless, bring a generous quantity of water, salted with 1½ tablespoons of coarse salt per quart of water, to a rolling boil. Add the beans, young ones, first snapped and stringed if necessary, and boil them, uncovered, over high heat, until they are crisp-tender, testing often as they cook. A fine, small green bean will cook in 4 or 5 minutes; larger beans will necessarily take longer cooking, but the object is to boil them for the minimum time possible. Not only color but flavor and vitamins will be preserved.

Drain the beans in a colander, then turn them out into a bowl of ice water, and leave them there for 10 seconds. This operation not only stops their cooking, it also rinses them of the large amount of salt in the cooking water which has played its part in their rapid cooking without discoloration.

NOTE: *There is nothing the matter with a good, young, fresh American green bean. But there are varieties of beans grown in France that are altogether incomparable in their color, size, flavor, and texture. As far as we know, these varieties are not marketed in the United States, but there is no reason why you cannot grow them yourself. Bean plants are indigenous to our continent, not to Europe! A source for seeds is listed on page 295. Ed.*

HOW TO COOK ASPARAGUS:

As we all know, the whole asparagus stalk rarely gets eaten; the tip is tender, the base is stringy and is left on the plate. Here is a way to improve matters; it depends on a homemade asparagus cooker:

Wash the asparagus, cut off all the woody part of the bottoms of the stalks, and peel the asparagus, running the knife from close to the tip downward to the bottom.

The homemade cooker is a tall tin can, such as a fruit-juice can, in which you have poked holes all over the bottom and sides with an ice pick, turning it into a virtual sieve. Stand the asparagus in this (tying them together loosely if the can is too big for the amount of asparagus).

Put the tin can in a tall, narrow stockpot, and pour in enough boiling water to come one-third of the way up the asparagus; boil for 3 to 5 minutes, depending on the size of the asparagus. Then add more boiling water to come two-thirds of the way up, and boil for the same length of time. Finally, add water to the top of the tips and boil again.

If the asparagus is fresh and of medium size, each stage of the cooking will be about 3 minutes, so that the tough part of the stalk gets 9 minutes of cooking, the middle 6 minutes, and the tip 3 minutes.

NOTE: *This pragmatic system for cooking asparagus solves the problem of the even cooking of French* white *asparagus particularly, which is inclined to be stringier at the base than our green asparagus. For green asparagus, rather than cutting off the bottoms of the stalks, break them off at the point at which they will allow themselves to break. (White asparagus usually won't break except so near the tips that too much goes to waste.) Peel the green asparagus as described above, and they may be cooked lying flat on their sides unless you have a tough batch, in which case progressive cooking, upright in a steamer, home-made or otherwise, will help. Ed.*

Poaching in *Cuisine Minceur*

Poaching does not mean "cooking in water," with all that conjures up of dismal and discouraging diet cooking. And yet, for certain foods, cooking in water is the natural and appropriate way.

A lobster cooked in well-salted water, in approximation of seawater, expresses its natural flavor better than in many an elaborate preparation.

Vegetables cooked in rapidly boiling water and dressed at the end of the cooking with just a small piece of fresh butter and minced fresh *fines herbes* are in themselves a delicious dish. To serve them this way, you must get into the habit of rinsing vegetables quickly so as not to give them time to lose their minerals in the rinsing water. Cook most of them as instructed for green beans on page 26.

Moreover, the cooking water often becomes a bouillon that can be saved to make, for example, soups.

When a fatty food is poached, its fat will melt and rise to the surface of the liquid where it can be removed with a skimmer, a small ladle, or absorbent paper.

Finally, poaching is a method of cooking that makes food particularly digestible.

Marinades

Marinades are an alchemy handed down from an earlier age. They were first of all an ingenious means of preserving meats, retarding spoilage and also considerably enhancing flavor at the same time. Today, these *bains épicés* ("spice baths") are still useful to flavor both meat and game. They tenderize game (wild boar, deer, etc.) and impart a vigorous taste of the hunt to domestic beef and lamb. During the process of slowly impregnating the meat with the flavors of a marinade, you must keep it in a cool place and turn it frequently.

Often, the marinade is also used as the cooking liquid and in the final preparation of the sauce that will accompany the marinated meat.

THE TRADITIONAL UNCOOKED MARINADE: The ingredients for *la marinade crue* are 1 onion, 2 shallots, ½ carrot, and a 3-inch piece of celery, all these vegetables peeled and thinly sliced.

Thyme, bay leaf, 1 clove of garlic, 2 cloves, 6 peppercorns, 6 whole grains of coriander, and a good pinch of salt.

And, 2 cups of white or red wine, ⅝ cup of vinegar, and ⅜ cup of oil.

In a deep dish, such as a baking dish, of a size just to hold the piece of meat comfortably, spread a bed of half the sliced vegetables. Put in the meat, and spread the rest of the vegetables over it. Add the wine, white or red depending on the final recipe, the vinegar, the herbs and spices, and then the oil.

THE TRADITIONAL COOKED MARINADE: The cooked marinade, *la marinade cuite*, accelerates the process of tenderizing meat. It is made with the same ingredients as the preceding uncooked marinade. But first, in a saucepan, heat a little olive oil, and in it cook the sliced vegetables gently until they give off some of their liquid. Then add the wine, vinegar, and herbs and spices, and simmer the marinade over low heat for 30 minutes. Let it cool completely before using.

MARINADES FOR FISH: In the South Pacific, raw fish is marinated, or macerated, in a little lemon juice and pepper which gives the effect of partial cooking, and the fish is eaten raw and very thinly sliced.

When fish are to be grilled, they may be macerated in a "short" marinade. The base is a little oil. The flavorings, depending on the fish and the effect wanted, are thin slices of peeled lemon, thyme, bay leaf, fennel, parsley stems, basil, thinly sliced onion, minced shallot, salt, pepper, saffron, etc.

MARINADES IN CUISINE MINCEUR: Because they require not fat, or very little, marinades come into their own in *cuisine minceur*. They are valuable allies, tenderizing, spicing, and compensating, in this light cooking, for the absence of the richer elements to which we are accustomed. There are specific examples of the use of marinades in my *minceur* recipes.

Meanwhile, to use marinades generally in *cuisine minceur*:
If the marinade contains oil, carefully wipe off the meat or fish with a cloth or absorbent paper before you cook it. If the marinade is to serve as the base for an accompanying sauce, degrease it, and then simmer it to evaporate the alcohol content of the wine that has been used, keeping only its aroma.

A resolutely *minceur* marinade: *L'infusion*
The wine that usually serves as the base for a marinade can be replaced by an infusion of water or stock in which have been simmered aromatic herbs such as rosemary, thyme, marjoram, basil. Such infusions are of course not very powerful. Their most rewarding use is in cooking various white meats *à la vapeur*, in flavored steam. You will find a number of such dishes among the *minceur* recipes.

Les fonds, les liaisons & les sauces
STOCKS, LIAISONS & SAUCES

The renown of French cuisine is born of its sauces. The metaphors with which the literature of cooking has attempted to describe the nature of sauces have drawn upon the vocabularies of alchemy and magic, botany and horticulture, chemistry and architecture—indeed, any vocabulary including that of poetry.

The *saucier*, sauce chef, is a magician dealing in alchemy, his craft a culinary sleight-of-hand from which well-made stocks emerge to become the roots from which sauces, like plants, grow. Their *liaisons*, unctuous and voluptuous, are the catalysts which cause sauces ultimately to come into being. Such is the strength of these processes that finally the results, the great sauces of France, must be described as the cornerstones of cuisine.

There follow the three great stocks, the principles of the *liaisons* of sauces, and six classic sauces.

The Three Great Stocks

Commercially produced canned stocks of real excellence—whether of veal, chicken, or fish—do not exist in France, any more than they do in the United States. To a Frenchman, this is a gross omission in his own country, for were they available and properly made, French housewives could sensibly achieve a sometime dream—to concoct the sauces they eye with envy and apprehension in the books of *grande cuisine*.

Until commerce finally remedies the situation, take heart. A fine stock is not really so difficult—no more so than the annual ritual of canning, preserving, and jam- and jelly-making which has once again become popular. I invite you, ladies—and gentleman—to supposedly "waste" a few weekend afternoons in making a supply of the three great stocks.

If you follow faithfully and methodically the instructions in the recipes, you will conquer successfully the somewhat mysterious pinnacle of Great Sauces and will be proud of yourself and pleased with the compliments you receive.

NOTE: *With this said, Michel Guérard has nevertheless studied with some concern the time-consuming and inconvenient aspects of making large quantities of veal, chicken, and fish stocks in a home kitchen. For this book he first created the simplified* fond de veau II *on page 36 and the rich* fumet de poisson II *on page 43. And he worked with several cans of American-made chicken broth which he freshened up simply by simmering the broth with fresh vegetables and giblets—as many American cooks also do— to make the* fond de volaille II *on page 40. He also approved our similar experiment for the shortcut fish* fumet *made with bottled clam juice on page 44.*

A great convenience in both the simplified veal stock and the rich fish fumet *is the addition of chicken-bouillon cubes. However, very few chicken-bouillon cubes in the United States are worth the foil they are wrapped in. They have a stale and salty flavor that will improve nothing to which they are added. Nevertheless, there are good instant chicken-broth products available. Some imported ones are discussed in the notes on page 37 in the simplified veal stock recipe.*

One of the important processes in making a good stock is the careful skimming of all the fat and scum that rise to the surface as the stock simmers, especially at the beginning. Because the vegetables are very finely cut up (in order to extract the maximum flavor from them), and because they float on the surface of the liquid, it is difficult to skim without also removing vegetables. We tried two simple remedies. One was to tie the diced vegetables in a piece of cheesecloth. The other was simply not to put the vegetables in until the other ingredients had simmered for a while and had been skimmed of a fair amount of scum; after that, we simply let the skimming go unless there was an obvious need for it. Ed.

1

Fond blond de veau I
LIGHT-BROWN VEAL STOCK

To make about 1 quart of stock:

2 pounds, in all, of veal knuckle and veal bones, cut into
     fairly small pieces (prevail on the butcher to do
     this for you)
2 ounces of ham, trimmed of all fat
1 pound of lean stewing beef (beef shank), cut in pieces
3 medium-size carrots, scraped and cut into ¼-inch dice
¼ pound of fresh mushrooms, stems trimmed, rinsed,
     and cut into ¼-inch dice
1 medium-size onion, peeled and minced
1 shallot, peeled and minced
1 clove of garlic, crushed
⅜ cup of dry white wine
3 quarts of cold water, or to cover well
2 tomatoes, halved and seeded
1 tablespoon of tomato paste
4-inch piece of celery
1 teaspoon of dried chervil, or several sprigs of fresh
     chervil or parsley
¼ teaspoon of dried tarragon, or sprig of fresh tarragon
Bouquet garni

In a roasting pan in a very hot oven (475° F.), brown the veal bones and knuckle, without any fat (*à sec*), for 15 minutes. With a large kitchen spoon, turn the pieces over several times as they brown.

Add the ham, stewing beef, carrots, mushrooms, onion, shallot, and garlic. Heat in the oven for another 5 minutes, or until the vegetables wilt but have not begun to brown.

Transfer everything to a soup kettle. Add the white wine and, on top of the stove, boil for 15 minutes to evaporate the alcohol. Then add the cold water and the tomatoes, tomato paste, celery, chervil, tarragon, and *bouquet garni.* Simmer the stock gently, partially covered, over low heat for about 3 hours. During this time, skim off periodically the scum and fat that rise to the surface.

Strain the stock—there should be about 1 quart— through a large, fine-mesh strainer into the container in which it will be stored. Let cool, then store, covered, in the refrigerator. For a perfectly fat-free stock, merely wait until it is well chilled; the hardened fat on the surface is then easy to remove.

Veal stock is used as the cooking liquid in recipes for dishes that are served in the "sauce" in which they are cooked, such as stews, fricassees, *coq au vin,* etc. It is an ingredient in many other kinds of preparations as well.

2

Demi-glace

To arrive at a more concentrated veal stock, it may be bound very lightly and then reduced in the following manner:

Dissolve 1 tablespoon of potato flour or arrowroot in 3 tablespoons of water or dry white wine. Bring the quart of veal stock to a boil, and, beating constantly with a large whisk, gradually pour the mixture into the stock and continue whisking until a perfectly smooth blending, or *liaison,* is achieved.

Then, simmer the stock gently again until it is reduced by half, or to about 2 cups. During this simmering, more scum will rise to the surface which must be skimmed off.

One can achieve the richness of a *demi-glace* without the arrowroot binding simply by simmering the stock longer, over very low heat, still skimming it often.

Demi-glace is used as the medium to extend a pan sauce that is started first with a wine or a liquor such as brandy. The wine or brandy is used to deglaze the skillet or sauté pan in which meat has been cooked, dissolving the caramelized juices in the pan, and is heated, reduced, and brought to sauce consistency with the addition of *demi-glace*. It is also used as a sauce base itself, as in sauce périgueux (19).

3

Glace de viande

The ultimate perfection is to continue to reduce the stock to a *glace de viande*, which coats a spoon with a clinging, shining layer of liquid that has been reduced down to a tenth of the original quart, or to about 3/8 cup.

Glace de viande is used in discretely small quantities in sauces. It will give life, in the French words, to a *sauce muette et sans charme* (speechless and without charm) and make it mellow and generous in flavor.

NOTE: Prepare a supply of veal stock or *demi-glace* in advance, for use in several recipes, not just one. It should be stored in glass or plastic containers and will keep 8 days in the refrigerator—and much longer in the freezer. *Glace de viande* may be "sterilized"—

that is, put in a small screw-top Mason jar which is immersed in boiling water and boiled for 60 minutes. It then does not have to be refrigerated.

(*If you wish to put up supplies of stock or* demi-glace *to keep not under refrigeration, we recommend the advice in the book* Putting Food By *by Hertzberg, Vaughan & Greene: Pressure-process pint jars of stock for 20 minutes, quart jars for 25 minutes, at 10-pounds pressure or 240° F. Ed.*)

4

Fond de veau II
SIMPLIFIED VEAL STOCK

To make about 1 quart of stock:

- 1 tablespoon of olive oil
- 1 large carrot, scraped and cut into ½-inch dice
- 1 large onion, peeled and cut into ½-inch dice
- ¼ pound of fresh mushrooms, stems trimmed, washed, and coarsely chopped
- 1 calf's foot, cut into 8 pieces (*see Note*)
- 1 large tomato, halved and seeded
- ½ ounce of dried mushrooms (morels, *cèpes*, or *shiitake* mushrooms; *see page 297*)
- 1 teaspoon of tomato paste
- 1 teaspoon of *arôme Patrelle* (*see Note*)
- *Bouquet garni*, including 1 clove
- 2½ quarts of cold water, or to cover well
- 3 cubes of Knorr-Swiss instant chicken bouillon (*see Note*)
- 1 level teaspoon of potato flour or arrowroot

NOTE: *If you cannot get a fresh calf's foot from your butcher, you may be able to get a pig's foot, or ask him for a veal knuckle and have him cut it into sev-*

eral pieces for you. Blanch it for 1 minute in boiling water before adding it to the vegetables in the soup kettle.

Arôme Patrelle is a commercial product not unlike our old-fashioned Kitchen Bouquet, but considerably more agreeable in flavor. Since the chief purpose of this ingredient is to give the stock a little color, ½ teaspoon of a good soy sauce will do as well; do not use more than ½ teaspoon, as it is much saltier than the other products.

Knorr-Swiss instant chicken-bouillon cubes are sold in many specialty shops and even in some supermarkets. They are virtually the same thing as French Maggi chicken-bouillon cubes, with which this recipe was originally made. You may find the Maggi brand in specialty shops as well. Or, you may use 1½ quarts of a clear canned chicken broth and 2 cups of water instead of the bouillon cubes and 2½ quarts of water. Ed.

Heat the olive oil in a medium-size kettle, add the carrot, onion, and fresh mushrooms, and lightly brown the vegetables in the hot oil. Then add all the remaining ingredients except the potato flour or arrowroot.

Simmer the stock, partially covered, over low heat for 2½ hours. During this time, skim off periodically the scum and fat that rise to the surface. Then strain the stock—there should be close to a quart—through a fine-mesh strainer into a saucepan.

Bring the stock back to the boil. Dissolve the level teaspoon of arrowroot in a little cold water and, with a whisk, beat this mixture briskly into the hot stock.

The veal stock is finished! And it is already close to a *demi-glace*. It is remarkably good; before using it, extend it with 1 cup of water if you wish.

Let the stock cool, then store, covered, in the refrigerator. The next day remove the last of the fat that has hardened on the surface.

5

Fond blanc de volaille I
CHICKEN STOCK

To make about 3 quarts of stock:

- 6 pounds of chicken carcasses (*see Note*), cut up, or a large stewing hen
- 3 large carrots, scraped and sliced
- ½ pound of fresh mushrooms, stems trimmed, rinsed, and sliced
- 3 shallots, peeled and minced
- 2 leeks, most of the green parts cut off, well washed
- 1 medium-size stalk of celery
- 1 large or 2 small cloves of garlic, crushed
- 1¼ cups of dry white wine
- 4½ quarts of cold water, or to cover well
- 2 medium onions, peeled, two of them stuck with a clove each
- Bouquet garni

NOTE: *A restaurant kitchen evidently will have a constant supply of chicken carcasses which can thriftily be made into stock; the home cook cannot count on this. It is convenient—and more economical than buying a whole bird—to buy chicken wings and backs from a market that sells chicken in parts. Ed.*

Put the cut-up chicken carcasses—or wings and backs, or the stewing hen—in a soup kettle with the carrots, mushrooms, shallots, leeks, celery stalk, and garlic. Add the white wine and boil for 15 minutes to evaporate the alcohol.

Then add the cold water, the onions, and the *bouquet garni*. Simmer the stock gently, partially covered, over low heat for about 3 hours. During this time, skim off periodically the scum and fat that rise to the surface.

Strain the stock—there should be about 3 quarts—through a large, fine-mesh strainer into the container in which it will be stored. Let cool, then store, covered, in the refrigerator. When the stock has chilled, remove the last of the fat that will have hardened on the surface.

Chicken stock is used as the cooking liquid in recipes for dishes which are cooked without browning or coloring (*à blanc*), such as chicken fricassees, poached chicken, and *blanquette de veau*. It is the base of many soups and is used for cooking vegetables such as rice and braised lettuce. It is a real convenience to have plenty of chicken stock on hand in your refrigerator or freezer.

6

Fond blanc de veau
WHITE VEAL STOCK

This stock is prepared in exactly the same way as chicken stock, or *fond blanc de volaille*, using, instead of chicken carcasses, the same weight in veal bones and veal knuckle; these must be blanched for 1 minute in boiling water before they are put in the soup kettle with the vegetables and wine. But, personally, I prefer the more subtle flavor of chicken stock.

7

Fond blond de volaille
LIGHT-BROWN POULTRY STOCK

Conversely, one can make a light-brown stock with poultry exactly as one makes light-brown veal stock, or *fond blond de veau*, using, instead of veal bones and veal knuckle, the carcasses not necessarily of chicken but, for instance, of duck, and adding a little more tomato to the recipe.

This type of stock is used in small quantities as the cooking liquid (*mouillage court*) in various types of poultry recipes.

8

Fond de volaille II
SHORTCUT CHICKEN STOCK

To make 3 cups of stock:

3½ cups of canned clear chicken broth
1 cup of water
1 medium onion, peeled and coarsely chopped
1 small carrot, scraped and coarsely chopped
1 medium stalk of celery, coarsely chopped
1 leek, green part discarded, well washed, and thinly sliced
1 or 2 large fresh mushrooms, stems trimmed, rinsed, and coarsely chopped
Several sprigs of parsley
½ bay leaf
Pinch of dried thyme or a small sprig of fresh thyme

If you are making a chicken dish the same day, you may also have available the *abattis,* that is, the gizzard (cut it up), heart, and neck, plus wing tips and fresh chicken bones that you might otherwise throw away. Add these to the ingredients if convenient.

Combine everything in a saucepan, and simmer, partially covered, over low heat for ½ hour. Strain the stock through a fine-mesh strainer, let it cool, then store, covered, in the refrigerator.

When chilled, even this simple stock will probably have a thin layer of hardened fat on the surface which should be removed.

NOTE: *This stock is significantly different from the real thing in that it contains no gelatin. Ed.*

Fond ou fumet de poisson I
FISH STOCK

To make about 1 quart of stock:

2   pounds of heads and bones of fresh white fish
      (*see Note*), evenly broken up
2   tablespoons of butter
2   tablespoons of peanut oil
1   large onion, peeled and thinly sliced
4   medium-size fresh mushrooms, stems trimmed, rinsed,
      and thinly sliced
1   shallot, peeled and minced
⅜   cup of dry white wine
5   cups of cold water, or to cover well
Bouquet garni, including plenty of fresh parsley stems

NOTE: *The French recipe calls for the bones and heads of specific fish, such as Dover sole in particular for its superior flavor, turbot, brill* (barbue), *and whiting* (merlan). *However, what really matters is that the fish be fresh and their flesh white and that you not use the trimmings of oily fish such as salmon, mackerel, bluefish, etc. Flounder or lemon sole will do for sole, halibut for turbot, grey sole for brill* (*which is rare in our waters*), *but the freshest local white fish by any name are what you want. Ed.*

Unless the fish bones and heads are absolutely fresh, soak them for 15 minutes in cold water, then drain before putting them in the soup kettle.

In the kettle, gently heat the butter and oil, add the vegetables and fish bones and heads, and cook all together over low heat for 5 minutes without letting them color. Add the white wine and boil for 15 minutes to evaporate the alcohol. Add the cold water and *bouquet garni,* and simmer slowly, partially covered, for 20 minutes. During this time, skim off periodically the scum that rises to the surface.

Strain the fish stock—there should be about 1 quart—through a fine-mesh strainer into the container in which it will be stored, pressing down lightly on the bones and vegetables in the strainer with a ladle or spoon. Let cool, then store, covered, in the refrigerator.

Fumet de poisson is used in recipes for poaching fish in a small amount of liquid (*mouillage court*) and for braising fish. It is used for many other preparations as well.

10

Glace de poisson

To make a concentrated stock, or *glace de poisson,* proceed as for making *glace de viande.* Simmer the strained stock over very low heat, again skimming carefully and often. The *glace* is finished when it has simmered down to about ⅜ cup of syrupy, shining glaze. Store in the refrigerator in a small screw-top jar.

Glace de poisson, like *glace de viande,* is added to sauces in small quantities to heighten their flavor.

11

Fond ou fumet de poisson II
RICH FISH STOCK

To make about 3½ cups of stock:

1 tablespoon of olive oil
1 large carrot, scraped and cut into ½-inch dice
1 large onion, peeled and cut into ½-inch dice
¼ pound of fresh mushrooms, stems trimmed, washed, and coarsely chopped
Bones of 6 fresh flounder or lemon sole, broken up
1 calf's foot, cut into 8 pieces (*see Note on page 36*)
Bouquet garni with plenty of fresh parsley stems and 5 peppercorns and 1 clove
3 quarts of cold water, or to cover well
3 cubes of Knorr-Swiss instant chicken bouillon (*see Note on page 37*)

Heat the olive oil in a medium-size kettle, add the carrot, onion, and mushrooms, and lightly brown the vegetables in the hot oil. Then add all the remaining ingredients.

Simmer the stock, partially covered, over low heat for 2½ hours. During this time skim off periodically the scum and fat that rise to the surface. Then strain the stock—there should be about 3½ cups—through a fine-mesh strainer into the container in which it will be stored.

Let cool, then store, covered, in the refrigerator. Later, remove any more fat that may harden on the surface.

Fish stock made this way is extraordinarily rich and flavorful. Before using it, you may extend it with 1 cup of water if you wish.

12

Fumet de poisson III
SHORTCUT FISH STOCK

To make 1 pint:
- 1 teaspoon of olive oil
- 1 small carrot, scraped and finely diced
- 2 shallots, peeled and minced
- ¼ cup of dry white wine
- Two 8-ounce bottles of clam juice
- 1 cup of water
- 2 fresh mushrooms, stems trimmed, rinsed, and sliced, or 1 small dried *shiitake* mushroom (*see page 298*), soaked and cut in strips
- *Bouquet garni,* including 1 clove and 4 peppercorns

In a saucepan, heat the olive oil, add the carrot and shallots, and cook over medium heat, stirring often, until the vegetables begin to color. Add the white wine and simmer for several minutes to evaporate the alcohol. Then add all the remaining ingredients, bring to a boil, and simmer, partially covered, for 20 minutes.

NOTE: *This stock is significantly different from the real thing in that it contains no gelatin. Ed.*

The Principles of the Liaisons of Sauces

NOTE: *In this summary, as in the previous chapter, classic processes are described that often cannot be used in* cuisine minceur. *They are explained in order to show the theory and some of the practice that continue to apply in* cuisine minceur *and what new methods must replace some of the old. Ed.*

It is much easier to make successful sauces if you understand how they work and why. The objective is to bind and enrich a light stock or liquid to make a thickened sauce. Classically, this is done in the following ways:

BINDING WITH FLOUR: This is being done less and less today. Nevertheless, handled with finesse, it could be said that this is better for you than the enrichment of sauces with outlandish quantities of butter and reduced cream. However, my personal views about sauces lead me not to make much use of either of these methods even in *cuisine gourmande* and very rarely in *cuisine minceur*.

Cooked *liaisons* with flour: *Les roux*
These are among the several ways of binding a liquid through the action of starch in flour. Whether the *roux* is to be brown, light-brown, or white, it is made with equal amounts, *by weight*, of flour and butter —though you can choose to use half the amount of butter and achieve a less rich sauce.

The flour may be wheat, corn, rice, barley, or potato flour. The liquid may be milk, chicken, veal, or beef broth or stock, fish *fumet* or stock, red or white wine, etc.

A standard example, to make a *roux blanc* for 1 quart of sauce:

    5 tablespoons of butter (2½ ounces)
    ½ cup of white wheat flour (2½ ounces)
    1 quart of liquid

The process, well known to all, is to melt the butter, add the flour, and stir very briskly with a whisk until, thanks to the elasticity of the gluten in the flour, you get a smooth, light paste which you then simmer very gently for 5 or 10 minutes. The mixture is not allowed to color at all.

The *roux* is allowed to cool a little. The liquid, boiling hot, is poured over the *roux* and beaten with the whisk to eliminate all lumps. The mixture is brought back to a boil and simmered for 20 minutes. Heavy at first, the sauce will become lighter as it cooks.

Traditional uses for *roux blanc* are for *sauce béchamel* and for chicken and fish *velouté* sauces.

For a *roux blond,* the butter and flour are allowed to color together lightly. For a *roux brun,* they are allowed to brown. They must be stirred often with the whisk. The remainder of the process is the same.

An improvement can be made in the *roux brun* by first spreading the flour on a baking sheet and letting it brown lightly in the oven (*farine torréfiée*). The butter then will not have to cook as long for the *roux* to achieve its color.

Similar in spirit to the *roux* is the technique of dusting with flour (or browned flour) the pieces of meat that are sautéed and browned in fat before liquid is added to make *ragoûts,* stews, *estouffades* (very slowly cooked stews), and brown fricassees.

Uncooked *liaisons* with flour: *Liaisons à crue et à froid*

With potato flour: When a sauce seems too thin, it can be bound with a mixture of potato flour dissolved in cold water or white wine. Pour the mixture gradually into the boiling sauce, beating rapidly with a whisk.

With *beurre manié* or *crème maniée:* Again for a sauce that seems too thin, cream together either butter or *crème fraîche* with flour (which amounts to the same thing as an uncooked *roux*) in the proportion of 1 part flour to 2 parts butter or cream. Beat the mixture bit by bit into the simmering sauce with a whisk until you achieve the consistency you want. The sauce starts to thicken almost immediately.

BINDING WITH EGG YOLKS: The yolks are first beaten with a whisk (cream may then be added) and beaten into a cupful of the hot liquid to be thickened into a sauce. This mixture is then stirred into the saucepan of hot liquid. Continue heating the sauce, still whisking, but of course do not attempt to boil it to make it thicken further. Above 160° F., the yolks will begin to harden and the sauce will curdle.

Traditional uses for *liaisons* with egg yolks are in *velouté* soups, *sauce poulette,* *blanquettes,* etc.

Cuisine minceur liaison with egg yolks:
Le sabayon léger

Beat together with a whisk egg yolks and cold water in the proportion of 4 egg yolks to ⅜ cup of water (or 2 yolks to 3 tablespoons of water). As air is beaten into the mixture, it takes on considerable added volume. When it has foamed up as much as it will, whisk it rapidly, off the heat, into the hot soup or sauce you want to thicken. The egg yolks, in suspension with the water, "set" when they come in contact with the hot liquid and give it added volume and an effect of great lightness.

This is the principle of **Sabayon de saint-pierre (94)**.

BINDING WITH THE BLOOD OF THE MEAT: This is done with the blood of pork and game, and also of fish and lamprey eel, and with lobster coral and tomalley. The principle is the same as in the standard *liaison* with egg yolk, with the blood or coral and tomalley (all sometimes mixed with *crème fraîche*) replacing the yolks. The sauce is not allowed to boil.

Traditional uses are in *coq au vin, civets* of game and fish, *matelotes* (freshwater fish stews), and lobster *à l'américaine*.

BINDING WITH FAT: This includes butter, cream, and *foie gras*.

Liaison with butter or cream: *Liaison au beurre ou à la crème fraîche*

The expression is *monter une sauce au beurre,* or "lift a sauce with butter." The aim is not only to thicken but especially to enrich the sauce. The method is, over very low heat, to swirl one by one small pieces of cold butter into the hot sauce by gently rotating the bottom of the pan over the heat.

One may also boil the sauce over brisk heat after adding butter. The sauce is then more shiny, less creamy.

To thicken a sauce with cream, simply bring sauce

and cream to a boil together and simmer until the sauce is as reduced as you want it.

Liaison au foie gras
Similar to a *liaison* with butter. In an electric blender, purée together a mixture of 2 parts *foie gras* and 1 part *crème fraîche*. Off the heat, beat the *foie gras* mixture into the hot sauce with a whisk.

BINDING BY EMULSION: This also includes the use of fat. *Liaison* by emulsion is the successful marriage of two ingredients that do not mix of their own accord, such as water and oil, cream, or butter, for which a third ingredient such as egg yolk or mustard serves as matchmaker or catalyst to make the union possible.

The best-known cold emulsified sauce is mayonnaise. The famous sauces emulsified over heat are *sauce béarnaise* and hollandaise and their derivatives, and also *beurre blanc*. Many cooks find these sauces capricious to make. The classic recipes, of course, do not apply in *cuisine minceur*, but the techniques of the originals are described in the section on great basic sauces that follows to make clear the derivation of the methods for the *minceur* versions.

BINDING WITH VEGETABLE PURÉES: A valuable procedure in *cuisine minceur*. The *liaison* is made with a precise amount of very finely puréed cooked vegetables (easily done in an electric blender). Depending on the recipe, the vegetables may either be cooked with the meat or fish for which they will later bind the sauce, or they may be cooked separately. These *purées de liaison* have a high vitamin content and the vitamins are all the more easily absorbed because the cellulose in the vegetables is broken down in the puréeing process.

The subtle and flavorful vegetable mixtures of which these *liaisons* are composed are based on aromatic harmonies that are very new. **They are one of the fundamental principles of my** *cuisine minceur* which you will find applied in a great many of my recipes.

It is also possible to create other original harmonies with judicious combinations of fruits and vegetables.

BINDING WITH YOGURT AND FROMAGE BLANC (173): The *fromage blanc* has zero or almost zero fat content. You will see later that this type of *liaison* is also one of the techniques that makes *cuisine minceur* possible. Neither yogurt nor *fromage blanc* can be used to excess, however. Yogurt imparts too distinct an acid taste of its own. *Fromage blanc* of appropriately low fat content gives a slight impression of dryness to the texture of a sauce, though this can be gotten around to some extent.

Six Classic Sauces

Here are recipes dear from time immemorial to the cooking of France—a choice selection that offers a six-pointed star, an architectural hexagon, a half-dozen culinary spotlights to illuminate the traditions of our cuisine. Mayonnaise, *béarnaise*, hollandaise, *beurre blanc, sauce américaine, sauce périgueux*—all these are well-known to Americans, and their original forms illustrate the techniques and appreciation of ingredients with which their *minceur* adaptations can be made.

13

Sauce mayonnaise

This sauce is not to be used in *cuisine minceur,* but the technique is fundamental and applies as well to **sauce mayonnaise minceur** I (32) and II (33). *To make about 1 cup:*

1 egg yolk
1 teaspoon of light-colored mustard (Dijon)
¼ teaspoon of salt
A grinding of white pepper, or a pinch of cayenne
¾ cup of oil (peanut, olive, or other oil, as you prefer)
A few drops of wine vinegar, or
    lemon juice if you are using olive oil

In a bowl and with a whisk, beat together the egg yolk, mustard, salt, and pepper. Then, drop by drop and then in a very thin stream, slowly add the oil, beating constantly as you pour. As the mixture thickens, add bit by bit either the vinegar or the lemon juice to thin out the sauce a little. When all the oil has been added, adjust the seasoning if necessary.

NOTE: The egg yolk and oil should both be at room temperature.

It is important to add the oil very slowly.

If the mayonnaise curdles: In another bowl, put a small spoonful of mustard and bit by bit whisk the curdled sauce into it.

Mayonnaise should be stored in a cool place, but preferably not in the refrigerator. Some oils (such as olive oil) will harden under refrigeration and the sauce will separate.

NOTE: *To make this mayonnaise in an electric blender, put into the container the egg yolk, mustard, 2 teaspoons of lemon juice, salt, pepper, and 3 tablespoons of the oil. Cover the container, turn on the blender at low speed, and almost right away lift off the cover and pour in the remaining oil in quite a rapid, steady stream. Allow 12 to 15 seconds to pour it in and for the last of it to be absorbed, and immediately turn off the blender. Taste for seasoning. Ed.*

14

Sauce béarnaise

This sauce and its variations are not to be used in *cuisine minceur* any more than is the preceding mayonnaise. But again, the technique is fundamental and applies to the two *minceur* versions, **sauce béarnaise Eugénie I** (38) and **II** (39). In *cuisine gourmande,* there are three ways to make a *béarnaise*— with clarified butter; with butter at room temperature (which I prefer because the fresh flavor of the milk solids in the butter is retained); and with either *crème fraîche* or sweet heavy cream (*crème fleurette*). Sweet cream makes a marvelously light *béarnaise*.

The usual version with butter at room temperature will serve to demonstrate the principle you need to understand in order to proceed with the *minceur* recipes.

To serve eight:

AROMATIC MIXTURE FOR REDUCTION:

    7 tablespoons of red-wine vinegar
    6 tablespoons of finely minced shallot
    1 teaspoon of crushed peppercorns
       (*poivre mignonnette*)
    2 tablespoons of minced fresh tarragon (*see Note*)
    1 teaspoon of minced fresh chervil or parsley (*optional*)
    A pinch of salt

5 egg yolks
10 ounces (2½ sticks) of unsalted butter, at room
    temperature and cut in pieces
More minced fresh tarragon and chervil or parsley
    (*optional*)

UTENSILS:

Small enameled or stainless heavy-bottomed saucepan
Bowls for separating eggs
Whisk
Saucepan of warm, not boiling water (*bain marie*)
Fine-mesh strainer

NOTE: When fresh tarragon is not in season, use 4
teaspoons of minced tarragon preserved in vinegar or
2 scant teaspoons of dried tarragon.

In the heavy-bottomed saucepan combine the vinegar, shallot, pepper, tarragon, chervil, and pinch of
salt. Simmer over medium heat, uncovered, for about
5 minutes, or until the liquid is reduced by about three
quarters; you should have a soft, juicy, but not liquid
"marmalade" left. Allow this to cool; in the meantime
separate the eggs, and lightly whisk the yolks.

Off the heat and with the whisk, beat the egg yolks
into the vinegar-shallot reduction. Put the saucepan
back over low heat, and heat, whisking constantly,
until the mixture thickens and becomes creamy. It
must not heat past lukewarm (test with your finger),
and it is thick enough when the movement of the whisk
exposes streaks of the bottom of the pan.

Now, still whisking, add the butter bit by bit; the
sauce is ready when the last piece of butter has been
absorbed and the whole is thickened but not heavy.
Set aside over warm water; beware of too hot water
in the *bain marie*.

The sauce may be served as is, or it may be strained
through a fine-mesh strainer, in which case you then
add a little more chopped fresh tarragon and chervil.

Note: The essential point in making a *béarnaise* is the whisking, which equalizes the temperature of the egg yolks as they coagulate and also beats air into the sauce to lighten it.

Some things may go wrong:

The egg yolks become too thick. The heat is too high; lower it and add a few drops of cold water.

The egg yolks foam but do not thicken. The heat is too low.

In the end, the sauce curdles. This can happen if it has cooled too much or if it has gotten too hot. If it is too cold, put a little hot water in a bowl and gradually whisk the sauce into it. If it is too hot, do the same thing with a little cold water in the bowl. This will rescue the sauce though it will not regain the lightness it should have had.

Note: *In making all emulsified sauces over heat, there is constant manipulation of the heat so that the sauces will not curdle or separate. The usual dodge of the amateur cook is to make the sauces over hot water; this is convenient, and it works, but it takes much longer than whisking the sauces over direct heat.*

Over direct heat, the tendency is to fiddle constantly with the control knob of the stove to control the heat, which is a nuisance and does not work very well. What chefs and experienced cooks know instinctively (and therefore often neglect to mention in their recipes) is that you can leave the heat at a moderate, or even surprisingly high, level and control the temperature of the sauce as you whisk it merely by holding the saucepan up away from the heat to lower the temperature, or by bringing the pan down closer to the stove to raise the temperature. This is a two-fisted, somewhat athletic operation, but more efficient than the less courageous methods. Exactly the same thing is done to make the creamy scrambled eggs for **Oeuf poule au caviar** *(54). Ed.*

15
Sauce hollandaise

A hollandaise is merely a *béarnaise* in which the vinegar-shallot reduction is replaced by cold water (1 teaspoon for each egg yolk), with lemon juice added at the end. Otherwise, the procedure is identical.

SAUCE MOUSSELINE:

A *mousseline* sauce is a hollandaise to which whipped sweet cream is added at the last.

16

Beurre blanc I
FOAMY BUTTER SAUCE

This is a cousin of the other emulsified sauces. The action of the whisk (or of its modern counterpart, the blender) in making emulsified sauces is—because of the way in which it homogenizes the ingredients—so fundamental that even the principal catalyst of the *liaison*, the egg yolk, may be dispensed with. This is what happens in traditional *beurre blanc* as made below and in **sauce beurre blanc minceur (40).**

To serve four or six:

   ¼ cup of dry white wine or water
   ¼ cup of white-wine vinegar
   2 tablespoons of finely minced shallot
   ½ pound (2 sticks) of cold unsalted butter, cut into 16 or more pieces; the butter must come straight from the refrigerator
   Salt and pepper

UTENSILS:

   Small enameled or stainless heavy-bottomed saucepan
   Small whisk

In the saucepan combine the water, vinegar, and shallot, and simmer over medium heat, uncovered, until the mixture has become a soft, juicy "marmalade." Allow this to cool to lukewarm.

Put the saucepan back over very low heat and whisk in the pieces of cold butter one at a time, adding each one just as the previous piece has about been absorbed. The mixture will become creamy. As you add more pieces of cold butter, you will find that you must whisk faster and that you must raise the heat a little to maintain the lukewarm temperature of the sauce. Add salt and pepper to taste before serving.

The *beurre blanc* may be strained through a fine-mesh strainer to remove the minced shallot, but personally I leave the shallot in to preserve the rustic authenticity of this sauce.

NOTE: *To hold the sauce briefly, put the saucepan in a pan of lukewarm, not hot, water.* Beurre blanc *will congeal if it is not given some warmth, but it will turn oily over hot water. Ed.*

17

Beurre blanc II
FOAMY BUTTER SAUCE

This is another method for the same *beurre blanc* which demonstrates that in addition to the action of the whisk, there is a spontaneous chemical reaction between the acid in the reduction and the butter, which also makes the butter foam.

The ingredients are the same as in the previous recipe. Instead of reducing the wine or water, vinegar, and shallot mixture to the usual "marmalade," reduce the liquid by about two thirds, or to just under 3 tablespoons. *(To see in advance how this will look, put 3 tablespoons of water in the saucepan before you make the sauce; the whole bottom of the pan should be covered with a shallow puddle. Ed.)*

Then: Have the reduced liquid boiling briskly over direct heat. Put the 2 sticks (½ pound) of cold butter in the pan—whole, not cut up. The butter will melt, of course, and as it does, the bubbling liquid will absorb it and thicken it simultaneously. All this must happen fast, so that the cold butter does not heat more than is necessary just to melt it.

To lighten the sauce, add at the last minute 4 tablespoons of cold water and whisk very rapidly. The *beurre blanc* will foam up still more.

NOTE: *Both these recipes will work with American butter, but they do take practice and, no matter what, you may still not achieve the thick creaminess you may remember from having had* beurre blanc *in France. There is no doubt that our commercial butter simply is not the same as the French (and some American butters will work better than others). Michel Guérard recommends a special, lightly salted butter from Brittany,* beurre demi-sel breton, *which has a particularly good flavor for making* beurre blanc.

You will, of course, use neither of the preceding recipes in cuisine minceur, *but the* sauce beurre blanc minceur *(40) begins with the same principle and it is delicious .Ed.*

18

Sauce américaine
LOBSTER SAUCE AMÉRICAINE

A spirited sauce with the perfume of the sea. *To make 1½ to 2 cups:*

    1 live lobster, about 2 pounds, cut up

MIREPOIX:
    1 tablespoon of olive oil
    1 tablespoon of peanut oil
    1 tablespoon of cold butter
    1 carrot, scraped and cut into ¼-inch dice

½ medium-size onion, peeled and cut into ¼-inch dice
2 shallots, peeled and minced
1 clove of garlic, unpeeled, crushed
Bouquet garni, including a sprig of tarragon

The cut-up lobster
Salt and pepper
3 tablespoons of armagnac or cognac
The *mirepoix*, above
3 ripe tomatoes, peeled, seeded, and diced
1 tablespoon of tomato paste
More salt and pepper
A pinch of cayenne
1 cup of dry white wine
1 cup of fish stock (9) (11) or water

LIAISON:

3 tablespoons of butter
The lobster tomalley and coral
½ teaspoon flour (*optional*)

UTENSILS:

Strong, rigid knife to cut up the lobster
2 small bowls
Sautoir, or large, straight-sided, not very deep saucepan,
     with a lid
Perforated spoon or skimmer
Heavy-bottomed saucepan
Whisk

The lobster must be cut up live. Whether you do this
yourself or have it done for you at the fish market,
it should be cut up as follows:

First cut off the tail at the point where it joins the
body, then cut off the claws. Crack the claws to make
it easier to remove the meat later. Cut the tail, crosswise, into several thick slices. Split the body lengthwise (do not remove the small claws), and remove
and discard the gritty sac at the back of the head.
With a spoon, scoop out and save in a small bowl all
the greenish tomalley and black coral.

To make the *mirepoix*, heat the oil and butter in
the *sautoir*, add the carrot, onion, shallots, garlic, and

bouquet garni. Cook the vegetables gently until they begin to soften but do not let them brown. With the perforated spoon, transfer them to a small bowl, draining them in the spoon to leave as much of the fat as possible in the pan.

Lightly salt and pepper the pieces of lobster, put them all in the *sautoir,* and heat, turning them often, until the shells turn red. Add the armagnac or cognac and cover the pan. The brandy should boil until it is reduced by three quarters, or almost completely evaporated, and has given over all of its perfume to the lobster.

Do not flame the brandy! In my opinion flaming is useless and will probably scorch the small claws, giving the sauce a disagreeable bitter taste.

Cover the lobster with the reserved vegetable *mirepoix* and the diced tomatoes. Add the tomato paste and season with salt, pepper, and the pinch of cayenne. Add the white wine and fish stock or water, and simmer, covered, over brisk heat for 10 minutes. Then remove the pieces of lobster, and simmer the sauce, uncovered, until it has reduced to a good consistency, or by about one third.

Strain the sauce through a fine-mesh strainer into the heavy-bottomed saucepan. With a fork, mash together to a smooth paste the ingredients of the *liaison*—butter, tomalley, coral, and flour. *(This paste may be made in the electric blender; augment the mixture with just enough of the sauce to make about ½ cup. Ed.)* With the whisk, beat this mixture energetically into the sauce, let the sauce boil for another 2 minutes, then pour it into a container for storage. Stir well before using. Shell the lobster meat and reserve it for another use, such as a lobster salad.

NOTE: You will see later that this sauce is an important resource in *cuisine minceur.* Like the three great stocks, it should be made ahead and refrigerated or frozen. It may also be "sterilized" like glace de viande (3).

Made with lobster, this sauce can be expensive. You can replace the regal lobster with the best fresh crab available in your area, adding also some bones of fresh sole or flounder. (In France, one would also add the heads of *langoustines* and *écrevisses*.) Naturally, this is only a makeshift version of the sauce and the result will not be as good.

NOTE: *Even though* sauce américaine *may be stored frozen, it is worthwhile to think ahead when you decide to make it and consider the use you will make of the amount the recipe yields. Store it in a screw-top preserving jar with cup measures indicated on the glass. These are the recipes in which it is used. Ed.*

Sauce homardière I (36)—	
Cold Lobster Sauce	¼ cup
Sauce homardière II (49)—	
Hot Lobster Sauce	½ cup
Gâteau de foies blonds de volailles (67)—	
Baked Mousse of Chicken Livers	⅜ cup
Homard rôti au four (86)—Baked Lobster	⅝ cup
Gâteau de homard aux truffes (87)—	
Steamed Lobster Cakes with Truffles	¾ cup
Court-bouillon de tous les poissons (97)—	
Poached Mixed Fish and Shellfish	¼ cup
Poulet en soupière aux écrevisses (117)—	
Poached Chicken in Tureens with Crayfish	½ cup

19
Sauce périgueux
TRUFFLE SAUCE

A sauce with the perfume of forest soil and humus. *To serve eight, or to make about 2 cups of sauce:*

1 cup of port
½ cup of armagnac or cognac
One 1¾- to 2-ounce can of Périgord truffles
    (*see page 299*)
The juice from the can of truffles
2 cups of demi-glace (2), well skimmed
Salt and pepper
3 tablespoons of cold butter (*optional*)

Heat a small saucepan, pour the port and armagnac into it, and boil until three-quarters of the liquid has evaporated. It should be reduced to about ⅜ cup. Meanwhile, drain the can of truffles, reserve the juice, and mince the truffles.

Add to the saucepan the minced truffles, the truffle juice, and the *demi-glace*. Season to taste with salt and pepper, and simmer over low heat for 15 minutes.

If the sauce is to be used as is, just before serving cut the butter into pieces and swirl them one at time into the hot sauce by rotating the bottom of the pan over the heat.

NOTE: In *cuisine minceur,* the same sauce is served without the butter, or it may sometimes be replaced by the following red-wine sauce:

20

Sauce au vin rouge de bordeaux
RED BORDEAUX SAUCE

To make about 2 cups of sauce:

   1½ cups of red bordeaux wine
   2 shallots, peeled and minced
   1 tablespoon of tomato paste
   2 cups of **demi-glace** (2)
   Salt and pepper

The procedure is the same as for *sauce périgeux,* except that the shallots are added to the wine while it reduces to ⅜ cup. Then add the tomato paste and the *demi-glace,* season to taste with salt and pepper, and simmer the sauce over low heat for 15 minutes.

NOTE: Both *sauce périgueux* and red bordeaux sauce are excellent for grilled *tournedos* or roast fillet of beef. *Sauce périgueux* is also used in small quantities as a component of other sauces.

To correct sauces that have gone wrong: For a sauce that is based on a flavorful stock but still seems somewhat flat, add an ingredient with an incisive taste that will wake it up, such as a squeeze of lemon juice or a drop of vinegar.

For a sauce that has acquired a slightly bitter or even acid taste, add a pinch of sugar or a dash of a fortified wine such as port, with, if necessary, a little cream.

The sauce lacks *charpente* and color. (*Charpente is a marvelous word for this, meaning literally the timber that is the framework of a building. What the metaphor is getting at is that you have not made a well-constructed stock—or some other reduced essence —with which to build your sauce. Ed.*) Add a little glace de viande (3) or glace de poisson (10), depending on the dish, a grinding of pepper, and sometimes a drop or two of armagnac or cognac.

Remember that it is often preferable when using wine in sauces to reduce them, by boiling, so as to diminish their volume and to evaporate their alcoholic content. For white wine, reduction lessens its acidity. For red wine, reduction makes its perfume stronger.

The same thing applies to brandies. However, fortified wines such as sherry or port, whose perfume is easily destroyed, usually do their work best unheated and added at the last minute.

Remember also for sauces based on a *roux* that any acid ingredient such as lemon juice must be added after the cooking and *liaison* of the sauce—in, for instance, a *blanquette* or *sauce ivoire*. Put in at the beginning, it will interfere with the action of the *liaison* and will thin out the sauce as well.

In emulsified sauces, on the contrary, lemon juice activates the coagulation of the egg yolks.

If the sauce contains milk, vegetables cannot be cooked in it because their acid content will curdle the milk. Exceptions are cabbage and cauliflower.

Part Two

Les soupes
SOUPS

21
Bouillon de légumes d'Eugénie
VEGETABLE BOUILLON

To serve four:

1 medium-size carrot, scraped
3 medium-size fresh mushrooms, stems trimmed, rinsed
½ leek, white part only, well washed
5-inch piece of celery stalk, or
      a piece of celery root half the size of the carrot
⅜ cup of drained, raw **diced fresh tomatoes** (130)
1 teaspoon of minced fresh parsley
1 teaspoon of minced fresh chervil
A pinch of minced fresh tarragon
5 cups of **chicken stock** (5) (8) (*see Note*)

UTENSILS:

Vegetable grater or cutter
Saucepan, with a lid
To serve: 4 heated individual soup tureens

NOTE: The combination of vegetables and herbs in this simple soup gives it freshness of flavor. This is a good way to treat a broth made of chicken-bouillon cubes (see page 37).
Cut the vegetables into small sticks 1 inch long and less than ⅛ inch thick. For the carrot and celery root,

it is easiest to cut them into 1-inch pieces and to grate them in a Mouli grater or other mechanical cutter.

Bring the stock to a boil, add the vegetables, and simmer the soup, partially covered, for 10 to 15 minutes; the vegetables should remain a little firm. Add the diced tomato, taste for seasoning, and serve in the heated tureens, sprinkled with the fresh herbs.

22

Soupe de tomates fraîches au pistou
FRESH TOMATO SOUP WITH BASIL

Serve hot or cold. To serve four:

3 firm, ripe tomatoes
1 medium-size carrot
½ leek, white part only, well washed
1 shallot
1 clove of garlic
1 teaspoon of olive oil
A sprig of thyme
½ bay leaf
1 tablespoon of tomato paste
5 cups of **chicken stock (5) (8)**, or water
1 teaspoon of salt
A pinch of pepper
Pistou: Enough minced fresh basil ground to a paste in a small mortar with 1 teaspoon of olive oil to make 2 teaspoons of the paste (*see page 298*)

UTENSILS:

Heavy-bottomed saucepan
Electric blender
Fine-mesh strainer
Small mortar and pestle
To serve: 4 individual soup tureens, heated or chilled

Wash, core, and cut up the tomatoes. Peel and slice coarsely the carrot, leek, shallot, and garlic. In the saucepan, heat the olive oil, add the sliced vegetables, and cook gently until they give off some of their liquid. Then add the thyme and bay leaf, tomatoes, tomato paste, chicken stock or water, and salt and pepper. Simmer, partially covered, over moderate heat for 20 minutes.

Remove the thyme and bay leaf. Purée the soup in the electric blender, then strain it through the fine-mesh strainer. Make the *pistou*. Reheat the soup, pour into the individual tureens, and at the last moment add a small spoonful of the *pistou* to each serving.

This is a delicious hot soup, but it is particularly good served chilled in the summertime. Store in the refrigerator after straining. Taste for seasoning. Add the *pistou* just before serving, and decorate each tureen with a small piece of fresh basil.

23

Crème d'oseille mousseuse
CREAM OF SORREL SOUP

To serve four:

¼ pound of fresh sorrel
2 teaspoons of olive oil
2 cloves of garlic, crushed with the flat of a knife and peeled
1½ teaspoons of salt
Pepper
1 quart of chicken stock (5) (8)
2 eggs

UTENSILS:

Saucepan
Electric blender
Bowl
Whisk
To serve: 4 heated individual soup tureens

Heat the olive oil in the saucepan, add the garlic, and let it color lightly. Add the chopped sorrel and salt and pepper, and stir to wilt the sorrel, then add the stock and simmer for 15 minutes. In the electric blender, purée the soup, half at a time, for 2 minutes. Return it to the saucepan and keep it warm—not quite at a simmer.

Just before serving, in the bowl whisk the eggs well until they double in volume. Then, whisking rapidly, gradually add them to the hot—but not close to boiling—soup. Continue whisking until the egg *liaison* has set just enough to hold without further whisking and heating. The soup should be thickened but very light.

24

Soupe de grenouilles
FROGS'-LEGS SOUP

To serve four:

> 24 small fresh or frozen frogs' legs, or 12 pairs
> 3½ cups of fish stock (9) (11)
> ⅜ cup of dry white wine
> 1 shallot, peeled and minced
> A pinch of minced fresh tarragon
> 1 bunch of water cress, rinsed and all the coarse stems removed
> 1 tablespoon of **fromage blanc** (173)
> 1 tablespoon of **crème fraîche** (172)
> Salt and pepper

UTENSILS:

> 2 enameled or stainless saucepans
> Perforated skimmer
> Electric blender
> Small whisk
> *To serve:* 4 heated individual soup tureens

In one saucepan, bring the fish stock to a boil. Add the frogs' legs, and remove them with the skimmer as soon as the liquid returns to a boil. (*If you can get only large frogs' legs, simply use fewer of them. Cook them only a little longer; do not overcook. Ed.*) Set them aside on a plate.

In the other saucepan, simmer together, uncovered, the white wine, shallot, and tarragon until the wine is reduced by more than half and the alcohol is entirely evaporated. Add the hot stock and the water cress (reserving a few perfect leaves for decoration), and simmer the soup for 7 minutes; in this short cooking time, the water cress will remain green. Purée the soup in the electric blender, and keep it hot.

By hand—you do not need a knife—pull all the meat of the frogs' legs off the bones. Apportion the meat among the 4 heated tureens.

Whisk together in a small bowl the *fromage blanc* and *crème fraîche*, whisk this mixture into the soup, taste for seasoning, and do not allow it to boil again. Pour the hot soup into the tureens, and float the reserved water-cress leaves on top like small lily pads.

25

Soupe à la grive de vigne
SONG-THRUSH SOUP

NOTE: *It is highly unlikely that we would find wild song thrush for sale in any American market—and wild-life conservationists would be up in arms if we could. Furthermore, the thrush in question must be a particular one that feeds on grapes, hence the name* grive de vigne, *or vine thrush. However, this recipe is interesting for a reason other than the exotic use of thrush, and that is its delicate garnishing and its flavoring with truffles. This is something you can do with any well-made poultry broth, which could be made with quail or simply with chicken. Ed.*

To serve four:

4 thrush
1 teaspoon of olive oil
1 carrot, scraped and coarsely chopped
1 onion, peeled and coarsely chopped
A *bouquet garni*, including 4 juniper berries if the broth
    is made with thrush or another game bird
2 quarts of cold water

GARNITURE:

¾ ounce of fresh *mousserons* (agaric mushrooms), or
    ¾ ounce of canned *nameko* mushrooms, drained
    (*see page 298*)
1 teaspoon of olive oil
1 medium carrot, scraped
1 small onion, peeled
3-inch piece of celery
4 or 5 fresh mushrooms, stems trimmed, rinsed
    All four of these *mirepoix* vegetables cut into
    ⅛-inch dice or smaller
Salt and pepper
A pinch of thyme flowers or dried thyme
1 teaspoon of juice from a can of truffles (*optional*)
2 tablespoons of **truffle sauce** (19) (*optional*)
The 8 raw breasts of the thrush (*see Note in the recipe*)
1 teaspoon of minced fresh chervil or parsley

UTENSILS:

Large saucepan for broth
Wooden spatula
Heavy-bottomed saucepan for *garniture*
Fine-mesh strainer
To serve: 4 heated individual soup tureens, with lids, or
    use circles of aluminum foil

The livers of the thrush are kept aside when the birds
are feathered and dressed. The breasts of the birds
are cut off and the 8 pieces of breast meat are set
aside for the *garniture*. The birds are then coarsely
chopped along with their livers.

The olive oil is heated in the large saucepan and the chopped birds, carrot, and onion are heated in this for 5 minutes and stirred frequently with the wooden spatula.

Then the cold water and *bouquet garni* are added and the mixture is brought to a boil. The surface is carefully skimmed, and the broth is kept at the lowest possible simmer for 1 hour and 15 minutes, until it is reduced by one half, or to about 1 quart.

However you achieve your quart of broth, the remaining instructions in the recipe apply. Ed.

While the broth is simmering, rinse the canned *nameko* mushrooms and drain.

Grease the heavy-bottomed saucepan with the teaspoon of olive oil, heat, and in it sauté the *mirepoix* of diced vegetables: Over medium heat, first put in the carrot, to cook 9 minutes; three minutes later, add the onion and celery, to cook 6 minutes; and three minutes after that, add the mushrooms, to cook 3 minutes—9 minutes' cooking time in all. Season lightly with salt and pepper and add the thyme. At this point, add the truffle juice and truffle sauce (*sauce périgueux*) if you are using them, bring the mixture to a simmer, and remove from the heat.

Strain the broth through the fine-mesh strainer and return it to its saucepan. Add the mushrooms and the *mirepoix* and truffle-sauce *garniture*, and simmer for 5 minutes. Taste for seasoning.

Just before serving, add the reserved breasts of the thrush and simmer for 1½ minutes. (NOTE: *Or add 8 small, thin slices of raw breast meat of chicken; simmer briefly, until the chicken has "set" all the way through. Do not overcook. Ed.*)

To serve, pour the soup into the heated individual tureens, sprinkle with the minced fresh chervil, and cover the tureens with their lids or with circles of aluminum foil.

26

Velouté aux champignons des bois
WILD-MUSHROOM SOUP

NOTE: *The original recipe requires dried morels, cèpes and mousserons, which are not available in America, though they are practical for this purpose in France. It is possible, delicious, and expensive to use imported canned morels and* cèpes; *for mousserons, an attractive substitute is canned Japanese* nameko *mushrooms. (See page 298).*

The following version of the recipe uses canned wild mushrooms only. Ed.

To serve six:

1 teaspoon of olive oil
1 medium-size onion, peeled and thinly sliced
1 small leek, white part only, well washed and thinly sliced
1 clove of garlic, peeled and cut in half
A scant ¼ pound of fresh mushrooms, stems trimmed, rinsed
1¾ ounces of canned morels
2½ ounces of canned *cèpes*
3¼ ounces of *mousserons,* or a 7-ounce can of *nameko* mushrooms, in all (1¾ ounces for the *velouté,* 1½ ounces for the *garniture*)
2 tomatoes, peeled, seeded, and cut in pieces

5 cups of chicken stock (5) (8)
Salt and pepper

Minced parsley
1 tablespoon of drained, raw diced fresh tomatoes (130)

UTENSILS:

Heavy-bottomed saucepan, with a lid
Electric blender
To serve: 4 heated individual soup tureens

Heat the olive oil in the saucepan, and in it first gently sauté the onion, leek, garlic, and fresh mushrooms.

Add the drained canned morels, *cèpes*, and 1¾ ounces of *nameko;* sauté all briefly together, and then add the tomatoes. Simmer, uncovered, for 5 minutes, stirring occasionally.

Now add the stock, season with salt and pepper, and simmer the soup, partially covered, for 30 minutes. Then purée it, a portion at a time, in the electric blender until the mushrooms are finely ground. Return this *velouté* to the saucepan, taste for seasoning, and keep it hot. Meanwhile, heat the remaining 1½ ounces of *nameko* in a little additional stock.

To serve, ladle the *velouté* into the heated tureens, and add the *garniture* of the whole *nameko,* minced parsley, and diced tomato.

27

Soupe de truffes
TRUFFLE SOUP

This is the *minceur* version of the celebrated truffle soup created by Paul Bocuse and made originally with fresh truffles. *To serve four:*

2-ounce piece of raw veal sweetbread
1½-ounce piece of raw chicken breast
Chicken stock (5) for poaching these

MIREPOIX:

½ teaspoon of olive oil
5 tablespoons of finely minced carrot
2 tablespoons of finely minced celery
6 tablespoons of finely minced fresh mushrooms
Salt and pepper
A pinch of thyme flowers or of minced fresh thyme leaves

1¾ ounces of truffles, thinly sliced (*see page 299*)
2 tablespoons of **truffle sauce (19)** (*optional*)
2 teaspoons of juice from the can of truffles
3 cups of hot **chicken stock (5)**

Saucepan

Small heavy-bottomed saucepan, with a lid

To bake and serve: 4 heated individual soup tureens, 4 circles of aluminum foil, kitchen string

SWEETBREAD AND CHICKEN:

Ideally, both the piece of veal sweetbread and of chicken breast should be braised, together, as in the recipe for **Ragoût fin d'Eugénie** (113). If you make the *ragoût*, think ahead, include the piece of chicken breast in the braising, and save out a 2-ounce piece of the sweetbread. However, to save time and to make this soup independently, simply poach the pieces of sweetbread and chicken breast in a little chicken stock for 10 minutes. Cut them both into ¼-inch dice.

MIREPOIX:

Coat the inside of the small saucepan with the olive oil, heat it, and add the diced carrot to cook, over moderate heat, covered, for 9 minutes; three minutes later add the diced celery, to cook for 6 minutes; three minutes later, add the mushrooms, to cook for 3 minutes—9 minutes' cooking time in all, covered throughout. The purpose is to have the vegetables give off their liquid, not to brown them. Add the salt and pepper and the thyme.

THE SOUP:

Preheat the oven to 450°–475° F.

Into each tureen, put a spoonful of the *mirepoix* of vegetables, 1½ teaspoons of the truffle sauce (*sauce périgueux*), ½ teaspoon of the truffle juice, and portions of the diced sweetbread, diced chicken, and sliced truffle. Add ¾ cup of the hot chicken stock to each tureen.

Cover the tureens with the circles of aluminum foil and tie these in place with string, as you would cover a jelly jar. Bake the tureens in the preheated oven for 10 minutes.

Let the privileged people with whom you share this *potage* discover for themselves the extraordinary aroma that emanates from it when they remove the foil from the tureen.

Les sauces
SAUCES

Cold Sauces

Sauce vinaigrette minceur I
FRENCH DRESSING

To serve four:

- 1 tablespoon of olive oil
- 5 tablespoons of chicken stock (5)
- 1 tablespoon of red-wine vinegar
- 1 tablespoon of lemon juice
- Salt and pepper

NOTE: For *vinaigrettes*, you should use real homemade stock, which has the gelatin content lacking in canned or bouillon-cube broths.

Combine the ingredients in a small bowl and mix well with a fork.

30

Sauce vinaigrette minceur II
FRENCH DRESSING WITH HERBS

To serve four:

    1 tablespoon of olive oil
    5 tablespoons of **chicken stock (5)**
    1 whole clove of garlic, peeled
    ½ teaspoon of minced fresh tarragon
    ½ teaspoon of minced fresh chervil or parsley
    2 leaves of fresh basil, minced
    1 tablespoon of sherry vinegar
    1 tablespoon of lemon juice
    Salt and pepper

Combine the olive oil, stock, garlic, and herbs in a
small bowl, and let them marinate together for 2
hours. Add the vinegar, lemon juice, and salt and
pepper, and mix well with a fork.

31

Sauce préférée
THE PREFERRED MINCEUR
SALAD DRESSING

To serve four:

    5 tablespoons of **fromage blanc (173)**
    2 tablespoons of wine vinegar
    1 tablespoon of soy sauce
    1 teaspoon of Dijon mustard
    1 teaspoon of minced fresh herbs (chervil, tarragon,
        parsley, chives)
    Salt sparingly to taste
    Pepper

Mix all the ingredients together in a bowl with a
whisk, or in an electric blender.

Sauce mayonnaise minceur I
LOW-CALORIE MAYONNAISE

This recipe makes a very light mayonnaise, which, however, should be used sparingly, as it does contain both egg yolk and oil. *To make about 1¼ cups:*

- 1 egg, separated
- 1½ teaspoons of light-colored mustard (Dijon)
- ¼ teaspoon of salt
- A grinding of white pepper, or a pinch of cayenne
- 2 tablespoons of peanut oil
- 2 tablespoons of olive oil
- 1 teaspoon of lemon juice
- 2 level tablespoons of **fromage blanc** (173)

The egg white, beaten

In a bowl and with a whisk, or with an electric beater, beat together the egg yolk, mustard, salt, and pepper. Then very slowly add the 4 tablespoons of oil, beating constantly. As the mixture thickens, add the lemon juice a few drops at a time to thin out the sauce a little. When all the oil has been added, gently stir in the *fromage blanc.*

NOTE: *The recipe may be prepared ahead to this point. Shortly before serving, beat the egg white, and fold it gently into the mayonnaise. Since you may not need the full quantity of the recipe at one time, you may fold only half the beaten white into half the quantity of mayonnaise, and save the remaining sauce to use another time with a freshly beaten white. See* **sauce mayonnaise** (13) *concerning refrigeration. Ed.*

Sauce mayonnaise minceur II
LOW-CALORIE MAYONNAISE WITH PURÉED VEGETABLES

The recipe is the same as for the previous mayonnaise except that, at the end, you add only 1 tablespoon of *fromage blanc* and you add if you have them on hand:

- 1 heaping teaspoon of **carrot purée** (137)
- 1 tablespoon of **onion purée** (146)

Fold in the beaten egg white at the very end, as before.

NOTE: *The possibilities for experimenting with vegetable purées in mayonnaise* minceur *are many. You need to remember that the purées must be cooked and that they must not contain excess liquid. Fresh herbs will blend better if they are first blanched in boiling water and minced. Ed.*

Sauce Créosat
COLD VEGETABLE SAUCE FOR GRILLED BEEF

To make 1 cup:

VEGETABLES:
- 5 tablespoons of diced cucumber
- 2 tablespoons of diced green pepper
- ⅝ cup of diced onion
- 2 tablespoons of diced tomato, drained

SEASONINGS:

1 teaspoon of olive oil
3 tablespoons of red-wine vinegar
½ teaspoon Worcestershire
½ teaspoon of Dijon mustard
1 tablespoon of minced sour gherkins (*cornichons*)
1 scant tablespoon of pickled capers
1 whole clove of garlic, peeled and split
A sprig of thyme
½ bay leaf
Salt and pepper

The vegetables should all be cut into ¼-inch dice, or smaller. Combine them in a bowl. In another bowl, blend all the seasonings together with a fork, as for a *vinaigrette*. Add this sauce to the vegetables, mix well, and store in the refrigerator in a covered container to marinate at least 3 days before using.

35

Sauce grelette
TOMATO CREAM SAUCE FOR SALAD

To serve ten:

1¼ pounds of firm ripe tomatoes
6 tablespoons of **fromage blanc** (173)
1 tablespoon of **crème fraîche** (172)
1 teaspoon of finely minced parsley
½ teaspoon of finely minced tarragon
1 tablespoon of ketchup
2 teaspoons of armagnac or cognac (*optional*)
Lemon juice
2 teaspoons of salt
White pepper

Prepare the tomatoes as for raw **diced fresh tomatoes** (130). Dice them not too coarsely, and drain. In a bowl, beat together with a whisk the *fromage blanc* and *crème fraîche*. Add the chopped herbs, ketchup, armagnac or cognac, and the lemon juice to taste, and whisk again. Then stir in the diced tomatoes, and season with the salt and a good pinch of white pepper. Store in a covered container in the refrigerator.

The sauce may be served from a bowl set in another bowl of cracked ice.

36

Sauce homardière I
COLD LOBSTER SAUCE

To make about 1½ cups:

1 recipe low-calorie mayonnaise (32)
4 tablespoons of lobster sauce américaine (18)
A spoonful of vegetables, diced, from court-bouillon (83)
½ teaspoon of minced fresh tarragon
½ teaspoon of minced fresh chervil or parsley

1 egg white, reserved from making the mayonnaise

UTENSILS:

Little saucepan
Bowl
Small whisk

In the little saucepan, over low heat, simmer the lobster *sauce américaine* until it is reduced by about half, let cool, and chill in the refrigerator.

Make the mayonnaise, but do not add the egg white. Whisk in the *sauce américaine* and the minced herbs, and refrigerate. Shortly before serving, beat the egg white and fold it gently into the *sauce homardière*. Depending on what you use this sauce with, the diced vegetables may be either sprinkled over the dish or stirred into the sauce when you add the *sauce américaine* and the herbs.

37

Sauce vierge
MINCEUR TOMATO SAUCE

To serve four:

Raw diced fresh tomatoes (130) made with 3 firm,
   ripe tomatoes
3 tablespoons of olive oil
4 level tablespoons of fromage blanc (173) (*optional*)
1 teaspoon of Dijon mustard
1 teaspoon of Worcestershire sauce
1 clove of garlic, unpeeled, crushed
2 tablespoons of minced fresh chervil
2 tablespoons of minced fresh parsley
1 tablespoon of minced fresh tarragon
8 coriander seeds, crushed in a mortar
Salt and pepper

Starting with the olive oil, mix all the following ingredients except the salt and pepper together well
with a fork, then add the diced tomatoes, and season
to taste. This sauce is not cooked—it is only heated
over hot water.

38

Sauce béarnaise Eugénie I
LOW-CALORIE BÉARNAISE SAUCE

To serve eight:

AROMATIC MIXTURE FOR REDUCTION:
4 tablespoons of red-wine vinegar
6 tablespoons of finely minced shallot
1 teaspoon of crushed peppercorns
   (*poivre mignonnette*)
1 tablespoon of minced fresh tarragon

1½ cups of raw **diced fresh tomatoes** (130), drained
1 tablespoon of **mushroom purée** (136)
1 teaspoon of minced fresh chervil or parsley
Salt to taste

LIAISON:

5 tablespoons of cold water, in all
2 egg yolks
2 tablespoons of olive oil

UTENSILS:

Two small enameled or stainless heavy-bottomed
    saucepans
Bowls for separating eggs
Whisk
Saucepan of warm, not boiling water (*bain marie*)

In the first saucepan combine the vinegar, shallot, pepper, and tarragon. Simmer over medium heat, uncovered, for about 5 minutes, or until the liquid is reduced by about three quarters; you should have a soft, juicy, but not liquid "marmalade." left. Allow this to cool and in the meantime separate the eggs and lightly whisk the yolks.

At the same time, in the second saucepan, simmer the diced raw tomatoes until all the excess liquid has evaporated.

Off the heat, add to the vinegar-shallot reduction 1 tablespoon of the cold water and, with the whisk, beat in the egg yolks. Put the saucepan back over low heat, and heat, whisking constantly, until the mixture thickens and becomes creamy. It must not heat past lukewarm (test with your finger), and it is thick enough when the movement of the whisk exposes streaks of the bottom of the pan.

Now, still whisking, add the olive oil and then, gradually, the remaining 4 tablespoons of cold water. Heat and whisk until the sauce has a good consistency, then stir in the simmered tomatoes, the mushroom purée, and the chervil. Taste for seasoning. Set the saucepan aside over warm water until you are ready to serve the sauce.

Sauce béarnaise Eugénie II
LOW-CALORIE BÉARNAISE SAUCE
WITH STOCK

To serve eight:

AROMATIC MIXTURE FOR REDUCTION:

4 tablespoons of red-wine vinegar
6 tablespoons of finely minced shallot
1 teaspoon of crushed peppercorns
   (*poivre mignonnette*)
1 tablespoon of minced fresh tarragon

HAVE READY TO FINISH THE SAUCE:

1½ cups of raw **diced fresh tomatoes** (130), drained
1 teaspoon of tomato paste
1 teaspoon of minced fresh chervil or parsley
Salt to taste

LIAISON:

1 tablespoon of cold water
2 egg yolks
2 tablespoons of olive oil
½ cup of hot **chicken stock** (5) (*see Note*)

UTENSILS:

Two small enameled or stainless heavy-bottomed
   saucepans
Bowls for separating eggs
Whisk
Saucepan of warm, not boiling water (*bain marie*)

NOTE: *For this sauce, you should use real homemade
stock, which has the gelatin content lacking in canned
or bouillon-cube broths. Ed.*

In the first saucepan combine the vinegar, shallot,
pepper, and tarragon. Simmer over medium heat, uncovered, for about 5 minutes, or until the liquid is
reduced by about three quarters; you should have a
soft, juicy, but not liquid "marmalade" left. Allow this
to cool and in the meantime separate the eggs and
lightly whisk the yolks.

At the same time, in the second saucepan, simmer the diced raw tomatoes until all the excess liquid has evaporated.

Off the heat, add to the vinegar-shallot reduction the tablespoon of cold water and, with the whisk, beat in the egg yolks. Put the saucepan back over low heat, and heat, whisking constantly, until the mixture thickens and becomes creamy. It must not heat past lukewarm (test with your finger), and it is thick enough when the movement of the whisk exposes streaks of the bottom of the pan.

Now, still whisking, add the olive oil and then, gradually, the hot chicken stock. Heat and whisk until the sauce has a good consistency, then stir in the simmered tomatoes, the tomato paste, and the chervil. Taste for seasoning. Set the saucepan aside over warm water until you are ready to serve the sauce.

40

Sauce beurre blanc minceur
LOW-CALORIE FOAMY BUTTER SAUCE

To serve four:

    ¼ cup of dry white wine
    ¼ cup of white-wine vinegar
    2 tablespoons of finely minced shallot
    4 tablespoons (½ stick) of cold butter, in one piece;
        the butter must come straight from the refrigerator
    1 teaspoon of crème fraîche (172)
    ½ cup of fromage blanc (173)
    Salt and pepper

UTENSILS:
    Small enameled or stainless heavy-bottomed saucepan
    Small whisk

In the saucepan combine the wine, vinegar, and shallot, and simmer over medium heat, uncovered, until the liquid has reduced by about two thirds, or to just under 3 tablespoons. *(To see in advance how this will look, put 3 tablespoons of water in the saucepan before you make the sauce; the whole bottom of the pan should be covered with a shallow puddle. Ed.)*

Then: Have the reduced liquid boiling briskly over direct heat. Put the piece of cold butter in the middle of the pan and add the teaspoon of *crème fraîche.* The butter will melt, of course, and as it does, the bubbling liquid will absorb it and lightly thicken it simultaneously; the cream helps this process as well. Stir only when the butter is more than half melted, and when it is all melted set the pan aside to cool to lukewarm.

Now whisk in the *fromage blanc* and taste for seasoning. *(You may reheat the sauce very gently over hot water, but not for long. Ed.)*

41

Sauce coulis de tomates fraîches
FRESH TOMATO PURÉE SAUCE

Served hot or cold. To make 1 quart:

2 pounds firm, ripe tomatoes, peeled
1 tablespoon of olive oil
3 shallots, peeled and chopped
1 clove of garlic, unpeeled, crushed
1 tablespoon of tomato paste
Bouquet garni
2¼ cups of chicken stock (5) (8)
Salt and pepper

UTENSILS:
Kettle of boiling water
Bowl of ice water
Heavy-bottomed stainless saucepan
Electric blender

To peel the tomatoes, plunge them into boiling water for 15 seconds and then plunge them into cold water so that the tomato just under the skin will not begin to cook. (*An easy way to do this is to put the tomatoes on a rack in the kitchen sink, stem ends up. Pour boiling water over them, which goes quickly down the drain. Turn the tomatoes over, pour boiling water over them again, and transfer them to the bowl of ice water. Ed.*) They are now very easy to peel. After peeling, cut the tomatoes in half crosswise, and gently squeeze them in the palm of your hand to eliminate the seeds and excess juice.

Heat the olive oil in the saucepan and in it gently cook the shallots. Add the garlic, tomatoes, tomato paste, *bouquet garni,* and chicken stock. Simmer over moderate heat for 20 minutes.

Remove the *bouquet garni,* purée the tomato sauce in the electric blender, and season it lightly to taste with salt and pepper. If the sauce is too thin, pour it back into the saucepan and simmer it again until it is reduced to a good but not heavy consistency.

42

Sauce coulis d'asperges
ASPARAGUS PURÉE SAUCE

To serve four or more:

¾ pound of fresh green or white asparagus, or
    10½-ounce can of white asparagus
½ cup of chicken stock (5) (8)
1 teaspoon of salt
A pinch of pepper
1 teaspoon of crème fraîche (172) (*optional*)

UTENSILS:

Asparagus cooker (*see page 27*)
Electric blender
Small enameled or stainless saucepan or double boiler

If you are using fresh green or white asparagus, cook them according to the instructions on page 27. Or, heat the canned asparagus in their own juice and drain them. Cut the asparagus into 1-inch pieces (discard any stringy parts that may remain at the bases), and purée them in the electric blender with the chicken stock, salt and pepper, and cream. Taste for seasoning and keep warm over hot water.

43

Sauce coulis d'artichauts
ARTICHOKE PURÉE SAUCE

To serve four or five:

3 small artichokes, or 1½ to 1¾ pounds in all
2 quarts of water
2 tablespoons of coarse salt
Juice of 1 lemon
½ cup chicken stock (5) (8)
1 teaspoon of crème fraîche (172)
Salt and pepper

UTENSILS:
Enameled or stainless kettle with a lid
Electric blender
Small enameled or stainless saucepan or double boiler

Wash the artichokes, cut off the stems, and cook the artichokes, covered, for 45 minutes in boiling salted water acidulated with the lemon juice. Put them in cold water to cool.

Remove all the leaves and scoop out the chokes. Cut the artichoke bottoms in pieces and purée them in the electric blender with the chicken stock and cream. Taste for seasoning and keep warm over hot water.

44

Sauce au persil
PARSLEY SAUCE

To serve four:

A large bunch of parsley, preferably the flat Italian
  variety
2 shallots, peeled and finely minced
1 cup of stock (*see Note*)
2 teaspoons of **mushroom purée** (136)
2 tablespoons of **fromage blanc** (173)
Lemon juice
Salt and pepper

UTENSILS:

Enameled or stainless saucepan
Strainer
Electric blender

NOTE: *To serve with meat, use* veal stock (1) (4);
to serve with seafood, use fish stock (9) (11). *Ed.*

Remove all the stems from the parsley and use only
the leaves. In the saucepan, cook together over low
heat the parsley, shallots, and stock for 15 minutes.
Strain the mixture and reserve the stock. Put the parsley and shallots in the electric blender and add the
mushroom purée, *fromage blanc,* and a squeeze of
lemon juice. Blend well, and thin the purée with some
of the stock. Taste for seasoning and keep the sauce
warm.

Sauce à la crème d'ail
GARLIC CREAM SAUCE

To serve four:

12 cloves of garlic, peeled
1½ cups of water
3 medium-sized mushrooms, stems trimmed, rinsed, and
    cut in half
½ teaspoon of salt
A pinch of nutmeg
½ cup of nonfat dry milk
1 teaspoon of glace de viande (3)
2 teaspoons of chopped parsley
Squeeze of lemon juice (*optional*)

UTENSILS:

Saucepan
Small heavy-bottomed saucepan
Electric blender

In the saucepan, blanch the garlic in unsalted boiling water three times, changing the water each time. In the heavy-bottomed saucepan, combine the 1½ cups of water and the garlic, mushrooms, salt, and nutmeg. Simmer all together, covered, over low heat for 15 minutes. Then stir in the dry milk, and simmer for another 5 minutes.

Add the *glace de viande* and parsley, and purée the sauce in the electric blender. Then add the lemon juice, taste for seasoning, and keep warm.

46

Sauce aux champignons des bois
WILD-MUSHROOM SAUCE

NOTE: *In its original form, this sauce serves as a substitute for truffle* **sauce périgueux** *(19) and is made with equal parts of dried morels,* **cèpes,** *and mousserons (agaric mushrooms). We found it impractical to attempt the original because none of these mushrooms are available dried; see page 297. The following adaptation, made with Japanese mushrooms, was very successful as a sauce in itself, but it does not serve as a substitute for truffle sauce as the original intends. Since the adaptation was a success, we searched the book for a particular dish in which it might be used. We came up with* **Poulet en soupière aux écrevisses** *(117), in which you have both* **sauce homardière,** *which is not simple to make, and live crayfish, which are not easy to obtain. Poulet en soupière made with the following sauce is merely an accident that we stumbled upon, but it seems worth suggesting because the sauce is so easy to make and the* **en soupière** *method of cooking a small bird is also so simple.*

The recipe yields 2 to 2½ cups and may be divided by one half. Ed.

To serve six:

¾ ounce of dried *shiitake* mushrooms, soaked and
   drained (*see page 298*)
2 cups of **veal stock** (1) (4)
2 tablespoons of port
1 tablespoon of **mushroom purée** (136)
1 tablespoon of **fromage blanc** (173)
½ lemon
Salt and pepper

UTENSILS:
   Saucepan
   Fine-mesh strainer
   Electric blender

Remove the stems of the soaked and drained *shiitake* mushrooms, cut the mushrooms into narrow *julienne* strips, and cut the longer strips in half. In the saucepan, simmer together the mushrooms, veal stock, and port over low heat for 10 to 15 minutes, until the liquid is somewhat reduced.

Strain the sauce into the electric blender. Add the mushroom purée and *fromage blanc,* and blend. Add lemon juice to taste, season with salt and pepper, and blend briefly again. Return the sauce to the saucepan, add the mushrooms, and reheat over low heat.

47

Sauce à la pomme
APPLE AND LEMON SAUCE

To serve four:

    3 medium-size or 2 large apples (about ¾ pound)
    2 lemons, to make ¼ cup of lemon juice and
        2½ tablespoons of diced lemon peel
    3 tablespoons of chicken stock (5) (8)
    Salt and pepper
    Powdered cinnamon (*optional*)

UTENSILS:

    Small fine-mesh strainer
    Enameled or stainless heavy-bottomed saucepan,
        with a lid
    Little saucepan
    Electric blender
    Bowl

Peel, quarter, and core the apples. (*We used 2 large Golden Delicious apples. Ed.*) Peel off the skins of the lemons in thin strips, then squeeze the lemons, strain the juice, and measure out ¼ cup. In the heavy-bottomed saucepan, cook the apples in the lemon juice, covered, for 20 minutes.

Meanwhile, cut the lemon peel into *julienne* strips as fine as pine needles, then cut these crosswise into tiny dice; cut enough to make 2½ tablespoons of dice. In the little saucepan, boil them in plain water for 7 or 8 minutes, and drain them in the fine-mesh strainer.

In the electric blender, combine the chicken stock and the cooked apples, purée the sauce, and pour it into a bowl. Add the cooked lemon peel, add salt and pepper to taste (and a very small pinch of cinnamon if you wish), and reheat the sauce when it is needed. Serve with grilled poultry.

48

Sauce sabayon au vin rouge
FOAMY RED-WINE SAUCE FOR FISH

To serve four:

¼ cup of red wine (such as a bordeaux)
¼ cup of fish stock (9) (11) (12)
4 turns of the pepper mill

SABAYON:

2 egg yolks
6 tablespoons of cold water

UTENSILS:

Small heavy-bottomed saucepan
Small bowl
Small whisk

Heat the saucepan, add the red wine, fish stock, and pepper, and boil the mixture until it has reduced by one half.

In the bowl, beat together the egg yolks and cold water with the whisk until the mixture expands in volume and is foamy. Off the heat, whisk this *sabayon* rapidly into the hot wine-and-stock mixture, and cook over low direct heat or over hot water, still whisking, until the yolks have set. *(If the sauce thins out when you take it off the heat, it needs longer cooking; of course do not allow it to boil, but the egg-yolk liaison is slower to take hold than you might expect. It will work faster, whisked well, over direct heat than over hot water; it is convenient, however, to make the sauce in the top of a small double boiler, over the direct heat, and to have the bottom of the double boiler ready with hot, but not boiling water if the sauce will have to be kept warm before serving. Ed.)*

49

Sauce homardière II
HOT LOBSTER SAUCE

To serve four or five:

3 tablespoons of dry white wine
5 teaspoons of armagnac or cognac
1 cup of fish stock (9) (11) (12)
½ cup of lobster sauce américaine (18)

MIREPOIX:

2 small carrots, scraped and cut into ⅛-inch dice
2 tablespoons of finely diced onion
1 teaspoon of olive oil
Salt and pepper

LIAISON:

2 tablespoons of mushroom purée (136)
2 level tablespoons of fromage blanc (173)
1 teaspoon of crème fraîche (172) *(optional)*
½ teaspoon of minced fresh tarragon, or a pinch of dried tarragon

A pinch of thyme flowers or dried thyme

UTENSILS:

2 small saucepans
Wooden spatula
Electric blender
Small whisk

In the first saucepan, boil together the white wine and the armagnac or cognac until the mixture is reduced by three quarters, or to about 4 teaspoons. Add the fish stock and reduce again by half, or to about ½ cup. Add the lobster sauce (*sauce américaine*) and keep warm over hot water.

Meanwhile, prepare the carrots and onion. In the second saucepan, heat the olive oil, add the vegetables, and cook gently over low heat, stirring occasionally with the wooden spatula. Season this *mirepoix* lightly with salt and pepper.

In the electric blender, purée together the mushroom purée, *fromage blanc, crème fraîche,* minced tarragon and ⅓ cup of the sauce. Add this *liaison* to the remaining sauce and beat well with the whisk. Then add the *mirepoix* from the second saucepan, add the thyme, and heat again but do not allow the sauce to boil.

Les entrées

FIRST COURSES

Oeufs au plat à l'eau
BAKED EGGS STEAMED IN WATER

To serve one:

  2 eggs (or 1 egg)
  1 tablespoon of water
  Salt and pepper

UTENSILS:

  Saucer
  2 flameproof baked-egg dishes, inside diameter 6 inches

Preheat the oven to 450° F.
  Break the eggs into the saucer. In one of the egg dishes, over high heat, bring the water to a boil. Remove the dish from the heat, slide the eggs into it, and invert the second dish over them to serve as cover (or use an ovenproof lid). Bake the eggs in the preheated oven for 3 or more minutes, or to your taste; the whites must be uniformly set, but the yolks not set enough to change color at their rims. Add salt and pepper only after the eggs are done.

NOTE: *One egg cooked this way is good for a minceur breakfast. With a vegetable-purée sauce (see Index) poured in a ribbon around two baked eggs, you have a good luncheon dish. Ed.*

51

Oeufs pochés
POACHED EGGS

Very fresh eggs
Simmering water
3 tablespoons of vinegar per quart of water

UTENSILS:

Several small cups
Large shallow saucepan
Perforated spoon
Shallow baking dish three quarters full of ice water
Dry cloth
To reheat: Kettle of boiling water

Break the eggs into separate cups. In the saucepan, bring the water and vinegar just to a simmer. (Do *not* add salt; it interferes with the setting of the egg white.) Slip the eggs in, one or two at a time, as convenient, and poach them for 3 minutes each. With the slotted spoon, lift them out as they are done, and put them in the dish of ice water.

To serve hot immediately, leave the eggs in the ice water for only 10 seconds and transfer them to the dry cloth to drain. Trim the whites neatly.

NOTE: *To serve cold, let the eggs cool completely in the cold water. If they are to be held for long, or to be coated with aspic, refrigerate them in the water, covered. Drain and trim before using.*

To hold and serve hot later: Let the eggs cool completely in the cold water, and refrigerate in the water, covered. Drain and trim, and empty the baking dish. Return the eggs to the dish, pour boiling water over them, let them stand for a minute or two to heat through, then transfer them to a dry cloth to drain before serving. Ed.

Oeuf glacé à la ratatouille
RATATOUILLE AND EGGS GLAZED WITH ASPIC

To serve four:

Ratatouille niçoise (135)
4 chilled poached eggs (51)
1 teaspoon of gelatin
½ cup of chicken stock (5)
Fresh chervil leaves or minced parsley

UTENSILS:
Sieve lined with a cloth
Little saucepan (butter warmer)
Cake rack and plate
To serve: 4 small chilled plates

Make the *ratatouille* and refrigerate it. Poach the eggs and refrigerate them. And make a small quantity of aspic: Soak the gelatin in a little water until it is soft. Strain the chicken stock through the cloth-lined sieve into the little saucepan. Add the soaked gelatin to the stock, and stir the mixture over low heat until the gelatin is completely dissolved. Refrigerate the aspic, stirring it occasionally, until it is syrupy.

Meanwhile, drain and trim the chilled poached eggs, place them on the cake rack over a plate, and keep them cold. Then, with a small spoon, mask each egg with a little of the aspic, refrigerate them until the layer of aspic sets, and repeat this procedure two or three times until the eggs are nicely glazed.

Spoon a bed of the *ratatouille* onto the chilled plates, put the eggs in the middle, and decorate them with the chervil leaves or sprinkle them with the minced parsley.

53

Cresson à l'oeuf poché
WATER-CRESS PURÉE WITH POACHED EGGS

To serve four:

Water-cress purée (139)
4 hot poached eggs (*see page 96*)
8 canned white asparagus tips, or
   8 fresh green asparagus tips
4 slices of truffle (*optional*)

UTENSILS:

Enameled or stainless saucepan for water-cress purée
2 saucepans
Perforated spoon
To serve: 4 heated plates

Make the water-cress purée (*purée mousse de cresson II*), but do not add the lemon juice and *crème fraîche* in the recipe yet. Poach the eggs.

Shortly before serving, heat the canned asparagus tips, or cook the fresh asparagus tips, and keep them warm. Reheat the poached eggs. Reheat the water-cress purée, add the lemon juice and *crème fraîche*, and spoon the purée onto the heated plates. Put the poached eggs in the middle, and decorate each one with a slice of truffle on top and an asparagus tip on either side.

Oeuf poule au caviar
SCRAMBLED EGGS WITH CAVIAR

To serve four:

    4 very fresh eggs
    2 teaspoons of **fromage blanc (173)**
    1 teaspoon of finely minced onion
    1 teaspoon of minced chives
    Salt and pepper
    1 ounce, or 4 generous teaspoons, of Iranian Sévruga
        caviar (*see page 293*)

UTENSILS:

    Finely serrated knife
    Bowl
    Fine-mesh strainer
    Small heavy-bottomed saucepan
    Whisk
    To serve: 4 egg cups on 4 small plates

With the serrated knife, carefully saw off the round ends of the four eggs. Empty only three of the eggs into the bowl and put the contents of the fourth one aside for another use. Wash all the shells and their caps carefully in hot water, and set them cut sides down on a cloth to dry (NOTE: *This is not really very hard to do, but all four shells may not be cut perfectly at the first try. We suggest that it is more convenient, if you use eggs for something else a day or two before, to cut some or all four shells is advance. Wash them, save them in a little cold water in the refrigerator, and rinse them again and let them dry before using. Ed.*)

Beat together the 3 eggs and strain them to remove any scraps of shell and the filaments in the whites. In the heavy-bottomed saucepan, scramble the eggs over moderate heat, beating constantly with the whisk, until they become a thick, almost smooth cream. (See page 53). Remove the pan from the heat and, still beating with the whisk, add the *fromage blanc*, onion, and chives, and season to taste with salt and pepper.

Spoon the scrambled eggs into the egg shells, add a spoonful of caviar to each shell, and set the caps on top; the caviar should be just visible under the cap. Set in the egg cups and serve immediately.

55

Huître à la poule
OYSTERS WITH EGGS AND BASIL SAUCE

To serve four:

4 large oysters on the halfshell
4 poached eggs (51)
Basil sauce (*see page 149*)
4 shrimp (*see Note on page 129*)
1 generous teaspoon of caviar (*see page 293*) (*optional*)

UTENSILS:

3 small saucepans
To serve: The oyster halfshells set in saucers filled with coarse salt

Poach the shrimp in *court-bouillon* (see page 148) or in a mixture of water and dry white wine. Remove the oysters from their shells, saving their liquor in a small saucepan. Wash the halfshells.

Make the sauce and keep it warm. Poach the eggs, let them cool in cold water for 1 minute, then drain and trim them. Poach the oysters in their liquor at very low temperature for 1 minute—the heat must be such that you can put your finger in the liquid.

To serve: Place a poached egg in each oyster shell, put an oyster on each egg, and mask them with the basil sauce (*sauce de homard au pistou*). The shrimp go on top, surrounded by just a little caviar put on a few grains at a time with a small coffee spoon. (*Be* sure the oyster shells are stable on their bed of salt in the saucers; the shells of American varieties of oysters are not as easy to handle as the flat belons or marennes that would be used in France. Ed.)

56

Caviar d'aubergine
EGGPLANT CAVIAR

To serve four:

2 eggplants, about ½ to ¾ pound each (*see Note*)

FOR THE STUFFING:

6 medium-size fresh mushrooms, stems trimmed, rinsed, and cut into ¼-inch dice or smaller
1 shallot, peeled and finely minced
1 clove of garlic, peeled and finely minced
3 heaping tablespoons drained, raw **diced fresh tomatoes** (130)
2 tablespoons of diced canned pimientos
3 or 4 tablespoons of minced fresh chervil or parsley

LIAISON:

1 egg yolk
Lemon juice to taste
1½ teaspoons of salt
A pinch of pepper
4 teaspoons of live oil
4 teaspoons of **fromage blanc** (173)

Small leaves of fresh chervil or parsley
8 perfect lettuce leaves

UTENSILS:

Small baking dish
Nonstick skillet
Bowl
Small whisk, or an electric beater
To serve: 4 salad plates

NOTE: *If you cannot get eggplants as small as ½ pound (the best place to get them is in your own garden), an eggplant weighing about 1 pound will do well enough. Split it in half as for the small eggplant, and though they will not look as well, cut the halves in two, crosswise, after stuffing them. Also, the baking time at the beginning of the recipe—30 minutes to 1½ hours—depends on the shape of the eggplant, the long narrow ones cooking much faster than the round, egg-shaped ones. Ed.*

Remove the eggplant stems, if they still have their stems, blanch them in boiling water, split them lengthwise, and set them aside. Wash the eggplants.

Put a few tablespoons of water in the baking dish, add the eggplants, whole, and bake them in a 350° F. oven for 30 minutes to 1½ hours, turning them several times. Let the eggplants cool, then cut them in half lengthwise, and scoop out the pulp with a spoon; be careful not to break the skins.

In the nonstick skillet, sauté the diced mushrooms, salting them lightly, until they are soft, and let them cool.

In the bowl, beat together with the whisk, or with an electric beater, the egg yolk, lemon juice, and salt and pepper. Then, as for a mayonnaise, beat in the olive oil, and then beat in the *fromage blanc*. Add to this sauce the eggplant pulp and all the ingredients of the stuffing, and mix well.

Fill the eggplant skins with the mixture, shaping them more or less as they looked originally. Arrange them on the lettuce leaves, decorate them down the centers with a row of chervil or parsley leaves, and put the reserved split stems back where they came from at the small end of each eggplant shell.

57

Gâteau d'herbage à l'ancienne
CABBAGE LEAVES STUFFED WITH GARDEN GREENS

To serve four:

8 or more leaves of green cabbage

FILLING:

A generous ¼ pound of spinach
2 ounces of sorrel leaves
2 ounces of Swiss chard leaves
2 large leeks, white part only, well washed
Boiling salted water
Bouquet garni

LIAISON:

1 whole egg
½ cup of milk made with nonfat dry milk
A scant ½ teaspoon of minced fresh tarragon
A scant ½ teaspoon of minced fresh chives
½ teaspoon of minced fresh parsley
½ onion, minced
Salt and pepper

UTENSILS:

Large saucepan
Bowl
Baking dish about 7 inches in diameter and
    1½ inches deep
Aluminum foil
Baking pan for *bain marie*
To serve: Heated round platter

Trim off the ribs of the cabbage leaves and the stems of the spinach, sorrel, and Swiss chard. Cut the leeks into thin slices.

Bring the salted water to a boil in the saucepan with the *bouquet garni*. In it blanch the cabbage leaves for 4 minutes, and spread them flat on a cloth to drain. Blanch separately, for 4 minutes each, the spinach and Swiss chard, and drain, squeezing out all excess water. Cut them up coarsely. Blanch the leeks for 9 minutes and drain.

In the bowl, beat the egg lightly with a fork only long enough to break it up. Add the milk and chopped herbs and onion, season with salt and pepper, and mix.

Preheat the oven to 425° F.

Line the baking dish with the cabbage leaves. They must cover the bottom and sides of the dish with enough extra beyond the dish so that, when the leaves are folded back over the filling, they will completely enclose it.

Add in layers the spinach, sorrel, Swiss chard, and leek, alternating with portions of the egg-and-milk mixture. Fold the cabbage leaves back over the filling, and cover the baking dish with aluminum foil. Bake in a pan of hot water (*bain marie*) in the preheated oven for 1 hour and 15 minutes. Remove the stuffed cabbage from the oven and let stand for 10 or 15 minutes so that it will keep its shape when it is unmolded.

Before unmolding, tip off any excess liquid, then unmold onto the heated platter.

58

Gâteau de carottes fondantes au cerfeuil
CARROT CAKE WITH CHERVIL

To serve four:

1 pound of young carrots, scraped and cut into slices
less than ¼ inch thick
2 tablespoons of butter
1 cup of **chicken stock (5) (8)**
1 teaspoon of salt
A pinch of pepper

¼ pound of mushrooms, rinsed, stems trimmed,
and minced
½ shallot, minced
1 teaspoon of olive oil (*optional*)

LIAISON:
2 eggs
3 tablespoons of grated Swiss cheese (or *gruyère*)
2 tablespoons of coarsely chopped fresh chervil or
parsley

1 teaspoon of soft butter
Sprigs of fresh chervil or parsley

Asparagus purée sauce (42), or
Artichoke purée sauce (43)

Heavy-bottomed saucepan, with a lid
Small nonstick skillet
Bowl
Pastry brush
Round Kugelhopf or ring mold (1-pint capacity)
Aluminum foil
Baking pan for *bain marie*
To serve: Heated round platter

Heat the butter in the saucepan, add the carrots, and let them color lightly without becoming soft. Then add the chicken stock and salt and pepper. Simmer the carrots, covered, for 5 minutes, then uncover and cook over moderate heat for 15 minutes; the liquid should be evaporated but the carrots should not be dry.

Meanwhile, in the nonstick skillet, or a skillet greased with 1 teaspoon of olive oil, sauté the minced mushrooms and shallot.

Preheat the oven to 425° F.

Remove the carrots to a chopping board, and chop them coarsely with a knife. With a fork beat the eggs lightly in the bowl, add the carrots, mushrooms, Swiss cheese, and chervil, and mix together gently.

With the pastry brush, very lightly butter the mold and put in the carrot mixture. Cover the mold with the aluminum foil, and bake it in a pan of hot water (*bain marie*) in the preheated oven for 25 to 30 minutes, or until the carrots are completely set. Unmold it onto the platter and pour in a ribbon around it the sauce you have chosen to use. Decorate the center with the sprigs of chervil.

59

Gâteau moelleux d'asperges
BAKED ASPARAGUS CUSTARDS

To serve four:

2 pounds of asparagus (*see Note*)
2 eggs
1 egg yolk
1½ teaspoons of salt
A pinch each of pepper and nutmeg
Butter (*optional*)

Asparagus purée sauce (42), or
Artichoke purée sauce (43)

1 tablespoon of peeled, seeded, and diced tomato
2 teaspoons of minced parsley

UTENSILS:
Electric blender
Sieve
Bowls
Saucepan
Whisk
Pastry brush
4 soufflé molds or ramekins, insider diameter 3½ inches,
    1½ inches deep
Baking pan for *bain marie*
Aluminum foil
To serve: 4 heated plates

NOTE: *We made this successfully with fresh green
asparagus and they made a very pretty dish. But in*

*France the recipe would be made with white aspara-
gus and the* gâteau *would have more definite character and flavor. See page 292. Ed.*

Peel the asparagus, and cut or break off the tough
parts of the stalks. Cook the asparagus in boiling
salted water (see page 27). Drain them, save out
12 percent 4-inch tips, and cut the rest into pieces.
Purée these in the electric blender; if there are tough
fibers left in the purée, strain it through the sieve.
Then, in the saucepan, over low heat, reduce the purée
if necessary, until there remains about 2 cups. Let the
purée cool.

Preheat the oven to 400° F.

In a bowl, lightly beat together with a fork the 2
eggs, egg yolk, salt, pepper, and nutmeg. With the
whisk, beat the eggs into the asparagus pureé.

With the pastry brush, very lightly butter the insides
of the molds or ramekins. (The butter will be virtually
eliminated when they are unmolded. However, to
keep the custards from sticking, you may simply
moisten them with water.) Put the asparagus mixture
in the molds, and bake them in a pan of hot water
(*bain marie*) in the preheated oven for 1 hour. After
30 minutes, cover them with aluminum foil if the
surface shows signs of browning.

To serve, reheat the asparagus tips in salted water.
Unmold the asparagus custards onto the heated plates.
Pour in a ribbon around them the sauce you have
chosen to use, and add to each plate 3 asparagus tips,
side by side, decorated with a ribbon of tomato dice
arranged across them. Sprinkle the sauce with the
minced parsley.

60

Tourte aux oignons doux
ONION TART

To serve four:

8 or more leaves of green cabbage, ribs trimmed off

FILLING:

1 large carrot, scraped and cut into ¼-inch dice
1 teaspoon of olive oil (*optional*)
1 pound of mild onions, peeled, thinly sliced, then diced
Salt and pepper
¼ pound of fresh mushrooms, stems trimmed, rinsed,
    and cut into ¼-inch dice
Pinch of thyme or thyme flowers

LIAISON:

1 egg
¾ cup of milk made with nonfat dry milk
Salt and pepper

Fresh tomato purée sauce (41), or
Artichoke purée sauce (43), or
Asparagus purée sauce (42) made with white asparagus

UTENSILS:

Heavy-bottomed saucepan, with a lid
    (nonstick if you wish)
Wooden spatula
Bowl
Baking dish about 7 inches in diameter and
    1½ inches deep
Aluminum foil
Baking pan for *bain marie*
To serve: Heated round platter

In the saucepan, cook the carrots until they give off their liquid, stirring often with the wooden spatula to keep them from sticking; the process is easier if you add 1 teaspoon of olive oil. Cook for 5 minutes, then add the onions and season with salt and pepper. Cook together, covered, over low heat for 15 minutes, stir in the mushrooms and the thyme, and cook another 10 minutes. Spoon out excess liquid if necessary.

Meanwhile, blanch the cabbage leaves in boiling salted water for 4 minutes, and spread them flat on a cloth to drain.

In the bowl, beat the egg lightly with a fork only long enough to break it up. Add the milk, season with salt and pepper, and mix.

Preheat the oven to 425° F.

Line the baking dish with the cabbage leaves. They must cover the bottom and sides of the dish with enough extra beyond the dish so that, when the leaves are folded back over the filling, they will completely enclose it.

Add the cooked vegetables to the egg-and-milk mixture. Pour this filling into the baking dish, fold the cabbage leaves back over the filling, and cover with aluminum foil. Bake in a pan of hot water (*bain marie*) in the preheated oven for 50 minutes. Remove the *tourte* from the oven and let it stand for 10 or 15 minutes so that it will keep its shape when it is unmolded.

Before unmolding, tip off any excess liquid, then unmold onto the heated platter. Pour in a ribbon around the *tourte* the sauce you have chosen to use.

61

Tarte de tomates fraîches au thym
FRESH TOMATO AND SPINACH TARTS WITH THYME

To serve four or five:

Enough fresh spinach to provide about 20 handsome
leaves
1 quart of cooked **diced fresh tomatoes (130)**, made
with about 3 pounds of firm, ripe tomatoes (*see
Note*)
Salt and pepper
4 or 5 small sprigs of thyme, or small pinches of dried
thyme

UTENSILS:

To cook and serve: 4 or 5 individual ovenproof baking
dishes or blini pans (*see color picture 2*), 4½ to
5 inches in diameter

NOTE: *The recipe for cooked diced fresh tomatoes
specifies that the tomatoes be "coarsely" chopped. For
this tart they will be best if, after they are peeled,
halved, and seeded, you then cut each half into 6 or 8
pieces and cook them rather briefly, 15 instead of 30
minutes. They will need to be drained; you may reduce the juice to a thin sauce and add this back to
the tomatoes if you wish before filling the tarts. Ed.*

Preheat the oven to 425° F.

Cut off the stems of the spinach, blanch the leaves a few at a time in boiling water for 2 minutes each, and spread them out flat on a dry cloth to drain. Line the baking dishes or blini pans with the spinach leaves; they must cover the bottom and sides with enough extra beyond the dishes so they can be folded back over the filling.

Drain the tomatoes of excess liquid if necessary, and taste for seasoning. Spoon them into the tarts and put the sprigs of thyme in the centers. Fold back the spinach leaves, completely covering the tomatoes or not, as you prefer. Bake the tarts in the preheated oven for 15 minutes. At the last, add a spoonful more of cooked tomato for color if the spinach covers all the filling. Serve in the baking dishes or pans.

62

Soufflé aux tomates fraîches
INDIVIDUAL FRESH-TOMATO SOUFFLÉS

To serve four or five:

1 quart of fresh tomato purée sauce (41)
½ teaspoon of minced fresh tarragon
1 tablespoon of gelatin
Soft butter
6 egg whites

UTENSILS:

Saucepan
2 large bowls
Small pastry brush
Large egg whisk (balloon whisk)
Small whisk
Rubber spatula
To bake and serve: 4 or 5 small soufflé molds, inside
    diameter 4 inches, 1½ inches deep (1-cup capacity)

Add the tarragon to the quart of fresh tomato sauce and reduce the sauce over brisk heat by about two thirds; you need 1½ cups. Meanwhile, soften the gelatin in a little water. Stir the gelatin into the reduced sauce, stir over heat until it has completely dissolved, pour the mixture into one of the large bowls, and let it cool completely.

Preheat the oven to 425° F. With the pastry brush, very lightly butter the inside of the soufflé molds.

Beat the egg whites: Separate them into a large bowl, and with the egg whisk beat them slowly at first to break them up. When they start to turn white, beat faster, and speed up the beating. Beat until, when you lift up the whisk, the whites form a soft peak on the end of it. Do not let them get too stiff. (You may also use an electric beater.)

Add about one-quarter of the whites to the cooled tomato mixture, and blend them in smoothly with the small whisk. Then add the remaining whites and gently fold them in with the spatula.

Fill the soufflé molds: Spoon in the soufflé batter just to the tops of each mold, and level it off with the side of a spatula or the back of a knife. With your thumb, go around the edge of the mold to separate the top of the soufflé batter from it, making a small trench ½ inch wide; this will help the soufflé to rise.

Lower the oven heat to 375° F. and bake the soufflés for 10 to 12 minutes. Serve immediately.

NOTE: You may add a touch of *fantaisie* by putting a poached egg inside the batter of each soufflé, but not in a menu where egg yolk is used as an ingredient in another dish.

OTHER VEGETABLE SOUFFLÉS:

Soufflés may be made with any of the purées in the chapter on vegetables. For the 1½ cups of reduced tomato sauce, substitute the same amount of vegetable purée. The tomato soufflé must be made with gelatin, but for the others you may substitute 2 egg yolks for the gelatin if you do not mind the extra calories.

63

"Hure" de saumon au citron et au poivre vert
SALMON ASPIC WITH LEMON AND GREEN PEPPERCORNS

To serve ten:

SALMON AND SEASONINGS:

1-pound piece of salmon, skinned, filleted, and all bones
  removed
1 cup of dry white wine
1 cup of fish stock (9) (11)
2 tablespoons of minced parsley
2 teaspoons of salt
⅛ teaspoon of pepper
3 eggs
5 lemons
4-ounce jar of canned pimientos, drained and diced small
4 tablespoons of drained green peppercorns
    (*see page 296*)
2 shallots, peeled and finely minced
2 teaspoons of minced fresh tarragon
2 teaspoons of minced fresh chervil or parsley

CLARIFIED FISH ASPIC:

1 quart of fish stock (9) (11)
1 medium-size onion
1 leek, white part only, well washed
3-inch piece of celery
2 fresh mushrooms, stems trimmed, rinsed
1 tomato
¼ pound of very lean ground beef
    (*see Note on page 116*)
4 teaspoons of lemon juice
2 teaspoons of dried tarragon
1 tablespoon of minced fresh chervil or parsley
2 teaspoons of salt
⅛ teaspoon of pepper
2 egg whites
2½ tablespoons of gelatin (2½ envelopes)
Salt and pepper

Tomato cream sauce for salad (35) (*optional*)

UTENSILS:

Oval flameproof baking dish
Large enameled or stainless saucepan
2 clean cloths
Fine-mesh strainer
Bowl
Oblong ceramic or porcelain mold, 6 inches long, 3½
    inches wide, and 4 inches deep (1½-quart capacity)

NOTE: Hure *is the word used for the pig's head from
which a* charcutier *(pork butcher) makes jellied headcheese, hence by extension is used here to describe
the salmon aspic made in a* charcutier's *oblong mold.
Ed.*

Put the mold in the refrigerator.

SALMON AND SEASONINGS:

Cut the salmon into strips about ¾ inch thick and ¾
inch wide. Marinate them in the baking dish with the
white wine, fish stock, parsley, and salt and pepper
for 1 hour.

Make the aspic, below.

Boil the eggs for 8 minutes, cool them under cold
running water, and shell. Separate the yolks and
whites and chop them separately.

Poach the salmon for 2 or 3 minutes, no more;
simply put the baking dish over direct heat, and bring
the marinade to a simmer. Drain the fish on a dry
cloth. Remove any fat and remaining bits of skin.

Peel the lemons, removing all the white inner skin.
Cut the lemons into small dice, discarding as many
of the white membranes as possible, and drain.

CLARIFIED FISH ASPIC:

Cut the onion, leek, celery, mushrooms, and tomato
into pieces. Put the vegetables in the saucepan and
add the ground beef, lemon juice, tarragon, chervil,
salt and pepper, and the egg whites first broken up
lightly with a fork. Stir in the fish stock, and bring

the mixture to a simmer; cook at a low simmer for 20 minutes.

Soak the gelatin in a little water until it is soft. Add it to the simmered stock and stir until it is completely dissolved. Taste for seasoning.

Line the strainer with a damp cloth, set over the bowl, and slowly pour in the hot aspic. Place in the refrigerator and stir occasionally to prevent it from setting.

Finish the preparation of the fish and seasonings, above.

NOTE: Added to the fish stock and vegetables, the whites of egg coagulate when the mixture is heated and rise to the surface in a thick layer to which small floating particles will cling, thus clarifying the stock. This process, however, depletes the flavor and aroma of the stock; the ground beef is added during the clarifying to compensate for the loss.

TO FILL THE MOLD:

During the entire operation, the cooled aspic in the bowl must be kept cool and at the consistency of oil—just at the point of setting. Have ready the strips of salmon and the seasonings—chopped whites and yolks of egg, diced lemon and pimientos, green peppercorns, and, mixed together, the minced shallots, tarragon, and chervil.

Pour a small ladleful of aspic into the chilled mold and sprinkle with a little of each of the seasonings; arrange a few strips of salmon, lengthwise, over them. Return the mold to the refrigerator until this layer of aspic has set. Repeat the operation, one layer at a time, until all the ingredients have been used up, ending with a layer of aspic. Cover the mold with aluminum foil and chill in the refrigerator for 24 hours.

To serve, dip the bottom of the mold briefly in hot water, and unmold onto a chilled platter; or, serve the "hure" de saumon directly from the mold. Cut it into slices ½ inch thick, and serve with or without the tomato cream sauce (sauce grelette).

64

Terrine de poissons aux herbes fraîches
FISH PÂTÉ WITH HERBS AND GREENS

To serve ten:

FISH:
¾ pound of boned and skinned salmon, in all, divided
  into a 4-ounce and an 8-ounce piece
4-ounce piece of boned and skinned porgy (*saint-pierre*),
  pike (*brochet*), or whiting (*merlan*)
4-ounce piece of a third, white-fleshed fish such as scrod
  (to substitute for *lotte*, or anglerfish)

GARNITURE:
4-ounce piece of salmon, above
4-ounce piece of the second fish, above
3 tablespoons of dry white wine
1 tablespoon of chopped parsley
½ teaspoon of salt
A pinch of pepper

A scant ½ pound of fresh mushrooms, stems trimmed,
  rinsed, and cut into ¼-inch dice
½ shallot, peeled and minced
1 teaspoon of olive oil (*optional*)

FORCEMEAT:
6 large spinach leaves without stems
¼ bunch of water cress, most of the stems removed
A dozen sorrel leaves
8-ounce piece of salmon, above
4-ounce piece of scrod, above
A small piece of garlic, minced
1 teaspoon of salt
A pinch of pepper
The leaves of a small branch of tarragon
½ cup of fresh chervil leaves or parsley leaves
1 egg white
½ beaten egg yolk
Clarified fish aspic (*optional; see page 115*)
Minced parsley (*optional*)

Tomato cream sauce for salad (35) (*optional*)

Small deep dish to marinate the fish
Skillet or nonstick skillet
Large saucepan
Colander
Electric blender
Oblong ceramic or porcelain mold, 6 inches long, 3½
    inches wide, and 4 inches deep (1½-quart capacity)
Aluminum foil
Baking pan for *bain marie*

GARNITURE:

Cut the 4-ounce pieces of salmon and of porgy, pike,
or whiting into strips not quite ½ inch wide. Put them
in the small deep dish to marinate in the refrigerator
with the white wine, chopped parsley, and salt and
pepper for 1 hour.

Sauté the mushrooms and shallot together; this may
be done in an ordinary skillet with the teaspoon of
olive oil, or in the nonstick skillet without oil. Remove
them when they have softened and given off some of
their liquid.

FORCEMEAT:

In the large saucepan, blanch together the spinach,
water cress, and sorrel in boiling salted water for 1
minute, and drain in the colander.

Cut the 8-ounce piece of salmon and the 4-ounce
piece of scrod or anglerfish into ½-inch dice. Purée
them in the electric blender, along with the egg white,
garlic, salt, and pepper, a few pieces at a time at
first, for 2 minutes. Add the blanched greens and the
tarragon and chervil, and blend another minute. Then
add the ½ beaten egg yolk and blend another 2
minutes.

Preheat the oven to 400° F.

Line the bottom and sides of the mold with the
forcemeat. Add a layer of the strips of marinated fish.
Add another layer of forcemeat, and continue until
the ingredients almost fill the mold, ending with a

layer of forcemeat. Cover with the aluminum foil and bake in the pan of hot water (*bain marie*) in the preheated oven for 50 minutes.

Let the pâté cool, cover it with a ¼-inch layer of liquid clarified aspic mixed with minced parsley, and store, covered, in the refrigerator.

The pâté may be served directly from the mold, cut into ½-inch-thick slices, or it may be unmolded onto a chilled platter before slicing. To cut neat, undamaged slices, use a knife dipped in boiling water. Serve with or without the tomato cream sauce for salad (*sauce grelette*), or with lemon.

65

Mousseline de grenouilles au cresson de fontaine
BAKED MOUSSE OF FROGS' LEGS WITH WATER CRESS

To serve four:

18 fresh or frozen frogs' legs of medium size,
    or 9 pairs, in all
2 sea scallops
1 *small* egg, lightly beaten
¼ cup of milk made with nonfat dry milk and water
2 tablespoons of **water-cress purée** (138)
½ teaspoon of salt
A pinch of pepper
Butter (*optional*)
1 cup of fish stock (9) (11) 12), or
    ½ cup of dry white wine plus ½ cup of water,
    seasoned with ½ shallot, minced, a small *bouquet garni*, and salt and pepper
Small sprigs of parsley, or water-cress leaves

Fresh tomato purée sauce (41), or
Artichoke purée sauce (43), or
Asparagus purée sauce (42)

UTENSILS:

Electric blender
Bowl
Small pastry brush
4 small ramekins or soufflé molds, inside diameter 3½ inches, 1½ inches deep (½-cup capacity)
4 pieces of aluminum foil
Baking pan for *bain marie*
Saucepan
To serve: Heated platter and/or 4 heated plates

With a small knife, bone 10 of the frogs' legs (simply scrape the tender meat off the bones). In the electric blender, purée together the frogs' legs meat and the scallops, and the beaten egg, milk, water-cress purée, and salt and pepper. *(You may strain this mixture through a coarse sieve if you wish. Ed.)*

Preheat the oven to 425° F.

With the pastry brush, very lightly butter the insides of the ramekins. (The butter will be virtually eliminated when the ramekins are unmolded. However, to keep the mousseline from sticking, you may also simply moisten the insides of the ramekins with water.) Put the mousseline mixture in the ramekins and cover with aluminum foil. Bake in a pan of hot water *(bain marie)* in the preheated oven for 10 to 12 minutes.

Meanwhile, in the saucepan poach the 8 remaining frogs' legs in the simmering fish stock, or seasoned white wine and water, for 2 minutes, or just until the meat has turned opaque all the way to the bone.

Tip off any excess liquid there may be in the ramekins and unmold the mousselines onto the heated platter. Pour in a ribbon around them the sauce you have chosen to use. Arrange the poached frogs' legs on the platter and decorate with the sprigs of parsley or the water-cress leaves. Or, present the *mousselines* on individual plates.

66

Petite terrine de loup chaude aux pointes d'asperges

HOT STRIPED-BASS PÂTÉS WITH ASPARAGUS TIPS

To serve four:

A 1½-pound striped bass, filleted, or about ¾ pound of fillets
¼ cup of dry white wine
1 teaspoon of minced shallot
1 teaspoon of minced fresh tarragon
Salt and pepper
2 egg whites
1¼ cups of milk made with nonfat dry milk and water
12 canned white asparagus tips, drained, or
    12 fresh green asparagus tips
Butter
4 small sprigs of tarragon

SAUCE:

1 teaspoon of olive oil
1 teaspoon of minced shallot
3 medium-size mushrooms, stems trimmed, rinsed, and quartered
The reserved white-wine marinade, above
3 tablespoons of nonfat dry milk
1 cup of fish stock (9) (11)
1 tablespoon of fromage blanc (173)
1 teaspoon of crème fraîche (172)

UTENSILS:

Oval baking dish
Electric blender
Pastry brush
4 small oval *terrines,* with lids, about 4½ inches long; or
    4 small soufflé molds 4 inches in diameter and 4
    pieces of aluminum foil (1-cup capacity)
Baking pan for *bain marie*
Heavy-bottomed saucepan
To serve: 4 heated plates

Put the bass fillets in an oval dish that will hold them compactly in one layer; add the white wine, spread the minced shallot and tarragon over them, and leave to marinate for 2 hours.

Reserve the marinade. Cut two-thirds, or ½ pound, of the raw fish into ½-inch dice, put this into the electric blender, and add the egg whites and salt and pepper. Blend for 2 minutes. Then, and not before, add the milk, and blend again for 2 or 3 minutes.

If you are using fresh asparagus tips, cook them in boiling salted water for 3 or 4 minutes, and drain. Trim the stem ends so that no stringy parts remain and the tips will fit easily into the *terrines* or molds.

Cut the remaining fish (¼ pound) into ¼-inch dice or a little smaller.

Preheat the oven to 425° F.

With the pastry brush, very lightly butter the insides of the *terrines* or molds. Fill them by half with the puréed fish mixture, add one-quarter of the diced fish and 3 asparagus tips to each one, and then add the remainder of the purée. Cover with the lids or aluminum foil, and bake the *pâtés* in a pan of hot water (*bain marie*) in the preheated oven for 15 minutes.

SAUCE:

Before putting the fish molds in the oven, start the sauce: In the heavy-bottomed saucepan, heat the teaspoon of minced shallot and the quartered mushrooms in the olive oil, without letting them color. Add the reserved white-wine marinade and simmer to evaporate the alcohol. Dissolve the nonfat dry milk in the fish stock, and add this to the saucepan. Simmer the sauce, covered, over low heat for 15 minutes, then add the *fromage blanc* and *crème fraîche*, and blend in the electric blender. Keep the sauce warm.

To serve, first unmold and allow any excess liquid to run off, then transfer to the heated plates, mask with the sauce, and decorate each serving with a small sprig of tarragon. Or, tip off any excess liquid, bring the *terrines* to the table, and unmold onto the plates there and serve the sauce from a sauceboat.

NOTE: A good substitute sauce is **sauce beurre blanc minceur** (40).

67
Gâteau de foies blonds de volailles
BAKED MOUSSE OF CHICKEN LIVERS

To serve four:
¼ pound of chicken livers (*see Note*)
1 teaspoon of salt
A pinch each of pepper and grated nutmeg
½ clove of garlic, peeled
1 *small* egg
½ teaspoon of truffle juice (*optional*)
1 cup of milk made with nonfat dry milk and water
½ teaspoon of minced fresh parsley
Butter (*optional*)

SAUCE:
⅜ cup of **lobster sauce américaine** (18), reduced to about 3 tablespoons
⅝ cup of **fresh tomato purée sauce** (41)

GARNITURE:
4 live crayfish (*optional; see page 293*)
2 black olives, cut in half

UTENSILS:
Electric blender
Small pastry brush
4 small ramekins or soufflé molds, inside diameter 3½ inches, 1½ inches deep (½-cup capacity)
4 pieces of aluminum foil
Baking pan for *bain marie*
Small saucepan for sauce
Saucepan for shellfish
To serve: Heated platter

NOTE: Foies blonds *means light-colored chicken livers and, in fact, when you see chicken livers in quantity at a market, they may often be of two colors, one dark red, the other a paler, more golden red; the latter are the more delicate in flavor and texture. Ed.*

Cut apart the two halves of the chicken livers, remove the filaments and any small greenish patches, and rinse the livers well under cold running water. Put them in the electric blender with the salt, pepper, nutmeg, garlic, egg, and truffle juice. Blend to a purée, then add the milk, blend again, add the chopped parsley, and blend again.

Preheat the oven to 425° F.

With the pastry brush, very lightly butter the insides of the molds. (The butter will be virtually eliminated when the ramekins are unmolded. However, to keep the mousse from sticking, you may also simply moisten the insides of the ramekins with water.) Put the chicken-liver mixture in the ramekins and cover them with the aluminum foil. Bake in a pan of hot water (*bain marie*) in the preheated oven for 20 minutes.

Meanwhile, in the small saucepan, reduce the lobster *sauce américaine*, then stir in the tomato purée sauce, heat together, and keep warm.

In the other saucepan poach the crayfish for 2 to 4 minutes, or for the time you judge best for their size; *do not overcook.* They may be poached in boiling salted water, or, better, in a mixture of ½ cup of dry white wine and ½ cup of water seasoned with a small *bouquet garni*, salt, pepper, and ½ chopped shallot.

Unmold the mousses onto the heated platter. Mask them with the lobster-flavored tomato sauce, decorate each one with half a black olive, and surround with the poached and well-drained shellfish.

Les salades
SALADS

68
Artichaut Mélanie
ARTICHOKE AND CARROT SALAD

To serve four:

3 freshly cooked or canned artichoke bottoms
12 freshly cooked green asparagus, or
    12 canned white asparagus
2 medium-size carrots, scraped
French dressing (29)
2 medium-size mushrooms, stems removed, rinsed, and
    cut into ¼-inch dice
½ apple, peeled and cut into ¼-inch dice
¼ cup of drained, raw diced fresh tomatoes (130)
Low-calorie mayonnaise (32)
A dozen leaves of a tender green lettuce such as Bibb
Minced parsley

UTENSILS:
Vegetable grater
Bowls
To serve: 4 chilled salad plates

Cut the artichoke bottoms into quarters. Cut the asparagus tips to about 3 inches long, and cut enough of
the tenderest parts of the stems into ¼-inch dice to
make a generous ¼ cup. Grate the carrots; you need

about 2 cups. Season, separately, the pieces of artichoke, the asparagus tips, and the grated carrots with a little French dressing (*sauce vinaigrette minceur I*).

In a bowl, combine the diced asparagus, mushrooms, apple, and tomato, and season this *garniture* with a little low-calorie mayonnaise (*sauce mayonnaise minceur I*). Add salt and pepper to taste.

With scissors, cut the lettuce into ½-inch strips (*chiffonnade*).

To serve: Arrange a bed of the *chiffonnade* on each chilled plate, put three pieces of artichoke in the middle, and over them apportion the diced *garniture* in mayonnaise. Add three asparagus tips to each plate, then add the grated carrots, and sprinkle minced parsley over all.

69

Salade des Prés à la ciboulette
FRUIT, MUSHROOM AND CHIVE SALAD

To serve four:

½ pound of young green beans
1 small grapefruit
1 apple
4 or 5 ounces of fresh or canned *cèpes*, or
   ¼ pound of fresh mushrooms
1 medium-size carrot, scraped and grated
Lettuce leaves
2 tablespoons of drained canned white "shoe-peg" corn
   kernels

French dressing (29), or
The preferred minceur salad dressing (31)

2 tablespoons of minced fresh chives

UTENSILS:
Stainless saucepan for the beans
5 bowls
To serve: 4 chilled salad plates

Cook the green beans until they are crisp-tender (see page 26), and refrigerate. Over a bowl to catch the juice, peel the grapefruit completely, removing all the white inner skin, and cut the sections out from between the membranes. Peel and core the apple and cut it into thin half-moon slices; put them to marinate with the grapefruit in the refrigerator.

If you have fresh *cèpes*, they are trimmed, washed, blanched for 1 minute in boiling salted water, then cut into thin slices. Or, drain and slice the canned *cèpes*. Or, use fresh mushrooms raw, stems trimmed, rinsed, patted dry, and thinly sliced.

Season each of the vegetables—green beans, *cèpes* or mushrooms, grated carrot, canned corn—in separate bowls with a little dressing (*sauce vinaigrette minceur I* or *sauce préférée*).

To serve, arrange lettuce leaves on the chilled plates. The green beans go in the middle in a mound. The grapefruit sections, apple slices, *cèpes* or mushrooms, and grated carrot are arranged in a ring around the beans, and the corn kernels and minced chives are sprinkled over all.

70

Salade de truffes au persil
TRUFFLE SALAD WITH PARSLEY

To serve two:

   ¼ cup of flat Italian parsley leaves
   1½ to 1¾ ounces of truffles
   1 small ripe tomato, peeled, seeded, and diced
   8 leaves of a tender green lettuce such as Bibb
   1 cooked artichoke bottom
   French dressing (29)

UTENSILS:
   6 small bowls
   2 small molds or ramekins, inside diameter 3½ inches,
      1½ inches deep (½-cup capacity)
   To serve: 2 chilled salad plates

Wash and stem the parsley and pat the leaves dry. Cut the truffles into thin slices; reserve 2 slices, and cut the rest into thin *julienne* sticks less than ⅛ inch thick. Prepare the diced tomato. Wash and dry the lettuce leaves, and cut them with scissors into strips ½ inch wide (*chiffonnade*). Cut the artichoke bottom into thin slices.

Season each of these ingredients, separately, with just a little of the French dressing (*sauce vinaigrette minceur I*).

Fill the molds or ramekins: Put in first the parsley, then the truffle *julienne,* then the tomato, and finish with the *chiffonnade.* Pack everything in quite firmly. Now unmold onto the chilled plates, ring the salads with the slices of artichoke, and put the 2 reserved slices of truffle on top.

71

Salade à la geisha
STUFFED-TOMATO SALAD WITH SEAFOOD AND BEAN SPROUTS

To serve two:

2 firm, ripe, medium-size tomatoes
Salt and pepper
2 ounces of freshly cooked or canned lump crab meat
1 small, thin-skinned grapefruit
½ small carrot, scraped
½ cup of fresh bean sprouts (*see Note*)
French dressing with herbs (30)
10 or 12 small leaves of curly chicory
6 fresh shrimp (*see Note*)
Minced fresh chervil or parsley

UTENSILS:

Small bowls
Vegetable grater
2 small saucepans
Strainer
To serve: 2 chilled salad plates

NOTE: *Fresh bean sprouts are no problem if you have access to an Oriental market. If you don't, canned bean sprouts will do, though they lack character and are too salty. Rinse them well, pat dry in a cloth, and refrigerate.*

The shrimp intended are small crevettes "bouquet," or crevettes roses, *which are marketed with their heads and decorative atennae on and which would be added to this salad unshelled. Unless you live in an area where shrimp are caught, you can get shrimp only with their heads removed; therefore it is best also to shell them after cooking. Ed.*

Peel the tomatoes (see page 239), slice off the round ends, and reserve these caps. With a small spoon, scoop out the seeds and cores, and with your hand gently squeeze out the excess juice. Set the tomatoes aside, sliced ends down, to drain.

Drain the crab meat if it is canned. Pick it over and dice it. Peel the grapefruit completely, removing all the white inner skin. Over a bowl, to catch the juice, cut out the sections of the grapefruit from between the membranes. Cut half of the sections into small dice, and save the rest, in the juice, for another use.

Grate the carrot. In a small saucepan, blanch fresh beans sprouts in boiling water for 5 seconds, and drain. Wash and dry the chicory.

Cook the shrimp in boiling salted water for 30 seconds to 1 minute, depending on their size, drain, and shell and devein them.

Keep all the ingredients cold in the refrigerator and assemble them shortly before serving:

Salt and pepper the insides of the tomatoes. Combine the diced crab meat and grapefruit, stuff the tomatoes with this mixture, and cover them with their caps. Dress the carrots and bean sprouts, separately, with a little of the French dressing (*sauce vinaigrette minceur II*). Arrange a bed of chicory leaves on the chilled plates, put the tomatoes in the middle, and ring them with the grated carrot and bean sprouts. Pour a little more dressing over the tomatoes, prop the shrimp up against them, and sprinkle a little minced chervil or parsley over all.

72

Salade pleine mer
SEAFOOD SALAD

To serve two:

A scant ½ pound of young green beans
1 fillet of sole or flounder weighing about 3 ounces
4 whole *langoustines* (small saltwater crayfish), or
    shrimp
2 scallops
2 live crayfish (*see page 293*), or 2 more shrimp
2 cups of fish stock (9) (11) (12)
4 shucked oysters (*optional*), with their liquor
4 shucked *palourdes* (*optional;* cherrystone clams are
    almost identical), with their liquor
The liquor of the oysters and clams

French dressing (29), or
Cold lobster sauce (36)

Lettuce leaves
Fresh chervil leaves or minced parsley

UTENSILS:
Saucepan for green beans
Enameled or stainless saucepan to poach seafood
Perforated skimmer or slotted spoon
Small stainless saucepan for oysters and clams (*optional*)
To serve: 4 chilled salad plates

NOTE: *As a salad,* salade pleine mer *is really a fine luncheon dish, the principle of which is comparable to that of* Le grand pot-au-feu de la mer (98) *in a later chapter—the use of a variety of shellfish, and at*

*least one fish, that are at their freshest and best
wherever you live at the season when you are shopping for them. Therefore, whatever is best at your fish
market is what you should use, including shrimp if
you wish, which are not mentioned in the French
recipe. Poach them last in the common pot of fish
stock, as their flavor is pervasive. Ed.*

Cook the green beans until they are crisp-tender (see
page 26), and refrigerate.

Cut the sole or flounder fillet diagonally into strips
(*goujonettes*) less than ¾ inch wide. Detach the tails
of the *langoustines* from their bodies and shell them,
or shell the shrimp.

In the saucepan, bring the fish stock to a boil, and
in it poach the fish and shellfish, one kind at a time,
for 1 to 2 minutes each, or as needed; do not overcook.
In another saucepan, poach the oysters and clams in
their simmering liquor for 30 to 40 seconds, turning
them all over once. As each batch of seafood is done,
remove with the skimmer or slotted spoon, and let
drain and cool on a dry cloth. Refrigerate everything
until the salad is to be assembled.

To serve: Season the green beans with a little
French dressing (*sauce vinaigrette minceur I*) or
cold lobster sauce (*sauce homardière I*). Arrange the
lettuce leaves on the chilled plates, mound the beans
in the middle, and sprinkle them with the chervil
leaves or minced parsley.

Cut the scallops crosswise into thin slices, and arrange them in a ring around the beans first, then add
the rest of the seafood. Spoon more sauce over it, and
top off each salad with a whole, unshelled crayfish or
one perfect shrimp.

73

Salade de moules au safran et aux coeurs de laitues
MUSSEL SALAD WITH SAFFRON AND HEARTS OF LETTUCE

To serve four:

- 1½ quarts of mussels in their shells, thoroughly scrubbed and rinsed
- ¼ cup of fish stock (9) (11) (12)
- 2 tablespoons of dry white wine
- ½ leek, white part only, well washed, cut into *julienne* strips
- 1 shallot, peeled and minced

SAUCE:

- 1 teaspoon of olive oil
- ½ shallot, peeled and finely minced
- 1 teaspoon of **crème fraîche (172)**
- A pinch of saffron
- The reserved cooking liquid, above

- 2 hearts of Bibb lettuce, cut in half, and a few perfect extra leaves
- Lemon
- 2 small stalks of celery, cut into thin *julienne* strips 2 inches long
- 2 tablespoons of drained, raw **diced fresh tomatoes (130)**
- ½ teaspoon of coarsely chopped fresh tarragon
- 4 mussels in their shells

UTENSILS:

- Large enameled or stainless saucepan, with a lid
- 2 bowls
- Strainer
- Small enameled or stainless saucepan
- *To serve:* 4 chilled salad plates

Scrub the mussels and prepare all the vegetables.

In the large saucepan, bring to a boil together the fish stock, white wine, leek, and shallot. Add the mussels, and cook, covered, for 6 minutes, or just until all the shells are open. Remove the mussels, and strain the cooking liquid and reserve it. Remove all the mussels from their shells except four, which will be used in their shells for decoration.

In the small saucepan, heat the olive oil, and add the ½ chopped shallot, *crème fraîche*, saffron, and about 6 tablespoons of the reserved cooking liquid. Boil for 1 minute, add the mussels, and let the mixture cool.

Arrange the lettuce leaves and hearts on the chilled plates, and season with a squeeze of lemon. Arrange the mussels on the lettuce, and spoon just a little of their sauce over each one. Decorate the salads with the *julienne* of celery, diced tomatoes, the four mussels in their shells, and the chopped tarragon.

74

Salade de poissons crus marinés
MARINATED RAW-FISH SALAD

To serve four:

5 or 6 ounces of firm-fleshed filleted raw fish— one or
more kinds, such as salmon and bass
1 tablespoon of olive oil
Salt and pepper
½ shallot, peeled and minced
2 teaspoons of green peppercorns, drained
1 lemon
1 head of tender green lettuce, such as Bibb lettuce
1½ ounces of ginger preserved in vinegar (*see Note*),
cut into very fine *julienne* strips
A spoonful of fresh huckleberries (*see Note*)

UTENSILS:

Narrow, flexible knife, very sharp
Chilled plate to marinate the fish
Small saucepan
Small strainer
Bowl
To serve: 4 chilled salad plates

NOTE: *Ginger preserved in vinegar is called* beni shoga *in Japanese grocery stores and has a brilliant orange color.*

The French recipe also calls for fresh airelles, *or* bilberries, *which are close relatives of* myrtilles—*in turn, approximately the equivalent of huckleberries. Wild blueberries would be delicious, and one could also use a spoonful of the smaller berries from a basket of cultivated blueberries, though these will be sweeter and less flavorful than the berries intended. Ed.*

With the sharp knife, cut the fish into slices so thin they are almost transparent. (*This is done on the flat of the fillet, at only a slight slant, the way smoked salmon is cut. Ed.*) Spread the slices on the chilled plate, dribble the oil over them, and sprinkle them evenly with a little salt and pepper, the minced shallot, and the green peppercorns.

Cut off the peel of the lemon in thin strips, and cut these into *julienne* sticks as fine as pine needles. Blanch them in boiling water for 1 minute, drain in the strainer, and cool them under cold running water. Wash and dry the lettuce, and with scissors cut the leaves into strips ½ inch wide (*chiffonnade*). In the bowl, toss the *chiffonnade* with lemon juice, salt, and pepper to taste.

Make a bed of the lettuce on each plate. Scatter over these the *julienne* strips of lemon peel and ginger, the berries, and the green peppercorns. Then arrange the slices of marinated fish on top, radiating from the centers like petals of flowers. Chill the salads in the refrigerator for at least 15 minutes before serving.

75

Salade de crabe au pamplemousse
CRAB MEAT AND GRAPEFRUIT SALAD

To serve four:

¼ pound of freshly cooked or canned lump crab meat
Scant ½ pound of very young green beans
12 canned white asparagus tips, or
    12 fresh green asparagus tips
1 small, thin-skinned grapefruit
Lettuce leaves, preferably a red variety such as oakleaf
Cold lobster sauce (36)
Minced fresh chervil or parsley

UTENSILS:

Saucepan
Bowls
To serve: 4 chilled salad plates

Drain the crab meat if it is canned. Pick it over. Cook the green beans until they are crisp-tender (see page 26). Cook the asparagus tips if you are using fresh ones. Peel the grapefruit completely, removing all the white inner skin. Over a bowl to catch the juice, cut out the sections of the grapefruit from between the membranes, and cut these into small dice. Wash and dry the lettuce. Keep all the ingredients cold in the refrigerator and assemble them shortly before serving.

Dress the beans with the lobster sauce (*sauce homardière I*). Arrange the lettuce on the chilled plates. Mound the beans in the middle, and set 3 asparagus tips upright in each mound. Dress the crab meat with lobster sauce, divide it among the four salads, and scatter over all the diced grapefruit, drained, and the minced chervil or parsley.

76

Salade d'écrevisses de rivière
CRAYFISH SALAD

To serve four:

1 quart of **court-bouillon** (83), or
    1 quart of salted water
32 live crayfish (*see page 293*), or
    32 small or medium-size shrimp (*see Note*)
A scant pound of very young green beans
12 canned white asparagus tips, or
    12 fresh green asparagus tips
Lettuce leaves (*see Note*)

SAUCES AND HERBS:

French dressing (29)
1 finely minced shallot
Cold lobster sauce (36)
A spoonful of the vegetables, diced, from the
    court-bouillon
2 teaspoons of fresh minced chervil or parsley

UTENSILS:

Large enameled or stainless saucepan
Colander
Bowls for ingredients and dressings
To serve: 4 chilled salad plates

NOTE: *This is a lovely salad in which to use fresh
shrimp. In this instance, there need be no apologies
if you do not use crayfish, though, of course, nothing
is as dazzling to see on the salad as the unshelled
crayfish used for* garniture.

The lettuce originally called for is trévise, *the dark-
red leaf seen in color picture 6. It is picked very young
in the vegetable garden at Eugénie-les-Bains and has
the texture of young romaine and some of the bitter-
ness of endive (see page 295). The most interesting
and rather tender lettuce in your garden or market
is what you should use. Ed.*

In the stainless saucepan, bring the *court-bouillon* or salted water to a boil, add the crayfish, and boil for 2 to 4 minutes (1 or 2 minutes for shrimp), or for the time you judge best for their size: *do not overcook*. Drain in the colander, let them cool, and shell and devein them. Save some of the vegetables for the sauce. If you are using crayfish, set aside 4 or 8 of them, unshelled, for decoration.

Cook the beans until they are crisp-tender (see page 26). Cook the asparagus tips if you are using fresh ones.

Make the French dressing (*sauce vinaigrette minceur I*), add the minced shallot, and divide the dressing among shellfish, beans, and asparagus to dress them each lightly.

Arrange the lettuce leaves on the chilled plates. Mound the green beans in the middle, decorate with 3 asparagus tips per plate, then arrange the shellfish on the salad, and, with a teaspoon, mask each one with a little of the lobster sauce (*sauce homardière I*). Finally, sprinkle over all the diced vegetables from the *court-bouillon* and the minced chervil. One or two unshelled crayfish top off each salad.

77

Salade de homard au caviar
LOBSTER SALAD WITH CAVIAR

To serve two:

2 small lobsters, not more than 1¼ pound each
Court-bouillon (83)
Scant ½ pound of young green beans
12 canned white asparagus tips
A spoonful of the vegetables from the *court-bouillon*
½ shallot, peeled and finely minced
Cold lobster sauce (36)
Lettuce leaves (*see Note on page 136*)
Fresh chervil leaves, or 2 teaspoons of minced parsley
¾ ounce of caviar (*see page 293*)

Large enameled or stainless saucepan
Saucepan
Bowls
To serve: 2 chilled salad plates

Bring the *court-bouillon* to a boil, put in the live lobsters, bring the liquid back to a boil, and boil the lobsters for 10 to 12 minutes, depending on their size. Remove the lobsters, let them cool, and shell them completely. The claw meat is kept whole and the tails are deveined and cut into 8 slices, or medallions, each.

Cook the green beans until they are crisp-tender (see page 26) and let cool. Drain the asparagus and cut off the tips to about 2½ inches long.

Dice the spoonful of vegetables from the *court-bouillon* and add them and the minced shallot to the lobster sauce (*sauce homardière I*). Dress the beans and asparagus, separately, with a little of the sauce.

Arrange the lettuce leaves on the chilled plates. Mound the beans in the middle, and prop two lobster claws, pointed ends up, in the top of each mound. Place the asparagus tips, tip ends up, around the beans, and add a few leaves of chervil or the minced parsley. Now ring the vegetables with the lobster slices, mask these with the sauce, and with a small spoon place a few grains of caviar on each one.

78

Salade de cervelles d'agneaux
LAMBS' BRAIN SALAD WITH CUCUMBER AND SORREL

To serve four:

2 lambs' brains, ready for cooking (*see Note*)
Water
Vinegar
Salt and pepper
Bouquet garni
1 small cucumber
A dozen and a half leaves of a tender green lettuce such
  as Bibb
A dozen and a half sorrel leaves, stemmed
3 pickled sour gherkins (*cornichons*), thinly sliced
1 tablespoon of capers
French dressing (29)
Low-calorie mayonnaise (32)
2 medium-size mushrooms, stems trimmed, rinsed
¼ cup of drained, raw diced fresh tomatoes (130)
Minced parsley

UTENSILS:

Saucepan
Bowl
Sieve
To serve: 4 chilled salad plates

NOTE: *Brains are prepared for cooking in the same way as sweetbreads (see page 299). A small calf's brains may be used instead of lambs' brains; it will need longer cooking. Ed.*

Rinse the brains one more time and leave them under cold running water for 15 minutes. In the saucepan, bring enough water to a boil to cover the brains well, and add 2 tablespoons of vinegar and 1 teaspoon of salt per cup of water, a good pinch of pepper, and the *bouquet garni*. Add the brains, bring the liquid back to a boil, and simmer them for 5 minutes. Off the heat, let the brains cool completely in the liquid, and refrigerate in the liquid.

Peel the cucumber, cut it in half lengthwise, scoop out the seeds with a teaspoon, and cut it into thin slices. Sprinkle with salt and refrigerate.

To assemble the salad: Drain the brains, trim them, and cut into thin slices. Wash and dry the lettuce and sorrel leaves, cut them into ½-inch strips (*chiffonnade*), and arrange on the chilled plates. Scatter over them the sliced *cornichons* and the capers. Drain the cucumber, season it with French dressing (*sauce vinaigrette minceur I*), and divide the slices among the four salads. Over the cucumber, arrange the brains in fans of neatly overlapping slices, and mask these lightly with the mayonnaise (*sauce mayonnaise minceur I*). Slice the mushrooms, cut the slices into small *julienne* sticks, and sprinkle these and the diced tomato and minced parsley over all.

79

Salade à l'aile de pigeon et au cerfeuil
GREEN SALAD WITH SQUAB AND FRESH CHERVIL

To serve four:

2 squab, trussed
1 quart **chicken stock (5) (8)**
Bibb or Boston lettuce
Chicory
⅓ cup drained, raw **diced fresh tomatoes** (130)
1 large fresh artichoke, cooked, or
       1 large canned artichoke bottom
12 fresh asparagus tips, cooked, or
       12 canned white asparagus tips
French dressing (29)
4 large fresh mushroom caps
1 lemon
4 teaspoons of canned drained white "shoe-peg" corn
   kernels

UTENSILS:

2 saucepans
Bowls
To serve: 4 chilled salad plates

Bring the chicken stock to a boil, add the squab, and simmer them for 8 to 10 minutes. The meat should remain slightly pink. Remove the birds and let them cool. (Reserve the stock for some other use.) Carve off the breasts, remove the skin, and cut the breast meat into thin slices (horizontally, with the grain). Carve off the legs, leaving second joints and drumsticks in one piece; these are not skinned.

If you are using fresh artichoke and asparagus, cook them according to the directions on pages 87 and 27. Slice the artichoke bottom thinly.

With scissors, cut the lettuce into ½-inch strips to make a *chiffonnade,* and chop the chicory coarsely. Slice the mushroom caps thinly and cut the slices into fine sticks or *julienne.* Peel off the skin of the lemon in very thin strips and cut the strips into *julienne* sticks as fine as pine needles.

Season, separately, the salad, artichoke slices, and asparagus tips with the dressing. Arrange the salad in a mound on each plate, and sprinkle with the diced tomatoes. Circle each mound with the slices of artichoke bottom, and add 3 asparagus tips to each plate. Put the squab legs on top of each salad, drumstick end up. Salt and pepper the slices of breast meat and arrange them in a close circle around the legs.

Over all, sprinkle the *juliennes* of mushrooms and lemon peel and the kernels of corn, and decorate with the chervil.

Les coquillages, crustacés & poissons
SHELLFISH & FISH

80

Huîtres au champagne
BAKED OYSTERS WITH CHAMPAGNE

To serve two:

> One dozen shucked oysters with their liquor
> 12 oyster halfshells, the shallow halves if they are deep
>   enough to hold both oyster and sauce, otherwise the
>   deep halves, well rinsed
> ½ cup of champagne or dry white wine
> 2 egg yolks
> 1 teaspoon of cold water
> 1 teaspoon of **crème fraîche** (172)
> Pepper

UTENSILS:

> Sieve lined with a cloth
> Shallow baking pan filled with coarse salt, ice-cream salt,
>   or fine white gravel
> Small heavy-bottomed saucepan for sauce
> Small whisk and bowl
> Small enameled or stainless saucepan for oysters
> *To serve:* Kitchen tongs and 2 deep saucers

Preheat the oven to 475°–500° F.

Through the cloth-lined sieve, filter the oyster liquor
into the stainless saucepan. Set the clean oyster shells

in the salt in the baking pan. Warm pan and shells over direct heat or, briefly, in the hot oven.

In the heavy-bottomed saucepan, boil the champagne until it is reduced by three quarters, or to about 2 tablespoons. Allow this to cool to lukewarm, and meanwhile separate the eggs and lightly whisk the yolks in the bowl.

Off the heat, whisk into the reduced champagne first the cold water and *crème fraîche* and then the egg yolks. Put the saucepan back over low heat, and heat, whisking constantly, until the mixture thickens and becomes creamy. It must not heat past lukewarm (test with your finger), and it is thick enough when the movement of the whisk exposes streaks of the bottom of the pan. Keep the sauce warm over lukewarm water.

In the stainless saucepan, bring the oyster liquor to a simmer, add the oysters, and poach them for 30 seconds, or until the edges just begin to curl, turning them all over once. Drain, reserving the cooking liquor, and place each oyster in a halfshell.

Whisk the hot oyster liquor bit by bit into the egg-yolk sauce, season with pepper from a pepper mill, and spoon a little of the sauce over each oyster. Bake them in the preheated oven for 30 seconds, or until the sauce is glazed and golden.

To serve, with the tongs transfer the halfshells to the saucers. *(We baked the oysters in two small, salt-filled baking dishes and served them in the same dishes, on heatproof mats. Ed.)*

81

Saint-jacques et belons aux truffes
SCALLOPS AND OYSTERS WITH TRUFFLES

To serve two:

  6 scallops (*see Note*)
  6 shucked oysters and their liquor

SAUCE:

1 teaspoon of salad oil
1 ounce of truffles cut into *julienne* sticks ⅛ inch thick
Pepper
¼ cup of milk made with nonfat dry milk and water
1 teaspoon of **crème fraîche** (172)
½ teaspoon of juice from the can of truffles
1 teaspoon of **mushroom purée** (136)
The oyster liquor, reserved from poaching the shellfish

VEGETABLE JULIENNE:

3-inch piece of a small carrot
3-inch piece of a small leek or large scallion, white part
    only, well washed
1 medium-size mushroom, stem trimmed, rinsed
3-inch piece of celery
    All these vegetables cut into *julienne* sticks as fine
    as pine needles and 1½ inches long

UTENSILS:

2 small enameled or stainless saucepans
Sieve lined with a cloth
Slotted spoon
Small nonstick skillet
To serve: 2 heated soup plates

NOTE: *We do not often see the shell-shaped roes of
scallops in our markets. If you do find them, add 2 or
4 to the dish; they have the brilliant orange-red color
of lobster coral when poached. Ed.*

In one saucepan, heat the oil, add the *julienne* of
truffles, sauté them briefly, and add pepper and the
milk, *crème fraîche,* and truffle juice. Simmer all together for 2 minutes and set aside.

Through the cloth-lined sieve, filter the oyster liquor
into the other saucepan. Bring to a simmer, and poach
the scallops in the oyster liquor for 4 minutes, turning
them each over once. Remove them with the slotted
spoon and keep them warm. Poach the oysters in the
liquor for 20 seconds on each side, remove, and keep
them warm with the scallops.

Add the mushroom purée and the poaching liquid

to the truffle mixture, which will salt the dish. This is meant to be a thin sauce. Keep it hot but do not let it boil.

At the last, in the nonstick skillet sauté the *julienne* of vegetables for 2 minutes.

To serve, apportion the scallops and oysters between the two heated soup plates, cover with the sauce, and sprinkle with the hot vegetables.

82

Homard, langouste ou écrevisses à la nage
LOBSTER, SPINY LOBSTER OR CRAYFISH IN COURT-BOUILLON

To serve two:

One 1½- to 1¾-pound live lobster (Atlantic lobster with large claws), or
One 1½- to 1¾-pound live spiny lobster (Pacific lobster without large claws), or
20 live crayfish (*see page 293*)
Court-bouillon for fish and seafood (83)
Parsley

UTENSILS:

Large enameled or stainless saucepan or kettle
Colander and bowl
Strong rigid knife
To serve: Heated deep platter for lobsters, or a bowl for crayfish

Bring the *court-bouillon* to a boil in the saucepan or kettle, plunge in the live lobster or crayfish and, as soon as the liquid returns to a simmer, time the cooking—12 minutes for a lobster of this weight and 2 minutes for crayfish (see Note). Remove them immediately. Strain the *court-bouillon* and reserve it and reserve the vegetables.

To serve lobster: Split it completely in half lengthwise, cutting from the bottom side. Remove and shell the claws of Atlantic lobster. Remove the gritty sac in the back of the head. Arrange the lobster halves and the claw meat in the heated platter, cover them with a generous spoonful of the vegetables, add a cupful of the hot *court-bouillon*, and sprinkle with minced parsley.

To serve crayfish: Mound the whole crayfish in a pyramid in the heated bowl, and decorate with sprigs of parsley.

NOTE: The vein in the crayfish may be cleaned by keeping the live crayfish for 12 hours in cold water to which nonfat dry milk has been added; this will clear out the gritty substance in the vein.

If cooked crayfish tails are to be used shelled in another recipe, pinch each shelled tail gently and pull out the vein from the tail end.

It is very important never to overcook lobster and crayfish, as this toughens them; they will be better even slightly undercooked. They should be allowed to rest for a short while after cooking and before serving. This "relaxes" the meat, which makes it even more tender.

NOTE: *Some American crayfish are larger than the European; they may need longer cooking. Ed.*

Nage: Court-bouillon pour crustacés et poissons
COURT-BOUILLON FOR FISH AND SEAFOOD

To make about 1½ quarts:

2 medium-size carrots
The white part of 1 leek, well washed
8-inch piece of celery
4 or 5 round spring or green onions, or
    1 medium-size white onion
2 shallots
2 cups of dry white wine
1½ quarts of water
2 tablespoons of coarse salt

SEASONINGS:

5 thin slices of lemon peel
2 whole cloves of garlic, unpeeled
25 green peppercorns (*see page 296*)
Bouquet garni composed of 6 parsley stems, ½ bay leaf,
    a small piece of fresh fennel, a sprig of thyme,
    and 1 clove

UTENSIL:

Large enameled or stainless saucepan with a lid

Wash and peel the vegetables, and cut them all into
thin slices less than ⅛ inch thick. In the saucepan,
over medium heat, cook the sliced vegetables, covered, for 5 minutes to make them give off their liquid.
Then add the wine, water, and salt, and the seasonings.

Simmer gently, covered, for 20 minutes. The vegetables should remain slightly firm; they are used in
certain sauces that accompany fish and seafood dishes.

Homard à la tomate fraîche et au pistou
LOBSTER WITH TOMATO AND BASIL SAUCE

To serve four:

4 small lobsters, not much more than 1 pound each
2 quarts of **court-bouillon (83)**

PISTOU (BASIL) SAUCE:

1 cup of **fish stock (9) (11) (12)** (*see Note*)
1 small carrot, scraped and coarsely chopped
1 small onion, peeled and coarsely chopped
⅓ cup of nonfat dry milk
1 tablespoon of **fromage blanc (173)**
1 tablespoon of **crème fraîche (172)**
1 teaspoon of tomato paste
Pistou: Enough minced fresh basil ground to a paste
     with a few drops of olive oil in a mortar to make
     1 teaspoon of the paste (*see page 298*)
¼ cup of drained, raw **diced fresh tomatoes (130)**
Salt and pepper

UTENSILS:

Enameled or stainless kettle
Small enameled or stainless saucepan
Small mortar and pestle
Electric blender
To serve: 4 heated plates

NOTE: *The name of the basil sauce above is* **sauce de homard au pistou**. *It may be used with a variety of fish and shellfish.*

For the fish stock, you may substitute dry white wine, or half white wine and half water. However, the acid in the wine makes the sauce tricky to handle. It will curdle the milk if you add the milk at the beginning—when the vegetables have simmered for 15 minutes. Wait to add it until after the sauce has been puréed in the blender with all the ingredients through to the tomato paste. Then, stir only 8 level teaspoons of nonfat dry milk to a paste with 2 table-spoons of water. Add this paste to the sauce in the blender along with the pistou, blend again, and be sure not to let the sauce boil when you reheat it.

We used this sauce, made with white wine and water, with great success on poached chicken. Ed.

In the kettle bring the *court-bouillon* to a boil, add the lobsters, and bring the liquid back to a boil. Boil the lobsters for 5 minutes, then take the kettle off the heat and let them cool to lukewarm in the *court-bouillon*.

SAUCE:

Meanwhile, in the small saucepan, simmer together the fish stock, carrot, and onion, covered for 15 minutes. Then stir in the nonfat dry milk, and cook for another 5 minutes, or until the vegetables are tender. Pour the mixture into the electric blender, add the *fromage blanc, crème fraîche,* and tomato paste, and blend. Add the *pistou* and blend briefly again. Return the sauce to its saucepan, add the diced raw tomato, and taste for seasoning. Reheat the sauce and keep it warm.

Remove the lobster tails from the bodies and shell them in one piece; devein them. Shell the large claws. Completely empty the bodies of the lobsters (and save all of this—it can be used to enrich a sauce américaine (18); lobster is expensive!).

To serve: With kitchen scissors, cut notches on both sides of the body shells; fit a shelled claw into each notch. Cut the tail meat into slices ¼ inch thick. On each plate, arrange a shell with overlapping slices of tail meat in a row behind it. Mask only the tail meat with the *pistou* sauce.

85

Homard au cresson
LOBSTER WITH WATER-CRESS PURÉE

To serve two:

2 small lobsters, not more than 1¼ pound each
½ recipe of **Water-cress purée** (139)

COURT-BOUILLON:

1½ quarts of water
2 cups of dry white wine
½ carrot, scraped and sliced
½ onion, peeled and sliced
Bouquet garni
2 tablespoons of coarse salt
20 black peppercorns

SAUCE:

3 tablespoons of dry white wine
1 shallot, peeled and finely minced
2 medium-size mushrooms, stems trimmed, rinsed,
     and finely minced
½ teaspoon of minced tarragon
Salt and pepper
8 level teaspoons of nonfat dry milk
⅓ cup of **fish stock** (9) (11)
1½ teaspoons of **fromage blanc** (173)
1½ teaspoons of **crème fraîche** (172)

2 teaspoons of olive oil

A dozen or more perfect water-cress leaves

UTENSILS:

Large enameled or stainless saucepan
Enameled or stainless saucepan and electric blender for
     purée
Small heavy-bottomed stainless saucepan, with a lid
Enameled skillet or nonstick skillet
To serve: 2 heated dinner plates

Have the lobsters cut up live at the fish market. The large claws are to be taken off and cracked, to make the meat easier to remove later, and the tails cut off in one piece. (Use, promptly, the bodies, claws, tomalley and coral to make or enrich a recipe of lobster sauce américaine (18).)

Make the water-cress purée. (*Reheat it and add the lemon juice and* crème fraîche *in the purée recipe just before serving. Ed.*)

In the large saucepan, bring all the ingredients of the *court-bouillon* except the peppercorns to a boil together, and boil for 15 minutes. Add the peppercorns and boil another 5 minutes. Then add the lobster claws and tails. Remove the tails in 3 minutes, or when they just start to turn red. Cook the claws for 5 minutes from the time the liquid comes back to a boil, take the saucepan off the heat, let them cool to lukewarm in the *court-bouillon,* and then shell them.

Meanwhile, remove the lobster tails from their shells in one piece.

SAUCE:

In the small saucepan, bring to a boil the 3 tablespoons of white wine, and add the shallot, mushrooms and tarragon. Add a little salt and pepper, and simmer, covered, for 2 minutes. Dissolve the dry milk in the fish stock, stir this into the saucepan, bring the mixture back to a simmer, and whisk in the *fromage blanc* and *crème fraîche.* Taste the sauce for seasoning, keep it warm over hot water, and do not allow it to boil again.

In the skillet, heat the olive oil and in it quickly sauté the lobster tails for about 4 minutes in all, 2 minutes on each side, or until they are just cooked through; do not overcook. (The tails may be sautéed in a nonstick skillet without the olive oil.)

To serve, spread a circle of the water-cress pureé in the centers of the heated plates. Arrange one tail with a claw on either side in the middle of each plate, mask the lobster with the sauce, and decorate with the water-cress leaves.

(In the more elaborate presentation in color picture 5, the lobster tails are sliced into medallions and arranged in a circle on the purée, with the claws upright in the center, ringed with the water-cress leaves. The sauce is poured in a ribbon around the purée instead of over the lobster. For this presentation, the sauce was puréed in the electric blender. Ed.)

86

Homard rôti au four
BAKED LOBSTER

To serve two:

One 1½-pound lobster
1½ quarts of court-bouillon (83)

REDUCED SAUCE BASE:

⅝ cup of lobster sauce américaine (18)
⅓ cup of dry white wine
1 teaspoon of lemon juice
6 tablespoons of finely minced shallot
2 teaspoons of minced fresh tarragon
2 teaspoons of minced fresh chervil or parsley
Salt and pepper
1 egg yolk, lightly beaten

FIRST SAUCE, FOR BAKING:

¾ of the reduced sauce base, above
½ of the tomalley and coral of the lobster
⅝ cup of fromage blanc (173)
Salt and pepper

SECOND SAUCE, FOR SERVING:

¼ of the reduced sauce base, above
½ of the tomalley and coral of the lobster
2 level tablespoons of fromage blanc (173)
1 teaspoon of crème fraîche (172)

Enameled or stainless kettle or large saucepan
2 small heavy-bottomed saucepans
Small whisk
Bowls and measuring cup
Sharp rigid knife
Electric blender
To bake and serve: Oval baking dish and a heated
    sauceboat

In the kettle, bring the *court-bouillon* to a boil, add the lobster, and bring the liquid back to a boil. Boil the lobster for 4 minutes, then take the kettle off the heat, let the lobster poach in the hot *court-bouillon* for another 5 minutes, then remove it.

REDUCED SAUCE BASE:

In one of the small saucepans, reduce the lobster *sauce américaine* by one half, or to a little over ¼ cup.

In the second small saucepan, combine the white wine, lemon juice, shallot, tarragon, chervil or parsley, and a little salt and pepper. Simmer over medium heat, uncovered, until you have a soft, juicy, but not liquid "marmalade" left. Allow this to cool. Then, off the heat, with the whisk beat in the egg yolk and the reduced lobster sauce.

Set aside one-quarter of this reduced sauce base in a small bowl to be used at the last in the second sauce, for serving. The remaining three-quarters is to be used in the first sauce, for baking. Keep both in a warm place.

With a sharp, rigid knife, split the lobster in half lengthwise, from the underside. Remove and discard the gritty sac at the back of the head. With a spoon, scoop out and save in a measuring cup all the green tomalley and red coral. Detach the large claws and shell them, keeping the pieces of meat whole. Place the claw meat over the spaces from which the tomalley and coral have been removed.

Preheat the oven to 475°–500° F.

If you have as much as ½ cup of tomalley and coral, purée the mixture in the electric blender. If not, mash them together to as smooth a paste as possible with a fork. Add just half of the mixture to the three-quarters of the sauce base in the saucepan, add the ⅝ cup of *fromage blanc*, mix well, and taste for seasoning.

Place the lobster halves in the baking dish, put 4 or 5 spoonfuls of water in the dish, and mask the lobster meat with the sauce for baking. Bake briefly in the preheated oven, just until the sauce is bubbling hot.

SECOND SAUCE, FOR SERVING:

Meanwhile, in one of the small saucepans, whisk together the remaining quarter of the sauce base, the remaining half of the tomalley and coral mixture, the 2 tablespoons of *fromage blanc*, and the teaspoon of *crème fraîche*. Just before serving, reheat, whisking well, and pour into the heated sauceboat.

87

Gâteau de homard aux truffes
STEAMED LOBSTER CAKES WITH TRUFFLES

To serve six:

A ½-pound piece of raw salmon, boned, skinned, and any fat removed (*see Note*)
1 teaspoon of salt
A pinch of pepper
1 egg
Milk made with ½ cup of water and 8 level teaspoons of nonfat dry milk

Court-bouillon (83), for poaching seafood and steaming lobster cakes

6 scallops
The tails of two 1½- to 2-pound lobsters (*see Note*)

¾ cup of **lobster sauce américaine** (18), in all

1 ounce of truffles, cut into chunky *julienne* sticks, plus 6 thin slices of truffles, in all

SAUCE:

The remainder of the reduced lobster sauce, above
1 teaspoon of tomato paste
1 teaspoon of port
1 teaspoon of minced fresh tarragon
Milk made with 1 cup of water and 5 level tablespoons of nonfat dry milk
Salt and pepper

UTENSILS:

Electric blender
Bowls
Saucepan for poaching
Small heavy-bottomed saucepan for sauce
Twelve 6-inch squares of aluminum foil
Fish poacher with a rack and several metal jar tops
To serve: 6 heated dinner plates

NOTE: *The recipe calls for 5 to 6 ounces of raw salmon, which is about what you will get from a ½-pound slice after boning and skinning, and the same amount of lobster meat, which is about what you will get out of the tails of the two lobsters. The lobsters must be cut up live, which your fish market will do for you. The practical thing to do is to make a supply of the lobster* sauce américaine *with the remainder of the lobsters, since this sauce, too, is called for in the recipe; the lobster meat cooked during the making of the sauce can be used for a salad or other dish.*

Another, luxurious form of the same recipe uses still another pair *of lobster tails for the forcemeat, in place of the salmon. If you are prepared to do this, poach the two extra tails in* court-bouillon *for 3 minutes, or*

just until they start to turn red, shell them, cut them into small chunks, and purée them in the electric blender as the recipe indicates for the salmon force-meat. Ed.

LOBSTER CAKES:

Cut the raw salmon into small chunks, and purée these in the electric blender for 2 minutes. Add the salt, pepper, and egg, blend another minute, and add the milk. Blend briefly once more, transfer this forcemeat to a bowl, and refrigerate.

In the saucepan, bring the *court-bouillon* to a simmer, and in it poach the scallops for 30 seconds to 1 minute, depending on their size. Remove them, and poach the lobster tails for 4 or 5 minutes. Shell and devein the tails, and cut both scallops and lobster meat into dice smaller than ½ inch Refrigerate.

In the heavy-bottomed saucepan, reduce the lobster *sauce américaine* by one half, or to about ⅝ cup. Let it cool completely.

Mix into the salmon purée the diced scallops and lobster, 2 tablespoons of the reduced lobster sauce, and the *julienne* of truffles. Shape this mixture into 6 round patties about 4 inches in diameter; they should be less than 1 inch thick. Place them each on a square of aluminum foil and cover with the remaining pieces of foil. The edges of the foil are *not* sealed. Refrigerate.

SAUCE:

In the electric blender, purée together the remaining ¼ cup of reduced lobster sauce and the tomato paste, port, and minced tarragon. Add the milk, blend again, taste the sauce for seasoning, and return to the small saucepan. Refrigerate.

NOTE: *The recipe may be prepared ahead to this point. Ed.*

Place the metal jar tops in the fish poacher, and set the rack on these to raise it up from the bottom. Pour in enough *court-bouillon* to come just to but not above the rack. Bring the *court-bouillon* to a boil, lower the heat to a simmer, and line up as many of the foil packets on the rack as it will hold. Steam them, covered, for 3 minutes. Lift out the rack, turn the packets over, steam them in the poacher for another 3 minutes, and lift out. The patties will have puffed up a little and have a tender and mellow consistency. Keep them warm while you steam the remaining packets in the same way.

While the lobster cakes are being steamed, reheat the sauce, but do not let it boil.

To serve, remove the pieces of foil, place the lobster cakes on the heated plates, pour a ribbon of the sauce around them, and decorate each one with a slice of truffle.

88

Truite en papillote à l'aneth et au citron
BAKED TROUT WITH DILL AND LEMON

To serve four:

    4 small fresh or frozen trout, ½ pound or less each
    Salt and pepper
    4 generous sprigs of fresh dill or fresh fennel
    1 shallot, peeled and minced
    Pale dry sherry
    Fish stock (9) (11) (12)
    Olive oil
    1 lemon, peeled so that all the white inner skin is cut
        away, and thinly sliced

UTENSILS:

    4 circles of aluminum foil
    Oval baking dish
    Scissors
    To serve: 4 heated plates

Buy the trout cleaned and scaled, heads left on.
    Preheat the oven to 450° F.

Season the insides of the fish with salt and pepper and put a sprig of dill or fennel in each one. Fold the circles of aluminum foil in half, and at the ends of the fold turn up and pinch the corners to make a sort of boat to hold the trout. Put the fish in their foil. Sprinkle them with the minced shallot, pour ¾ teaspoon of sherry, 1 tablespoon of fish stock, and ½ teaspoon of olive oil over each one, and cover them with the slices of lemon.

Close the foil by folding over the edges and pinching them together securely; the shape should be rather like that of an apple turnover. Place the *papillotes* in the baking dish, and bake the trout in the preheated oven for 8 minutes. *(This brief cooking time is for very small trout. We used thawed 10-ounce frozen trout, larger than a* minceur *portion should be, because they are readily available. They were prepared ahead in their* papillotes *and refrigerated until dinnertime. The baking time was then 16 to 18 minutes. Ed.)*

To serve, put the foil *papillotes* on the heated plates. With scissors, carefully cut all around the top side of the foil so it can be opened easily at table.

89

Escalope de saumon à l'oseille
SALMON SCALLOPS WITH SORREL SAUCE

To serve four:

A piece of salmon fillet weighing 1 pound (*see Note*)
Salt and pepper

SAUCE:

½ cup of fish stock (9) (11)
1 tablespoon of pale dry sherry
2 tablespoons of **demi-glace** (2), or
    2 tablespoons of **simplified veal stock** (4)
1 shallot, peeled and minced
3 medium-size mushrooms, stems trimmed, rinsed, and quartered

1 tablespoon of nonfat dry milk
An additional ¾ cup of fish stock (9) (11)
1 tablespoon of **mushroom purée** (136) (*optional*)
1 teaspoon of **crème fraîche** (172)
1 ounce of fresh sorrel leaves (about 2 dozen medium-
    size leaves)

UTENSILS:

8 small pieces of aluminum foil
Cleaver
Enameled or stainless saucepan
Electric blender
Kitchen scissors
Nonstick skillet
Large spatula
To serve: 4 heated plates

NOTE: *It is not very likely that you will be able to buy filleted salmon, since our fish markets normally sell this fish in crosscut slices. You can of course fillet a salmon you catch yourself. The fillet should not be from too large a fish, or it will be too thick for this method of cooking.*

We had no difficulty working with crosscut slices of salmon, two of them cut ¾ inch thick and weighing ½ pound each. Remove the bone, skin, and any visible fat yourself, cut them in half lengthwise, and flatten the pieces to about ¼ inch thick as for the fillet. Ed.

Cut the salmon fillet diagonally into 8 lozenges, which will each weigh about 2 ounces. For the rapid cooking method that will be used, they must be flattened; put them each between two pieces of aluminum foil and flatten them with the side of the cleaver (or of a large chef's knife).

SAUCE:

In the saucepan, combine the ½ cup of fish stock and the sherry, *demi-glace,* shallot, and mushrooms, and simmer all together over low heat until the liquid is reduced by half.

Dissolve the nonfat dry milk in the ¾ cup of fish stock. Add this to the reduced mixture in the saucepan, and simmer for 3 minutes. Then add the mushroom purée and *crème fraîche*, purée the sauce in the electric blender, and return it to the saucepan.

With the scissors, cut the sorrel into narrow strips.

NOTE: *The recipe may be prepared ahead to this point. Refrigerate the fish. The sauce is finished in 5 minutes, and the salmon is cooked in scarcely half a minute, just before serving. Ed.*

Add the cut raw sorrel to the hot fish-stock sauce, and cook them together at a low simmer for 5 minutes. Taste for seasoning.

Meanwhile, season the salmon scallops with salt and pepper, heat the nonstick skillet, and sear them in it quickly for 10 seconds on each side, or just until they are opaque all the way through, turning them with the spatula.

To serve, pour the sauce in the center of the heated plates first, and then add the salmon scallops. Serve immediately.

90

Merlan à la julienne de légumes
BAKED WHITING STUFFED WITH VEGETABLES

To serve two:

Two 1-pound whitings
Salt and pepper
Two-thirds of the *julienne* stuffing, below
½ shallot, peeled and minced
¼ cup of fish stock (9) (11) (12)
1 teaspoon of minced parsley

1 teaspoon of olive oil
1 small carrot
1 small piece of celery root
3 medium-size mushrooms

>All three of these vegetables cut into *julienne* sticks 1½ inches long and as fine as pine needles; the mushrooms must be cut with a knife, but the carrot and celery root may be grated in a mechanical vegetable cutter.

¾ teaspoon of salt
A pinch of pepper
A good pinch of minced fresh tarragon

SAUCE:

½ small carrot (about 1 ounce), chopped
1 large or 2 small mushrooms (about 1 ounce), chopped
3-inch piece of celery stalk, chopped
⅝ cup of fish stock (9) (11) (12)
8 level teaspoons of nonfat dry milk
1 teaspoon of crème fraîche (172) (*optional*)
One-third of the cooked vegetable *julienne,* above
½ teaspoon of port
Salt and pepper

UTENSILS:

2 heavy-bottomed saucepans, one with a lid
Electric blender
Small oval enameled cast-iron baking dish
Large spatula
To serve: 2 heated dinner plates

Have the whitings prepared for cooking at the fish market. They should be cleaned through the gills and then boned: A slit is made along the dorsal fine (on the back), and the fin is removed. The fillets are separated from the bones, the backbone is cut with scissors close to the head and tail, and the whole "frame" is removed, thus leaving the fish whole but with a pocket for stuffing.

JULIENNE STUFFING:

Heat the olive oil in one saucepan, and in it gently sauté the *julienne* of vegetables, starting with the carrots, to cook 9 minutes; three minutes later, the celery root, to cook 6 minutes; and three minutes later, the mushrooms, to cook 3 minutes—9 minutes' cooking time in all. Add the salt and pepper, cover, and over low heat braise the vegetables together for another 10 minutes. They should be cooked through but still firm.

Add the tarragon and let the mixture cool completely.

SAUCE:

In the other saucepan, combine the chopped carrot, mushroom, celery stalk, and ⅝ cup of fish stock, and simmer, covered, for 25 minutes. Then add the nonfat dry milk, stir well, and simmer for another 5 minutes. Add the *crème fraîche*, and purée the mixture in the electric blender. Return it to the saucepan, add one-third of the cooked vegetable *julienne* and the port, and taste for seasoning. Reheat this sauce while the fish is in the oven.

THE FISH:

Preheat the oven to 475° F.

Season the inside of the whitings lightly with salt and pepper, and stuff them with the remaining two-thirds of the vegetable *julienne*. Spread the minced shallot in the baking dish, add the ¼ cup of fish stock, and put in the stuffed fish. Bake them for 8 minutes, basting two or three times with the juices in the dish.

To serve, with the spatula transfer the fish to the heated plates, mask them generously with the hot sauce, and sprinkle with the minced parsley.

91

Carrelet au cidre
FISH BAKED IN CIDER

To serve two:

A 1¼- to 1½-pound flatfish (*see Note*)
Salt and pepper
½ cup of **fish stock** (9) (11) (12)
½ cup of cider (*see Note*)
1 tablespoon of **mushroom purée** (136)
2 teaspoons of minced shallot
1 teaspoon of minced fresh tarragon
1 small apple, peeled, cored, and cut into *julienne* sticks
    1½ inches long and no more than ⅛ inch thick; add
    to the apples 2 tablespoons of lemon juice
1 tablespoon of peeled, seeded, and diced raw tomato

UTENSILS:

Oval enameled cast-iron baking dish
2 large spatulas
To serve: The baking dish and/or 2 heated dinner plates

NOTE: A carrelet *is a flat, white-fleshed fish for which grey or lemon sole, flounder, hake, plaice, porgy, or scup may be substituted. Fish larger than the weight specified may of course be cooked in this way to serve more people, with a longer cooking time as needed until the flesh flakes at the gentle prod of a fork. Completely filleted fish may be baked this way as well, which is more convenient, but there will be some loss of flavor for lack of head, skin, and bones.*

In the fall of the year, there are many kinds of cider made in the United States, some very good indeed. What is needed here is a dry cider, that is, one not very sweet—which is not the easiest type to come by. It may be "hard," meaning fermented and mildly alcoholic, or "sweet" in the sense of fresh and not yet alcoholic. Ed.

Have the fish cleaned and scaled at the market, head and tail left on.

Preheat the oven to 425° F.

Salt and pepper the fish. Combine the fish stock, cider, and mushroom purée. Spread the minced shallot and tarragon in the baking dish, put in the fish, and add the stock-cider-mushroom mixture. Bake the fish, uncovered, for 15 to 20 minutes, basting two or three times with the cooking liquid in the dish. Halfway through the cooking time, or in about 7 minutes, spread the *julienne* of apples and lemon juice over the fish.

When it is done, remove the fish to a board, skin it, and lift off the fillets. Either return these to the baking dish for serving, or place them on the heated serving plates. Salt and pepper them lightly again, moisten with a little of the cooking liquid and apples, and sprinkle with the diced tomato.

92

Daurade cuite sur litière
BAKED SEA BREAM

To serve two:

Whole 1¼- to 1½-pound flatfish (*see Note*)

1 teaspoon of olive oil (*optional*)
½ medium-size carrot
½ small leek, white part only, well washed
½ onion, peeled
2 small mushrooms, stems trimmed, rinsed
    All these vegetables cut into ¼-inch dice
½ teaspoon of minced shallot
½ clove of garlic, peeled and minced
A sprig of thyme
½ bay leaf

⅓ cup of drained, raw **diced fresh tomatoes** (130)
⅜ cup of fish stock (9) (11) (12)
1 teaspoon of **crème fraîche** (172) (*optional*)
Salt and pepper
Minced parsley

Nonstick skillet (*optional*)
Flameproof oval baking dish
Fine-mesh strainer
Small stainless saucepan
Electric blender
To serve: 2 heated dinner plates

NOTE: *Sea bream, or daurade, is a flatfish that is not found in American waters. It resembles a porgy or scup, which the French call saint-pierre (see page 169), in that each side lifts off the bone in one fillet— as with round-bodied fish—rather than in two fillets as with turbot, sole, flounder, and other flatfish. We used a porgy to make this rustic dish, but any lean, white-fleshed flatfish may be cooked in the same way. Ed.*

Have the fish cleaned and scaled at the market, head and tail left on.

Preheat the oven to 425° F.

Heat the nonstick skillet, and add the carrot, leek, onion, mushrooms, shallot, garlic, thyme, and bay leaf. Cook the vegetables gently to make them give off their liquid, stirring occasionally. They should remain crisp-tender. (Or, you may heat the olive oil in the baking dish and cook the vegetables in this on top of the stove.)

Spread the vegetables in the baking dish, and add the diced tomato and the fish stock. Place the fish on top, and bake it in the preheated oven for 15 to 20 minutes. Baste it three or four times with the juices in the dish as it cooks. Remove the fish to a warm platter where it can be skinned, and keep it warm.

Strain the cooking liquid into the saucepan, reserving the vegetables, and boil it over high heat to reduce it by one quarter. Then pour it into the electric blender, add the *crème fraîche,* blend, and taste for seasoning.

Meanwhile, skin the fish and return it to the baking dish. *(Remove the head or not, as you wish. Ed.)*

Spread the vegetables over it, discarding the thyme and bay leaf, and add the reduced cooking liquid. Return the fish to the hot oven for a few seconds to reheat, sprinkle with the parsley, and serve from the baking dish.

93

Chapon de mer farci
BAKED STUFFED SCULPIN

To serve four:

A whole sculpin or other fish weighing about 2½ pounds (*see Note*)

STUFFING:

1 teaspoon of olive oil
1 tablespoon of minced onion
3 tablespoons of minced fresh mushrooms
1 teaspoon of minced fresh tarragon
1 teaspoon of minced fresh chervil or parsley
The liver of the fish, finely minced (*optional*)
Salt and pepper

1 tablespoon of minced shallot
1 cup of fish stock (9) (11) (12)
½ cup of dry white wine

SAUCE:

The cooking liquid, above
¼ cup of milk made with nonfat dry milk and water
1 tablespoon of **mushroom purée** (136)
1 teaspoon of **crème fraîche** (172) (*optional*)
2 tablespoons of drained, raw
     diced fresh tomatoes (130)
Salt and pepper
Minced fresh chervil or parsley

 2 heavy-bottomed stainless saucepans
 Aluminum foil
 Oval baking dish
 Bulb baster or large spoon
 Electric blender
 To serve: 4 heated dinner plates and a sauceboat

NOTE: Chapon de mer *is also called* rascasse, *the famous fish used in* bouillabaisse. *Called sculpin in this country, it is plentiful in our waters but not often marketed. This recipe, however, is appropriate for any fish that can be baked whole, excepting the use of the liver of the fish in the stuffing, which is not possible or desirable with many fish. Ed.*

Have the fish cleaned and scaled at the fish market, head and tail left on, and the liver of the fish reserved.

In a saucepan, heat the olive oil and in it sauté the onion for 2 minutes without letting it color. Add the mushrooms, tarragon, and chervil or parsley, and cook for another 2 minutes. Then add the minced liver of the fish, season with salt and pepper, mix well, and cook all together 1 minute. Let this stuffing cool, then refrigerate it.

Preheat the oven to 425° F.

Season the inside of the fish with salt and pepper, put in the stuffing, and, if necessary, wrap a strip of aluminum foil around the fish to hold it together. Spread the shallot in the baking dish, put in the fish, and add the stock and white wine. Bake the fish in the preheated oven for 25 to 30 minutes, or according to its weight and thickness. Baste it often as it cooks. Remove it to a warm platter where it can be filleted, and keep it warm.

Transfer the cooking liquid to a saucepan, and boil it to reduce it by one third. In the electric blender, combine the reduced liquid and the milk, mushroom purée, and *crème fraîche*, and blend. Return the mixture to the saucepan, add the diced tomato, taste for seasoning, and reheat this sauce but do not let it boil.

Meanwhile, skin and fillet the fish. Arrange the fillets on the heated plates, mask them lightly with the hot sauce, add a spoonful of the stuffing to each serving, and sprinkle with the chervil or parsley. Serve the remaining sauce from the sauceboat.

94

Sabayon de saint-pierre en infusion de poivre
BAKED PORGY WITH PEPPER SAUCE

To serve four:

Whole 2½-pound porgy (*see Note*)
½ shallot, peeled and minced
Salt and pepper
¾ cup of fish stock (9) (11) (12)
1 teaspoon of crushed pepper (*poivre mignonnette*)

SABAYON SAUCE:
2 egg yolks
3 tablespoons of cold water
½ cup of the reduced cooking liquid

UTENSILS:
Oval baking dish
Aluminum foil
Bulb baster or large spoon
Strainer
Small heavy-bottomed saucepan or small double boiler
Small bowl
Small whisk
Large spatula
To serve: 4 heated dinner plates

NOTE: *Saint-pierre is called porgy in the United States. On the North Atlantic coast, porgy is also known as scup and seldom weighs more than a pound; farther south, it is larger and called sheepshead. This recipe may be used for any whole, delicate, white-fleshed fish large enough to serve four that fillets well after cooking; the baking time will depend on the thickness of the fish. Porgies are rather flat; they may cook in less than 30 minutes. Ed.*

Have the fish cleaned and scaled at the fish market. The skin and head are left on.

Preheat the oven to 425° F.

Spread the minced shallot in the baking dish, put in the fish, sprinkle it with salt and pepper, and add the fish stock. Cover the dish with aluminum foil and bake a 2½-pound fish in the preheated oven for 20 to 30 minutes, or longer depending on how thick it is. Baste three or four times as it cooks.

Remove the fish to a warm platter where it can be filleted, and cover with the foil. Turn off the oven.

Strain the cooking liquid into the saucepan or the top of the double boiler, add the crushed pepper, and boil it over direct heat to reduce it while you fillet the fish. Skin the fish and lift the fillets off the bones. Moisten the fish with a spoonful or two of the hot cooking liquid, cover again with foil, and return to the turned-off oven.

Measure the reduced cooking liquid, pour ½ cup back into the saucepan or the top of the double boiler, and keep over low heat. In the small bowl, beat together the egg yolks and cold water with the whisk until the mixture expands in volume and is foamy. Off the heat, whisk this *sabayon* rapidly into the hot cooking liquid, then cook, still whisking, over low direct heat or over hot water, until the yolks have set. (*If the sauce thins out when you take it off the heat, it needs longer cooking; of course do not allow it to boil, but the egg-yolk liaison is slower to take hold than you might expect. It will work faster, if you whisk well, over direct heat. Ed.*)

With the spatula, transfer the fish fillets to the heated dinner plates, spoon the sauce over them, and serve immediately.

95

Bar aux algues, sauce vierge
BASS BAKED IN SEAWEED

To serve four or six:

One 1½- to 2-pound bass
Salt and pepper
Enough fresh seaweed to fill the casserole by more than
    half (*see Note*)
4 live crayfish (*optional; see page 293*)
½ cup of water

Minceur tomato sauce (37), or
    2 cups of cooked **diced fresh tomatoes** (130)
Water-cress purée (139)

UTENSILS:

Large cast-iron oval casserole with a lid, or a covered
    roasting pan, or a fish poacher with a rack and lid
To serve: Heated dinner plates

NOTE: *The seaweed used (see color picture 3) is often though not always used to pack live lobsters for shipping, therefore fish markets do sometimes have it, though they usually throw it away. If enough people create the demand for fresh seaweed, there is no reason why fish markets should not supply it. Many other whole fish could be cooked in the same way.*

Contrary to what we have read, we did not find that dried Oriental seaweeds were appropriate substitutes for the fresh. The dried seaweeds are to be eaten (this fresh one is not), they are of entirely different varieties, and of course they contain no seawater.

We did make one successful experiment using a Japanese seaweed called nishime kombu. *Two small strips of this were soaked in water for several hours. They swell to remarkable size, enough to loosely "bandage" around the fish from end to end. We then steamed the fish in a fish poacher with the rack raised up from the bottom with metal jar tops set under it, and used not water but fish stock in the bottom of the poacher. To remove the seaweed, cut it with scissors along the side of the fish. The bass was delicious, but the process was more trouble, less direct, than the Guérard original. Note, however, that a fish steamed this way, with or without seaweed, is excellent* minceur *fare with a well-seasoned* minceur *sauce. Ed.*

Have the bass cleaned, the head left on, and *not* scaled. The scales preserve the essential flavor in the meat of the fish, and they hold the skin together so that it is very easy to remove after cooking.

Season the inside of the bass with salt and pepper. Spread half the seaweed in the casserole, lay the bass and the 4 live crayfish on it, cover with the rest of the seaweed, and add the water. Cover the casserole, place over high heat, and cook the fish for 20 to 30 minutes.

Meanwhile, warm the tomato sauce (*sauce vierge*) to lukewarm over hot water.

To serve: First bring the fish to the table in the casserole to be admired before it is returned to the kitchen to be filleted. Remove the fish to a board, remove the skin, and lift off the fillets. Arrange them on the heated plates with *sauce vierge* on one side and water-cress purée on the other, and decorate with the scarlet crayfish.

NOTE: To my way of thinking, this a natural and rewarding way to cook a saltwater fish; it gains an added richness of the flavor of the sea. To heighten this naturalness of flavor, instead of using the usual black pepper inside the fish, use dried green peppercorns ground from a pepper mill (*see page 296*).

96

Turbotin clouté d'anchois à la vapeur de safran
TURBOT OR RED SNAPPER STEAMED WITH ANCHOVIES AND SAFFRON

NOTE: *Turbot and red snapper are not notably similar fish, but they have a distinction in common: A young ("chicken") turbot, turbotin, is considered one of the finest fish of Europe; so is red snapper considered possibly the finest fish caught in American waters. We therefore used red snapper here, instead of turbot— which, if you find it at all, will probably have been frozen—while you have a good chance of finding snapper completely fresh. Note also that this simple recipe is appropriate for any lean fish that fillets well after cooking, or for a piece of halibut, which resembles turbot. Ed.*

To serve four—or according to the weight of the fish:

    A 2½-pound chicken turbot (to serve four), or
        ⅔ pound of whole red snapper per person
        (*see Note*)
    2 salted anchovies (*see Note*)
    1 quart, or as needed, of fish stock (9) (11)
    A good pinch of saffron

SAUCE TO SERVE FOUR:

    1 cup of the saffron-flavored stock, above
    1 tablespoon of **mushroom purée** (136)
    1 teaspoon of **crème fraîche** (172)
    Salt and pepper
    4 large, perfect spinach leaves, stemmed
    2 or 3 tablespoons of peeled, seeded, and diced tomato

UTENSILS:

    Sieve and a small pointed knife for anchovies
    Fish poacher with a rack, and several metal jar tops
    Electric blender and saucepan for sauce
    Kitchen scissors and saucepan for spinach
    Knife and spatulas to fillet fish
    To serve: 4 heated dinner plates

NOTE: *If you have a turbot, it should be cleaned and skinned, but the head left on, at the fish market. The 2½-pound turbotin called for in the original recipe to serve four requires about 35 minutes' cooking time. Turbot is a wide, flat fish and you need for it a special, broad poacher or turbotière; or, it may be steamed in a roasting pan with the rack raised off the bottom with metal jar tops.*

A red snapper should be cleaned, the head left on, and not skinned, but it should be scaled. We made this recipe with a 2-pound snapper which served three people. The cooking time was 16 to 18 minutes over already simmering stock. The skin of red snapper is thin; the poacher rack should be oiled so that the skin will not tear when the fish is removed from it, tearing the meat of the fish as well.

The place to shop for salted anchovies is an Italian grocery store. Ed.

In the sieve, rinse the salted anchovies under cold running water for 10 minutes. Drain. With the small knife, slit the anchovies on both sides down the backbone. Lift off the 4 fillets, cut these each in half lengthwise, which will give you 8 pieces, and cut the pieces in half crosswise, which will give you 16 small pieces.

Now "lard" each side of the fish with 8 pieces of anchovy (or with 4 pieces per serving). Push the tip of the small knife into the side of the fish. *Under* the knife blade, poke the piece of anchovy into the fish, then hold the anchovy in place with your finger as you withdraw the knife. Season the fish on both sides with pepper but only a little salt, as the anchovies are still highly salted.

Place the metal jar tops in the fish poacher to raise the poacher rack up from the bottom, pour in enough fish stock to come just to the level of the jar tops, add the saffron, and bring the stock to a boil. Lightly oil the poacher rack, place the fish on it, lower the rack into the poacher, and cover. Steam a turbot, over moderate heat, for up to 35 minutes, or as needed for its thickness and weight. Steam a red snapper 8 to 9 minutes per pound.

Lift out the fish when it is done, and keep it warm.

To serve four, measure out 1 cup of the stock from the poacher, and combine it in the electric blender with the mushroom purée and *crème fraîche*. Blend, taste for seasoning, and pour this sauce into the small saucepan. With kitchen scissors, cut the spinach leaves into ¾-inch strips, blanch these in boiling salted water for 1 minute, drain, and add to the sauce. Just before serving, reheat the sauce without boiling it.

Skin the fish and, with the knife and spatulas, split and lift the fillets from the bones. To serve, cover the centers of the heated plates with the sauce, place portions of the filleted fish on top, and garnish with the diced tomato.

97

Court-bouillon de tous les poissons
POACHED MIXED FISH AND SHELLFISH

The term *court-bouillon* is used here in the literal sense, that of "short boiling" or brief cooking. *To serve four:*

SEAFOOD:

16 mussels in their shells, bearded, scrubbed, and well rinsed

12 shucked oysters and their liquor

4 scallops and their liquor, cut in half crosswise, or quartered, depending on their size

3 to 4 ounces of raw lobster (the meat of 1 large or 2 small tails), cut into ½-inch dice, or the same amount of canned lump crab meat, drained

¼ pound of skinned and boned scrod, to substitute for *lotte* (anglerfish), cut into 8 pieces

¼ pound of fillet of sole or flounder, cut diagonally into 8 "mini" fillets

VEGETABLE GARNITURE:

1 medium-size carrot, scraped and cut into *julienne* sticks ¼ inch thick and 1½ inches long

1 medium-size white turnip, peeled, and cut in the same way

8 to 10 young green beans, snapped, strung, and cut in half crosswise

¼ cup young shelled green peas

12 fresh green or canned white asparagus tips, cut 3 inches long (*optional*)

8 large stemmed spinach leaves

TO POACH THE SEAFOOD:

2 tablespoons of dry white wine

½ cup of fish stock (9) (11)

1 shallot, peeled and finely minced

The combined liquors of the oysters and scallops, above, filtered through a strainer lined with a cloth

¼ cup of milk made with nonfat dry milk and water

Pepper

SAUCE:

The combined poaching liquids, above

¼ cup of lobster sauce américaine (18)

1 tablespoon of mushroom purée (136)

Salt and pepper

UTENSILS:

2 saucepans for vegetables

Colander

Saucepan for mussels

Fine-mesh strainer

Board, shallow saucepan (*sautoir*) or large enameled or stainless skillet for seafood

Perforated spoon

Electric blender

Small saucepan for sauce

To serve: 4 heated soup plates

Have all the seafood prepared and refrigerated, the vegetables prepared, and the remaining ingredients and the utensils at hand.

Begin with the vegetables, as the seafood will afterward be cooked very rapidly. In one saucepan, boil the vegetables in salted water, putting them in in the following sequence: Carrot and turnip, to cook for 10 minutes; five minutes later, green beans, peas, and fresh asparagus tips, to cook 5 minutes—10 minutes' cooking time in all. (If you use canned asparagus tips, add them for only the last 2 minutes.) Set the vegetables aside to keep warm in their cooking liquid.

In another saucepan, blanch the spinach leaves in boiling water for 1 minute, and drain.

SEAFOOD:

In another saucepan, bring to a boil together the white wine, fish stock, and shallot. Add the mussels in their shells, cover, and cook for 6 minutes, or until the shells open. Remove the mussels and shell them.

Strain the mussel cooking liquid into the shallow saucepan or skillet. Add now the combined liquors of the oysters and scallops, the milk, and pepper from a pepper mill. In this new mixture, after bringing it to a simmer, poach the diced lobster or crab meat, and the scrod, sole, and scallops for 1½ minutes. Add the shelled mussels and the oysters, and cook all together another 30 seconds, turning all the oysters over once. Remove immediately from the heat; the seafood will continue to poach in its own heat.

SAUCE:

Pour the seafood cooking liquid into the electric blender, add the lobster *sauce américaine* and mushroom purée, blend, and taste for seasoning. Reheat this sauce in the small saucepan.

To serve: Drain the vegetable *garniture*. Arrange 2 spinach leaves in the bottom of each heated soup plate and, with the perforated spoon, apportion all the seafood among them. Pour the sauce, which should be fairly thin, over the seafood, and then add the vegetables.

98

Le grand pot-au-feu de la mer et ses légumes
SEAFOOD PLATTER WITH VEGETABLES

NOTE: *In a home kitchen, this lavish dish should be thought of as a weekend project for at least two people to cook together. Furthermore, an important principle is involved:* Le grand pot-au-feu de la mer *was created to make use in one festive dish of the widest variety of the best fish and shellfish available at a given moment in a particular place. Therefore, its composition at Eugénie-les-Bains changes as the seafood available there changes. So, far from following the list of ingredients exactly, you should on the contrary make your own selection of what is best and in season at your fish market in your locality. The only strict rule is that no fatty fish may be used, and you will then have a* minceur *feast that is a feast indeed.*

Yours will be, and should be, an entirely different pot-au-feu on East, West, Gulf, northern, or southern coasts. Cooking times for the fish will vary markedly. The following recipe should be read as your point of departure. It has not been changed from the original, as it is not possible to make adjustments that will fit every reader's circumstances, but a few suggestions for substitutions are made for guidance.

First prepare all the fish, shellfish, and vegetables to be ready for cooking. Make the three sauces; they may be kept warm in their separate saucepans set in a pan of hot water (bain marie), *or—with the exception of the red-wine* sabayon—*reheated at the last. Line up the utensils and the ingredients that are to be cooked in them. Everything is cooked briefly and very simply, but separately and simultaneously, which is why the* pot-au-feu *should be made by more than one person—as, of course, is done in a restaurant kitchen.*

You need in all about 1½ cups of fish stock (9) (11) (12)—or about 5 cups if you cook the vegetables

*in stock rather than salted water—and you need half
a recipe, or about 1 pint, of* **court-bouillon** *(83), both
prepared in advance. Ed.*

To serve four:

1 pound of filleted *bar* or *loup* (bass), cut into 4 equal
  pieces
½ shallot, peeled and minced
A bunch of parsley
Salt and pepper
½ cup of fish stock

4 small slices, about 2 ounces each, of *lotte* (anglerfish),
  or pieces of scrod, fillet of sole, flounder, or other
  white fish
¼ cup of red wine
½ cup of fish stock
Bouquet garni, including 4 peppercorns

16 mussels, scrubbed and rinsed
¼ cup of dry white wine
¼ cup of fish stock
½ shallot, peeled and minced
8 *langoustines* (small saltwater crayfish), or shrimp in
  their shells
2 cups of **court-bouillon**
4 *rougets de roche* (red mullet), ¼ pound each, or
  other small whole fish, cleaned and scaled
4 large shucked oysters, and 4 oyster halfshells

VEGETABLE GARNITURE:

8 pieces of carrot, trimmed into olive shapes
8 small white turnips, peeled and short stems left on, or
  8 pieces of white turnip, trimmed into olive shapes
4 small leeks or 8 large scallions, well washed, roots and
  most of the green tops cut off
12 asparagus tips 3 to 4 inches long
½ cucumber, peeled with a vegetable scraper, leaving
  ¼-inch strips of skin on the cucumber, cut into
  ½-inch slices
1 quart of fish stock or salted water

Parsley sauce (44), and
Minceur tomato sauce (37), and
Foamy red-wine sauce for fish (48)

UTENSILS:

3 saucepans for sauces
Baking dish
Aluminum foil
4 saucepans for seafood and vegetables
Colander
Perforated skimmer
To serve: 4 heated dinner plates and 3 heated sauceboats

Preheat the oven to 425° F. In the baking dish, which should be of a size to hold the bass fillets close together in one layer, spread the minced shallot and then a layer of parsley. Put the bass on top, season with salt and pepper, and cover with more parsley. Add the ½ cup of fish stock, and cover the dish with the aluminum foil. Bake in the preheated oven for 12 minutes.

In one of the saucepans, boil together for 5 minutes the ¼ cup of red wine and the ½ cup of fish stock, adding also the *bouquet garni*. In this poach the small slices of *lotte* or pieces of fish fillet until they are just done. Do not overcook, and set them aside off the heat in their cooking liquid.

In another saucepan, boil together for 5 minutes the ¼ cup of white wine, the ¼ cup of fish stock, and the minced shallot. Add the mussels in their shells, cover, and steam for about 6 minutes, or until the shells open. Remove the mussels from their shells and put them back into their cooking liquid.

In the third saucepan, bring the 2 cups of *court-bouillon* to a boil, add the *langoustines* or shrimp, and simmer for 1½ minutes, or according to their size. Drain the shellfish, reserving the *court-bouillon* and returning it to the saucepan. Bring it back to a simmer, and poach the oysters in it just until their edges curl.

Remove them with the skimmer, and set them aside off the heat in a few spoonfuls of the *court-bouillon*. Bring the *court-bouillon* back to a boil, add the 4 small red mullet, remove the saucepan from the heat, and let the fish poach in the hot liquid for 5 minutes.

In the fourth saucepan, boil the vegetables for the *garniture* in the quart of boiling fish stock or salted water. Put them in in the following sequence: carrots, turnips, and leeks or scallions, to cook 10 minutes; five minutes later, asparagus tips and cucumber slices, to cook 5 minutes—10 minutes' cooking time in all. Keep the vegetables warm, off the heat, in their cooking liquid.

To serve the *pot-au-feu*, with the skimmer lift the pieces of fish out of their cooking liquid, let the liquid drain off, and arrange them on the heated plates. Lift out the oysters and put them each back on a halfshell, arranging 4 mussels on each shell as well. Drain the vegetables in the colander, and arrange them on the plates. You have 4 pieces, or a multiple of four, of each ingredient with which to arrange four handsome servings like the one in color picture 9.

The sauces are served separately from the sauceboats, but you may also first put a spoonful of each sauce on the plates: on the bass, the parsley sauce; on the little whole fish, the tomato sauce (*sauce vierge*); on the slice of *lotte*, scrod, or sole, the redwine *sabayon* sauce.

Les viandes

MEATS

99

Grillade de boeuf "aux appétits"
**GRILLED FILLET OF BEEF WITH
SHALLOT AND GARLIC**

To serve four:

> 4 slices of fillet of beef weighing 4 ounces each
>   (*see Note*)
> 1 teaspoon of olive oil

GARNITURE "AUX APPÉTITS":
> 1 shallot, peeled and finely minced
> 1 small clove of garlic, peeled and finely minced
> 2 tablespoons of minced fresh parsley
> Juice of ½ lemon
> 2 teaspoons of olive oil
> Salt and pepper
> A little freshly grated nutmeg

UTENSILS:
> Charcoal grill or ridged cast-iron skillet (*see page 5*)
> *To serve:* 4 heated plates

NOTE: *To get the right thickness for 4-ounce slices,
the* tournedos *is the section of fillet of beef called for.
It is cut near but not at the very end of the rib end of
the whole fillet. The butcher will usually bard these lean
slices of beef, which of course must not be done here.
Indeed, any traces of fat should be removed. Ed.*

Combine the ingredients of the *garniture "aux appétits"* and let them marinate together.

Very lightly brush the *tournedos* with the olive oil. Heat the grill or the cast-iron skillet to very hot, and cook them rapidly to taste as described on page 5, turning them around once to sear them with crisscross grill marks, and turning them over once and turning them around again to make the same marks on the other side. When they are done, pat them with paper towels on both sides to remove as much oil and fat as possible.

Spoon the *garniture* onto the *tournedos* and serve immediately on the hot plates. A good accompaniment is **Normandy fruit and artichoke gratiné (134)**.

100

Grillade de boeuf au gros sel
FILLET OF BEEF GRILLED ON COARSE SALT

The *tournedos* may also be grilled without any oil or fat at all. Completely cover the bottom of a cast-iron skillet with a thin layer of coarse salt. Heat the skillet in a very hot (500° F.) oven until the salt crackles. Put the pieces of fillet in the skillet—they will not stick—and cook them over high heat on the top of the stove, turning them once.

101

Grillade de boeuf au poivre vert
GRILLED FILLET OF BEEF WITH GREEN PEPPERCORNS

Cook the *tournedos* as in either of the preceding recipes, and serve them with the sauce used for **Breast of duckling with green peppercorns (120)**, using **veal stock (1) (4)** instead of chicken stock.

102

Estouffade de boeuf aux petits légumes
CASSEROLE OF BEEF WITH VEGETABLES

To serve two:

10 ounces of stewing beef (chuck), trimmed of all fat and gristle and cut into 10 cubes (about ¾ pound before trimming)
1 cup of red wine
2 cups chicken stock (5) (8)

FOR BRAISING:
1 large leek, white part only, well washed, sliced
1 large carrot, scraped and sliced
2 small onions, peeled and sliced
2 medium-size mushrooms, stems trimmed, rinsed, and sliced, or 3 tablespoons of mushroom purée (136)
A small *bouquet garni*
1 teaspoon of salt
A pinch of pepper

GARNITURE:
8 small, round green or spring onions
8 pieces of carrot
8 pieces of white turnip
4 pieces of cucumber
All three of these vegetables trimmed into olive shapes
4 "cauliflowerets"

SAUCE:
A generous spoonful of the braising vegetables
⅝ cup of the strained braising liquid
4 level teaspoons of fromage blanc (173)
1 teaspoon of crème fraîche (172)

Minced fresh parsley

UTENSILS:

Small enameled cast-iron casserole, with a lid
Nonstick skillet
Saucepan
Perforated skimmer
Fine-mesh strainer
Electric blender
To bake and serve: The casserole and 4 heated plates

In the casserole, boil the wine until it is reduced by half to evaporate all the alcohol.

In the nonstick skillet, over brisk heat, sauté the pieces of beef on all sides to sear and seal the meat. *(It will not brown as it would in an iron skillet with fat. Ed.)*

To the wine in the casserole add the seared meat, braising vegetables, salt and pepper, and enough chicken stock to cover the ingredients well. Cook the *estouffade,* covered, just at a simmer either on top of the stove or in a moderate (350° F.) oven for 1½ hours, or until the meat is tender. I consider the oven best for this purpose.

About 20 minutes before the beef is done, boil the vegetables for the *garniture* (see page 300).

When the meat is done, remove it with the skimmer, and strain the sauce through the fine-mesh strainer. *(You may reduce it if it seems thin. Ed.)* Save a spoonful of the braising vegetables and put them in the electric blender. Add ⅝ cup of the strained braising liquid and the *fromage blanc* and *crème fraîche,* and blend. Return this sauce to the casserole and taste for seasoning. Drain the vegetables.

Return the meat to the casserole, place the *garniture* of vegetables on top, and sprinkle with the minced parsley.

103

Pot-au-feu de viandes en fondue
"FONDUE BOURGUIGNONNE" OF VEAL,
BEEF, LAMB AND VEGETABLES

To serve four:

One 5-ounce slice of veal ¾ inch thick (*see Note*)
One 5-ounce slice of fillet of beef ¾ inch thick
One 5-ounce slice of lamb ¾ inch thick (*see Note*)
1 tablespoon of soy sauce

1½ quarts of beef bouillon (*see Note*)
1 small piece of celery
1 clove of garlic, unpeeled
Bouquet garni, including 1 clove
8 small, round green or spring onions
4 small leeks, well washed, most of the green part cut off
16 pieces of carrot
16 pieces of white turnip
8 pieces of cucumber
      All three of these vegetables cut into olive shapes

SAUCES:

½ cup of fresh tomato purée sauce (41)
½ cup of parsley sauce (44)
½ cup of low-calorie béarnaise sauce (38) (39)

UTENSILS:

3 small saucepans for sauces
Baking pan for *bain marie*
Large saucepan
To serve: 2 deep serving dishes
      Fondue set—alcohol lamp, casserole, 4 long-
         handled forks
      3 small bowls for sauces
      4 plates and 4 small bowls or consommé cups

NOTE: *For the veal, the slice called for is cut from the*
noix *de veau,* a section of the leg. The lamb is also
cut from the leg, or *gigot. The slice of beef cut from*

the fillet will present no problem, but because meat is cut differently in France and the United States, for the veal and lamb it will be more convenient to buy ¾-inch-thick boned loin chops. Remove all fat.

For the beef bouillon, the staple article would be degreased broth of boiled beef—the classic pot-au-feu. But a substitute is certainly allowable. A formula made with Spice Islands products which Michel Guérard has had the opportunity to experiment with: For 1½ quarts of broth, 2 level tablespoons of Spice Islands beef-stock base, 1 level tablespoon of Spice Islands chicken-stock base, and 1½ quarts of boiling water. Ed.

Prepare the three sauces and keep them warm over hot water (*bain marie*).

Cut the veal, beef, and lamb as evenly as possible into ¾-inch cubes. Marinate them in a bowl with the soy sauce while you cook the vegetables.

In the large saucepan, bring the bouillon to a boil, add the celery, garlic, and *bouquet garni,* then add the other vegetables in the following sequence: onions and small leeks, to cook 15 minutes; five minutes later, carrots and turnips, to cook 10 minutes; three minutes later, cucumbers, to cook 2 minutes—15 minutes' cooking time in all.

Strain the bouillon into the fondue casserole, and put the vegetables in one of the serving dishes, discarding the garlic and *bouquet garni.* Put the cubes of raw meat in the second serving dish and the sauces in the small bowls.

To serve: The casserole of bouillon is set on the alcohol lamp in the center of the table, and each guest cooks his own pieces of meat on the end of his fondue fork in the boiling bouillon, dipping them into one of the sauces when the meat is done to his own taste (½ minute to 1 minute). Some of the bouillon may also be ladled out into bowls or consommé cups for each person.

104

Langue de boeuf à la fondue d'oignons
BABY BEEF TONGUE BRAISED WITH ONIONS

To serve four or five:

1 calf's tongue weighing 1½ pounds (*see Note*)
Salt and pepper
1½ cups of red wine
¾ pound of onions, peeled and thinly sliced
2 medium-size tomatoes, washed, cut in half, and seeded
Bouquet garni, including 1 clove of garlic, unpeeled and
    crushed
1 tablespoon of minced fresh tarragon, in all
1 tablespoon of minced fresh chervil or parsley, in all
1 cup of **chicken stock (5) (8)**

UTENSILS:
Large enameled or stainless saucepan
Small enameled or stainless saucepan
Small oval enameled cast-iron casserole, with a lid
Electric blender
To serve: Heated oval platter and 4 heated dinner plates

NOTE: *The French recipe calls for a tongue of baby
beef (langue de génisse). This is available, especially
in the West, where baby beef is mainly sold. But, for
minceur cooking, the fat content of even a small beef
tongue may be too high. Veal tongue is delicate and
lean. We had success with it. Ed.*

In the large saucepan, first parboil the tongue in
unsalted boiling water for 10 or 15 minutes.

In the small saucepan, simmer the wine until it is
reduced by half.

Preheat the oven to 400° F.

Sprinkle the tongue with salt and pepper and put it
in the casserole—which should be just a comfortable
fit for it. Cover the tongue with the sliced onions,
and add the tomatoes, *bouquet garni,* half the minced
tarragon and chervil or parsley, and the reduced red
wine and the chicken stock. Braise the tongue, cov-

ered, in the preheated oven for about 2 hours, or until very tender.

Remove the tongue from the casserole and skin it, removing also any pieces of gristle and bone at the root; keep it warm.

Discard the *bouquet garni* and garlic, and purée the braising liquid and vegetables in the electric blender. Keep this sauce warm in a saucepan; it should be moderately thick. Taste it for seasoning.

Cut the tongue into thin slices and arrange them close together on the heated platter to approximate its original shape. Pour the puréed onion sauce around it, and sprinkle the remaining minced tarragon and chervil or parsley over all.

105

Côte de veau "grillée en salade"
GRILLED VEAL CHOPS IN LETTUCE LEAVES

To serve four:

4 veal rib chops, well trimmed (*see Note*)

1 teaspoon of olive oil
1 small carrot, peeled and cut into ⅛-inch dice
1 small onion, scraped and cut into ⅛-inch dice
3 mushrooms, rinsed, stems trimmed, and cut into
   ⅛-inch dice
Salt and pepper
A good pinch of thyme flowers or chopped fresh thyme,
   or a small pinch of dried thyme
¾ cup of veal stock (1) (4), in all
1 heaping tablespoon of peeled, diced raw tomato
1 teaspoon of minced parsley
1½ tablespoons of mushroom purée (136)
12 or more perfect green lettuce leaves
¾ cup of fresh tomato purée sauce (41)

UTENSILS:

Heavy-bottomed saucepan, with a lid
Charcoal grill or ridged cast-iron skillet (*see page 5*)
To bake and serve: Oval baking dish and a sauceboat

NOTE: *The veal chops called for are called* côtes pre-mières, *which are rib chops cut from the ninth to twelfth rib. Ed.*

Grease the saucepan with the olive oil, heat, and in it sauté the diced vegetables: Over low to medium heat, first put in the carrots, to cook 9 minutes; three minutes later, add the onions, to cook 6 minutes; and three minutes after that, add the mushrooms, to cook 3 minutes—9 minutes' cooking time in all. Season lightly with salt and pepper and add the thyme.

Cover and cook gently for 2 minutes, then add half (⅜ cup) of the veal stock, the chopped raw tomato, and the parsley. Continue to cook, covered, for another 10 minutes. Add the mushroom purée, mix all together gently so as not to crush the cooked vegetables, and set aside to cool.

Blanch the lettuce leaves in boiling water for 1 minute and spread them out on a dry cloth.

Preheat the oven to 400° F.

Heat the grill or the ridged cast-iron skillet to very hot, and lay the chops on it. Quickly turn them around, then turn them over, then turn them around again. The purpose is to sear the chops with crisscross brown marks on both sides without really cooking them but to give them the flavor of grilled meat. Remove them immediately.

Cover each chop with a portion of the cooked vegetables, then wrap each one in lettuce leaves, 3 or more as needed per chop.

In the baking dish, first put the remaining ⅜ cup of veal stock, then add the chops, and bake them in the preheated oven for 15 minutes. Serve them directly from the baking dish and serve the tomato sauce from the sauceboat.

NOTE: *The chops may be prepared in advance except for the baking. To do this, however, let both the vegetable mixture and the "grilled" chops cool completely before assembling them. Ed.*

106

Escalope de veau grillée au coulis d'artichauts
VEAL SCALLOPINI WITH ARTICHOKE PURÉE SAUCE

To serve four:

- 4 veal scallopini, cut from the leg, weighing about 3½ ounces each
- 1 tablespoon of salad oil

GARNITURE:
- 16 small, round green or spring onions
- 16 pieces of carrot
- 16 pieces of white turnip
- 8 pieces of cucumber
  All three of these vegetables trimmed into olive shapes
- 1 tablespoon of minced parsley

Artichoke purée sauce (43)

UTENSILS:
- 2 saucepans
- Charcoal grill or ridged cast-iron skillet (*see page 5*)
- *To serve:* 4 heated dinner plates

Boil the vegetables for the *garniture* (see page 300). Heat the artichoke purée sauce and keep it warm.

With the pastry brush, lightly paint the scallopini with the oil. Heat the grill or the ridged cast-iron skillet, and quickly cook them on it for 2 minutes on each side. Turn them around once before you turn them over, and turn them around once again when you cook the second sides. The purpose is to sear the scallopini with crisscross brown marks on both sides.

Remove the meat from the grill and sponge them off with paper towels. Drain the vegetables.

To serve, mask the centers of the hot plates with the artichoke sauce, place the scallopini in the middle, and surround them with the vegetables of the *garniture*, which you sprinkle with the minced parsley.

107

Blanquette de veau
VEAL FRICASSEE

To serve two:

10 ounces of shoulder of veal, trimmed of all fat and
gristle and cut into 10 cubes (about ¾ pound before
trimming)
3 cups of chicken stock (5) (8)
1 leek, white part only, well washed
2 medium-size carrots, scraped
5-inch piece of celery
3 medium-size fresh mushrooms, stems trimmed, rinsed
Bouquet garni
1 teaspoon of salt
A pinch of pepper

GARNITURE:

4 small, round green or spring onions
4 pieces of carrot
4 pieces of white turnip
4 pieces of cucumber
All three of these vegetables trimmed into olive
shapes
4 fresh or canned button mushrooms

SAUCE:

A pinch of minced fresh tarragon
4 teaspoons of fromage blanc (173)
½ teaspoon of crème fraîche (172)
1 teaspoon of truffle sauce (19) (*optional*)
⅝ cup of the strained stock

UTENSILS:

2 saucepans, one with a lid
Strainer
Bowl
Electric blender
To serve: 2 heated dinner plates

NOTE: *Our veal requires blanching before it is cooked
to remove the scum that it throws off when it is sim-*

mered. Put it in enough cold water to cover it well, bring the water to a boil, and simmer for 2 or 3 minutes. Drain, rinse under cold running water, rinse the saucepan, and return the meat to the saucepan. Ed.

Coarsely slice the cooking vegetables and add them and the chicken stock to the blanched veal in the saucepan. Simmer, covered, for 1 to 1½ hours, or until the meat is tender.

About 20 minutes before the veal is done, boil the vegetables for the *garniture;* in one saucepan, cook them in boiling salted water, putting them in in the following sequence: onions, to cook 15 minutes; five minutes later, carrots, and turnips, to cook 10 minutes; five minutes later, mushrooms, to cook 5 minutes; and two minutes later, cucumbers to cook 3 minutes—15 minutes' cooking time in all. Keep them warm, off the heat, in their cooking liquid.

Remove the veal from the first saucepan, and strain the stock into the bowl. Put a spoonful of the cooking vegetables in the electric blender, and add the tarragon, *fromage blanc, crème fraîche,* truffle sauce (*sauce périgueux*) or mushroom sauce, and ⅝ cup of the hot stock. Blend for 1 minute. Drain the vegetables of the *garniture.*

Put the veal on the heated plates, cover with the sauce, and place the vegetables on top.

108

Blanquette de veau à la vapeur
STEAMED VEAL FRICASSEE

This recipe is the same throughout as the previous one, except that the veal is steamed over rather than cooked in the chicken stock. The best utensil to use is a two-piece steamer or *couscoussière* (see page 288). Put the stock and its vegetables in the bottom and the veal in the top of the steamer. Cook the veal, covered, at a low simmer for 1 hour, or until tender.

About 15 minutes before it is done, add the vegetables of the *garniture* in the same sequence as in the previous recipe. The sauce is made at the end in the same way.

109

Jarret de veau aux oranges
BRAISED VEAL WITH ORANGES

To serve four or five:

A veal roast cut from the heel of the round, weighing
  about 5¼ pounds with the bone *(see Note)*
1 tablespoon of olive oil

MARINADE:

1 large onion, peeled and thinly sliced
Juice of 2 oranges
Juice of 1 lemon
Bouquet garni, including 1 clove
A sprig of fresh basil
Salt and pepper

SAUCE:

The braising liquid
⅝ cup of chicken stock (5) (8)
¼ cup of vinegar
4 teaspoons of granulated sugar, or less to taste
1 orange

UTENSILS:

Deep oval dish
Large oval enameled cast-iron casserole, with a lid
Electric blender
Small saucepan
Small whisk
To serve: Heated deep oval baking or serving dish

The heel of the round is the bottom end of the leg of veal. It is crosscut by the butcher partway up the leg. The meatier side is then cut off lengthwise along the bone; you want the other, smaller side, with the bone. The cut is rich in gelatin. Or, less expensive and leaner is the hind veal shank (osso buco), which may also be used, cooks in about the same amount of time, but is awkward to slice. Ed.

Combine all the ingredients of the marinade. Pour it over the veal in the oval dish, and marinate the meat for 12 hours, turning it two or three times.

Preheat the oven to 425° F.

Remove the veal, wipe it off, and coat it with the olive oil. Heat the casserole, put in the veal, and let it color lightly, turning it until it is golden on all sides. Add the marinade, and bake the roast, covered, in the preheated oven for 1½ hours.

Meanwhile, dissolve the sugar in the vinegar.

Peel off the skin of the third orange in thin strips, and cut them lengthwise into *julienne* strips as fine as pine needles. Blanch these in boiling water for 2 minutes, drain them in a small sieve, and stop their cooking under cold running water.

Cut off all the white inner skin of the peeled orange, and cut out the sections between the membranes.

Remove the veal from its casserole and keep it warm; it will be easier to carve if it rests 20 minutes. In the electric blender, combine the braising liquid and the chicken stock, and blend. Reheat this sauce in a small saucepan, whisk in the sweetened vinegar and the orange rind, then add the orange sections. Taste for seasoning.

Carve the veal into thin slices, arrange them overlapping in a row in the heated oval dish, and pour the hot sauce and oranges around them.

110

Rognon de veau "en habit vert"
VEAL KIDNEY BRAISED IN SPINACH AND LETTUCE LEAVES

To serve two:

1 young veal kidney weighing 6 to 8 ounces
4 to 6 spinach leaves
4 to 6 lettuce leaves
Salt and pepper

FOR BRAISING:

1 teaspoon of olive oil
1 small carrot, scraped and sliced
1 small leek, white part only, well washed, sliced
½ onion, peeled and sliced
¾ cup of veal stock (1) (4)
Small *bouquet garni*

LIAISON:

1 teaspoon of **mushroom purée (136)**
½ teaspoon of **fromage blanc (173)**
½ teaspoon of Dijon mustard

UTENSILS:

Small enameled-iron casserole or saucepan, with a lid
Bowl
Fine-mesh strainer
Electric blender
Small saucepan
To serve: 2 heated dinner plates

Remove all the fat and the filament that encase the veal kidney if the butcher has not already done so, and cut out the kernel of fat at the root of the kidney.

Cut off the stems of the spinach, blanch the spinach and lettuce leaves a few at a time in boiling water for 1 minute each, and spread them out flat on a dry cloth to drain. Sprinkle the kidney with salt and pepper, and wrap it in the spinach and lettuce.

Heat the olive oil in the casserole, and in it cook the carrot, leek, and onion until they soften and give off some of their liquid. Add the wrapped kidney, veal stock, and *bouquet garni*, and braise the kidney, covered, over low heat, for 25 to 30 minutes, basting often with the juices in the casserole. (Do not overcook; when it is done, it should still be pink in the center.)

Remove the kidney, and strain the braising liquid through the fine-mesh strainer. (NOTE: *The liquid should be somewhat reduced; if it seems thin, put it in the small saucepan when you strain it, and simmer it while you unwrap and slice the kidney. Ed.*) Put the braising liquid in the electric blender, add the mushroom purée, *fromage blanc,* and mustard, and blend. Pour this sauce into the small saucepan and reheat it, but do not allow it to boil again.

Unwrap the veal kidney, and slice it very thinly. Pour a ribbon of the sauce around the inside edges of the heated plates; arrange the spinach and lettuce leaves in the center, and arrange the slices of kidney on top of them.

111

Foie de veau à la vapeur aux blancs de poireaux en aigre-doux
STEAMED CALF'S LIVER WITH
SWEET-AND-SOUR LEEKS

To serve six:

2 pounds of young, light-colored calf's liver, in one piece (*see Note*)
Salt and pepper
2 cups of chicken stock (5) (8)

MINCED GARNITURE:

1 teaspoon of olive oil
2 shallots, peeled and minced
1½ ounces of canned morels

1½ ounces of *mousserons,* or ½ ounce of dried
    shittake mushrooms, soaked and drained,
    to substitute for both morels and *mousserons*
    (*see Note and page 298*)
¼ pound of fresh mushrooms, stems trimmed,
    rinsed and quartered
4 ounces of cooked and boned meat from a fresh pig's
    foot, or 6 ounces of fine-quality headcheese, in one
    piece (*see Note*)
A pinch of thyme flowers, or a small pinch of dried
    thyme
1 tablespoon of port
3 tablespoons of veal stock (1) (4)
Salt and pepper to taste

24 small young leeks or large scallions, 3 to 4 inches
    long after trimming off roots and green tops
1 teaspoon of olive oil
Salt and pepper
¼ cup of water
⅜ cup of sherry vinegar
2 teaspoons of granulated sugar

SAUCE:

Minced *garniture,* above
Vinegar cooking liquid from the leeks, above
¾ cup of chicken stock, above, from the bottom of the
    steamer

UTENSILS:

Small heavy-bottomed saucepan, with a lid
Large sheet of heavy-duty aluminum foil
Couscoussière or two-piece steamer (*see page 288*)
Small oval casserole, with a lid
Bowls
Colander
Small saucepan
To serve: Deep oval, heated platter and/or 6 heated
    dinner plates

NOTE: *To cook evenly, the piece of liver should be
near to a center cut so that it does not have a tapered
end that will cook more quickly than the rest.*

If you use shiitake *mushrooms, at first do not cook them with the minced* garniture. *Rather, cut them, after soaking and draining, into thin* julienne *strips, cut these into shorter pieces (do not chop), and cook them gently for 2 minutes in a nonstick pan. Add them to the rest of the* garniture *after it is chopped.*

The intent of the cooked and boned meat of the pig's foot (which the author suggests be bought already prepared from the charcutier, *or pork butcher) is to have for the minced* garniture *a tender, gelatinous meat with just a trace of tender gristle. A good (possibly German) butcher can produce the pig's foot for you, but it will be a fair amount of trouble to cope with. We found that a fresh piece of headcheese from a superior delicatessen, melted down a bit to release the meat from its gelatin base and drained, did well enough. (Indeed, the meat from pigs' feet is sometimes used to make headcheese, illogical though it sounds.) Prepared headcheese may be highly seasoned; be careful not to overseason the* garniture. *Ed.*

Prepare all the vegetables, and line up all the ingredients of the recipe.

MINCED GARNITURE:

In the heavy-bottomed saucepan, heat the teaspoon of olive oil, add the minced shallots, the canned morels, drained, and *mousserons,* the fresh mushrooms, the meat from the pig's foot or headcheese, and the thyme. Cook all together gently, uncovered, for 4 minutes. Add the port, veal stock, and salt and pepper, and simmer over low heat, covered, for 10 minutes. Then chop the whole mixture finely with a large knife, saving any juice and returning it to the minced ingredients. Set aside and let cool.

THE LIVER:

Put the piece of liver on the sheet of aluminum foil, sprinkle it with salt and pepper, and cover it with the minced *garniture*. Wrap it securely in the foil, giving it the shape of a small rolled roast.

NOTE: *The recipe may be prepared ahead to this point. Ed.*

Pour the chicken stock into the bottom of the *couscoussière* or steamer, put the wrapped liver in the top section, cover, and bring the stock to a simmer. Cook the liver for 30 minutes, then remove it and let it rest for 15 minutes before slicing it.

THE LEEKS:

Meanwhile, in the oval casserole, heat a teaspoon of olive oil, add the leeks or scallions, and let them color lightly. Season with salt and pepper, add ¼ cup of water, cover, and cook over low heat for 10 to 20 minutes, or until they are almost tender. Then add the vinegar and sugar, and simmer for another 5 minutes, or until the liquid is reduced by half.

To serve: Scoop all the minced *garniture* off the piece of liver and leave it in the foil. Put the liver on the heated platter, slice it, and keep the slices together, neatly overlapping. Drain the leeks, saving their cooking liquid, and arrange them in a row of crosses on the liver (as in color picture 10). Keep the platter warm.

In the small saucepan, combine the minced *garniture,* the vinegar-flavored liquid in which the leeks have cooked, and ¾ cup of the hot chicken stock from the bottom of the steamer. Boil briskly for 1 minute, taste for seasoning, and pour the sauce around the liver.

NOTE: *The more elaborate presentation of this dish shown on an individual plate in color picture 10 is not very practical if you are serving six people and are to have the liver, leeks, garniture, and sauce all hot as they should be. If you want to do it, however, preferably with someone to help, the only important difference in procedure is that you strain the minced garniture out of the sauce. Pour the strained sauce around each slice of liver on the plates, rim the slices with the minced garniture, and then arrange the leeks or scallions on them. Ed.*

112

Gâteau de ris de veau aux morilles
BAKED MOUSSE OF SWEETBREADS
WITH MORELS

To serve four:

A scant ½ pound of veal sweetbread, in all
1½ ounces of canned morels, drained, in all
   (The sweetbread is divided up between the force-meat and the garniture. The morels are divided up between the garniture and the sauce. Ed.)

FORCEMEAT:

2-ounce piece of the raw sweetbread
½ pound of raw boned breast of chicken
½ egg white, or the white of a small egg
1⅜ cups of milk made with nonfat dry milk and water
1 teaspoon of salt
A pinch each of pepper and grated nutmeg
1 teaspoon of glace de viande (3)
1 teaspoon of crème fraîche (172) *(optional)*

GARNITURE:

Ingredients for braising *(see page 204)*, cut down by
   about one half
The remaining piece of sweetbread
3 fresh mushrooms, stems trimmed, rinsed
Two-thirds (1 ounce) of the morels
1 teaspoon of glace de viande (3)
1 teaspoon of juice from a can of truffles *(optional)*
Salt and pepper

2 fresh mushrooms, stems trimmed, rinsed
The remaining one-third (½ ounce) of the morels
¾ cup of the braising liquid, above
3 tablespoons of milk made with nonfat dry milk and water

4 slices of truffle (*optional*)

UTENSILS:

Electric blender
Small enameled cast-iron casserole for braising, with a lid
Nonstick skillet
Small saucepan for sauce
4 small soufflé molds or ramekins, inside diameter
      4 inches, 1½ inches deep (1-cup capacity)
4 pieces of aluminum foil
Baking pan for *bain marie*
To serve: 4 heated dinner plates

FORCEMEAT:

Prepare the sweetbread for cooking (see page 299), and cut off a 2-ounce piece. Cut this and the breast meat of chicken into small chunks. Purée them in the electric blender, starting with only a few pieces at first, and adding the egg white and a little of the milk as needed so the blades will turn. Blend 1 minute. Then add the salt, pepper, nutmeg, 1 teaspoon of *glace de viande,* the *crème fraîche,* and the remainder of the milk, and blend again. Pour into a bowl and refrigerate. (The forcemeat at this stage may be quite liquid.)

GARNITURE:

Braise the remaining piece of sweetbread as described on page 205 (cooking time, 25 to 30 minutes in all). Reserve the braising liquid.

Cut the braised sweetbread, the 3 fresh mushrooms, and about two-thirds of the morels into dice a little smaller than ½ inch. Heat the nonstick skillet, add the mushrooms and morels, and cook them briefly so they will give off their liquid. Add the diced sweetbread, 1 teaspoon of *glace de viande,* the truffle juice, and salt and pepper. Heat all together, mixing well, allow the mixture to cool, and refrigerate. Purée the braising liquid in the electric blender, and refrigerate.

NOTE: *The recipe is prepared ahead to this point. Ed.*

SAUCE:

Coarsely chop the 2 fresh mushrooms and the remaining morels. In the small saucepan, simmer them until they are cooked through in ¾ cup of the blended braising liquid, to which you also add the 3 tablespoons of milk. Purée this sauce in the electric blender and keep it warm.

Preheat the oven to 400° F.

Rinse the insides of the molds or ramekins with a little water so the forcemeat will not stick when the mousses are unmolded. Fill them almost half full with the forcemeat, add a generous spoonful of the diced *garniture*, then fill them almost to the top with the remaining forcemeat. Cover the molds with the aluminum foil and bake them in a pan of hot water (*bain marie*) in the preheated oven for 20 minutes.

To serve, first tip off any excess liquid there may be in the molds, then unmold them onto the heated plates. Pour a ribbon of the sauce around them, and decorate with the slices of truffle.

113

Ragoût fin d'Eugénie
SWEETBREAD RAGOUT EUGÉNIE

To serve four:

1 veal sweetbread weighing about ¾ pound
A piece of veal kidney weighing about 4 ounces

FOR BRAISING:

Salt and pepper
1 teaspoon of olive oil (*optional*)
1 small carrot, scraped and coarsely chopped
½ onion, peeled and coarsely chopped
2 small tomatoes, peeled and quartered
¼ cup of dry white wine
Bouquet garni
1 cup of chicken stock (5) (8)

VEGETABLE GARNITURE:

8 small, round green or spring onions
8 pieces of carrot
8 pieces of white turnip
8 pieces of cucumber
     All three of these vegetables trimmed into olive
        shapes
8 "cauliflowerets"

TO FINISH THE DISH, AND THE SAUCE AND LIAISON:

Scant ½ pound of fresh mushrooms, stems trimmed,
     peeled, and cut into ½-inch dice
1 ounce of canned morels, drained, and cut into
     quarters, or 2 large or 3 small dried *shiitake*
     mushrooms (*see page 298*), soaked, drained, and
     cut into ¼-inch strips
3 tablespoons of minced shallot

⅔ cup of the braising liquid, above
2 tablespoons of truffle sauce (19) (*optional*)
4 teaspoons of juice from a can of truffles (*optional*)

The diced kidney, above, sautéed
4 tablespoons of mushroom purée (136)

3 scant tablespoons of **fromage blanc** (173)
1 teaspoon of **crème fraîche** (172) (*optional*)

UTENSILS:

Small enameled cast-iron casserole, or a heavy-bottomed
Teflon saucepan, with a lid
Saucepan for vegetables
Colander
Nonstick skillet
Fine-mesh strainer
To serve: Casserole and 4 heated plates

Prepare the sweetbreads for cooking (*see page* 299).
Remove all the fat and filament that encases the veal
kidney if the butcher has not already done so, and
cut out the kernel of fat at the root of the kidney.
Cut the kidney into ½-inch dice. Line up all the ingredients of the recipe.

Salt and pepper the sweetbread (use a pepper mill).
In the casserole, heat the olive oil, add the sweetbread and the chopped carrot and onion, and let the
ingredients color lightly, turning the sweetbread several times. (You don't need the olive oil if you use
a nonstick pan.) After 5 minutes or more, add the
tomatoes, white wine, and *bouquet garni,* and simmer
to evaporate all the alcohol. Then add the chicken
stock, bring it to a boil, and braise the sweetbread,
covered, at a low simmer for another 15 minutes.
(*In all, the sweetbread will have cooked 25 to 30
minutes. Ed.*)

Meanwhile, boil the vegetables for the *garniture*
(*see page* 300).

In the nonstick skillet, sauté the mushrooms, morels,
and shallot, and cook all together for 5 minutes.

Remove the sweetbread from its casserole, and cut
it into ½-inch dice. Strain the braising liquid through
the fine-mesh strainer, and measure out ⅔ of a cup.
Return the sweetbread to the casserole, and add the
mushroom mixture, the ⅔ cup of braising liquid, and
the truffle sauce (*sauce périgueux*) and truffle juice.
Keep warm.

In the nonstick skillet, quickly sauté the diced kidney over brisk heat so the pieces will remain tender and slightly pink in the center.

Now gently stir into the sweetbread casserole the mushroom purée, *fromage blanc*, and *crème fraîche.* Taste for seasoning. Add the sautéed kidney and the *garniture* of vegetables, and mix together carefully so as not to damage the vegetables. Serve very hot, directly from the casserole.

114

Gigot d'agneau cuit dans le foin
LEG OF MILK-FED BABY LAMB BAKED IN HAY

To serve six:

A 2½- to 2¾-pound leg of lamb (*see Note*)
2 large fistfuls of fresh hay (*see Note*)
A sprig of fresh thyme
½ bay leaf
A sprig of fresh wild thyme (*see Note*)
Salt and pepper
½ cup of water
¾ cup of juice from a roast of lamb, free of all fat (*see Note and page 15*)
1 teaspoon of chopped fresh tarragon
2 mint leaves, chopped

UTENSILS:

Cast-iron oval casserole, with a lid
Small saucepan
To serve: Carving knife, heated platter, heated sauceboat

NOTE: *This is a beautiful recipe that grows directly out of Michel Guérard's situation at Eugénie-les-Bains, where the meadows all around the hotel naturally make available the aromatic grasses and plants such as wild thyme. The baby milk-fed lamb, agneau de lait, is raised locally. And in a restaurant kitchen with its continuous cycle of cooking, it is not impractical to expect to have on hand the juice from a previous roast of lamb; rather, it is well to have a use for it and not let it go to waste.*

Impeccably simple as this recipe is, it is obviously fraught with obstacles. Young milk-fed lamb is sold in New York City, for instance, and doubtless, though rarely, elsewhere. But then the city, where there is a demand for such luxuries, is no place to look for fresh hay, so one must bring the lamb to the country to cook it, or bring the hay to the city. All in all, the recipe is presented as an illustration of Michel Guérard's special kind of culinary imagination, with no notion that most readers can easily duplicate it. You will see, however, that with the materials at hand it is simplicity itself.

The meat is carved in slices parallel to the bone and with the grain, not across the grain toward the bone. Ed.

In the casserole, make a bed with a large fistful of the hay and add the thyme, bay leaf, and wild thyme. Place the leg of lamb on the hay, salt and pepper it, and cover it with another layer of hay. Add the water, and cook the lamb, covered, either on top of the stove or in a preheated 425° F. oven, for 40 minutes.

Meanwhile, in the saucepan heat the lamb juice, add the tarragon and mint, and let the herbs infuse in the juice off the heat. Reheat briefly at the last minute.

The roast is presented in the iron casserole and then carved into thin slices which are each lightly salted and peppered and arranged on the heated platter. The juice is passed separately in a sauceboat.

As accompaniment, serve **Confit bayaldi** (132)— Baked Zucchini, Eggplant and Tomatoes—or one or two vegetable pureés (see Index).

The lamb juice may be replaced by **fresh tomato purée sauce** (41) flavored with garlic.

Volailles & gibiers
POULTRY & GAME

115

Volaille "truffée" au persil
ROAST CHICKEN OR GAME BIRD WITH PARSLEY

To serve four:

2½-pound bird (chicken, guinea hen, or pheasant)
Salt and pepper
1 teaspoon of salad oil

PARSLEY GARNITURE:

5 tablespoons of minced parsley
1 tablespoon of minced chives
2 teaspoons of minced tarragon
2 shallots, peeled and finely minced
2 medium-size mushrooms, stems trimmed, rinsed, and finely minced
1 tablespoon of **fromage blanc (173)**
Salt and pepper

SAUCE:

¾ cup of **chicken stock (5) (8)**
1 clove of garlic, unpeeled and crushed
1 tablespoon of minced parsley

UTENSILS:

Small mortar and pestle
Small roasting pan
Fine-mesh strainer
Small saucepan
To serve: Heated deep oval baking or serving dish

In the mortar, mix together to a paste all the minced ingredients of the parsley *garniture* with the *fromage blanc* and with salt and pepper to taste.

Remove any excess fat inside the tail opening of the bird. Working from the neck opening, with your fingers—do not cut anything—gently separate the skin from the breast meat and all the way to the tops of the drumsticks. Spread the parsley mixture as evenly as possible between the skin and the breast meat and dark meat, and pat the skin back into place. Salt and pepper the inside of the bird, truss it, and paint the skin lightly with the oil.

Preheat the oven to 425° F. Roast the bird for 20 minutes, then turn the heat down to 350° F. and roast it for about another 40 minutes, or until the juices inside the bird run clear with no trace of pink. *(Do not baste it with fat that accumulates in the pan. If you wish, baste occasionally with a spoonful of hot chicken stock. Ed.)*

Remove the bird to a carving board and let it rest in a warm place. Discard as much fat as possible from the roasting pan. On top of the stove, over low heat, add to the pan the ¾ cup of stock and the garlic and tablespoon of minced parsley. Stir and scrape all the brown glaze into the sauce. Let it reduce by about one third, then strain it through the fine-mesh strainer into the small saucepan, taste for seasoning, and keep it warm.

To serve, quarter the bird, and present it in the heated oval dish with the juices from the carving board and the sauce poured over it.

116

Poulet au tilleul en vessie
CHICKEN STEAMED WITH ONIONS AND LINDEN BLOSSOMS

To serve four:

2½-pound chicken
Fresh linden blossoms, or linden tea (*see Note*)
¾ pound of onions, peeled and thinly sliced
1 tablespoon of pale dry sherry
Salt and pepper
1 quart of chicken stock (5) (8)

1 teaspoon of glace de viande (3) (*optional*)
1 teaspoon of crème fraîche (172) (*optional*)
½ apple, peeled, cored, and cut into ¼-inch dice
2 tablespoons of minced canned pimiento

UTENSILS:
Soft kitchen string
Plastic poultry-roasting bag (*see Note*)
2 saucepans
Saucepan or oval casserole large enough to hold the bird
    comfortably, with a lid
Large bowl
Slotted spoon
Electric blender
To serve: 4 heated dinner plates

NOTE: *A very old method of cooking is to encase food in a pig's bladder, which is first turned inside out and then tied so that it is almost hermetically sealed (see page 21). A bird, as in this recipe, will steam in its own juices, along with whatever herb, vegetables, or stock may have been added. In the words of the French manuscript, what is called for is* une vessie de porc, ou sa version actuelle, un sac plastique. *We opted for the easily found modern plastic bag, the heat-resistant type intended for roasting poultry. Be sure never to use any type of plastic bag that is not meant for use with high heat.*

Tilleul is the small blossom and its two attached leaves of the linden tree, sometimes called a "lime" tree; the tree itself is also called tilleul in France and is very common there. The fresh blossoms are intended in the recipe, but dried linden—linden tea—is readily available in herb and health-food shops, loose and in tea bags; the tea bags are even found in five-and-tens. We used 8 linden-tea bags stuffed inside the chicken, with good results. If you have fresh linden, use a good handful, or about ¾ ounce, and decorate the chicken at the last with a few of the leaves. Ed.

Put the linden-tea bags inside the chicken, and truss it. Put the bird in the plastic bag with the sliced onions, sherry, and salt and pepper. Tie the top of the bag with string, and let the bird marinate in the bag, in the refrigerator, until you are ready to cook it.

In a saucepan, boil the stock until it is reduced by three quarters, or to about 1 cup; a concentrated stock is needed. Add this to the plastic bag, and tie again securely. Close to the top, where the bag is tied, with a small pointed knife make 5 or 6 small slits.

Fill the large saucepan or casserole half full of boiling water, add the chicken in the bag, and simmer it, covered, over moderate to low heat for 1¼ hours. Then remove the bag to the bowl and slit it open. Remove the bird to a platter and keep it warm; remove the tea bags.

Turn all the juices and onions out into the bowl. With the slotted spoon, transfer the onions to the electric blender. Measure 1¼ cups of the remaining juices, add this to the blender, and add the *glace de viande* and *crème fraîche*. Blend, and pour this sauce into a saucepan.

The sauce is finished quickly, therefore start carving the chicken into quarters, removing all the skin. Over low heat, meanwhile, reheat the sauce to which you have added the diced apple, grapefruit, and pimiento. To serve, spoon the sauce onto the heated plates first and place the chicken on top.

117

Poulet en soupière aux écrevisses
POACHED CHICKEN IN TUREENS
WITH CRAYFISH

To serve four:

   Two 1¼-pound Rock Cornish hens (*see Note*), or
      one 2¼-pound chicken, trussed
   2 quarts chicken stock (5) (8)
   ½ pound of fresh snow peas, or
      1 package of frozen snow peas
   8 live crayfish (*see Note*)
   Boiling salted water

SAUCE:

   1 cup hot lobster sauce (49)
   ½ cup reserved chicken stock, above

UTENSILS:

   Deep saucepan for birds
   Saucepan for crayfish
   Colander
   Bowl of ice water
   Bowl for reserved stock
   To bake and serve: 4 deep individual soup tureens, 4
      circles of aluminum foil, kitchen string

NOTE: *A French 2¼-pound chicken is a short, chunky
bird which carves well into four compact quarters. We
feel American chickens of this weight are long and
bony in comparison for the purposes of this recipe
which is baked and served in rather small individual
tureens. The two Rock Cornish hens, each one quartered, make attractive portions in the tureens and allow
the four people served to have identical helpings of
both breast and second joint and leg. If you wish to
use a chicken, see the variation of this recipe,* Poulet
aux écrevisses (118).

   *On the face of it, this is a simple recipe; the cook-
ing method is exceptionally practical. The lobster*

sauce (sauce homardière) *which accompanies it, however, is not a simple matter, as it is based on the great classic lobster sauce,* sauce américaine, *and other prepared ingredients as well. There is no substitute for* sauce américaine. *Make it, and see the Note on page 58 concerning planning ahead for its use in other recipes.*

The addition of live écrevisses, *or crayfish, involves, for most people, getting these by air (see page 293) when they are in season. We recommend that you either send for a good shipment of crayfish and enjoy* Ecrevisses à la nage (82), *saving 8 or 12 for this or the following recipe, or that you skip them altogether and add no substitute. You could use medium-size shrimp in their shells, but their flavor is very different and too distinct to work well with the other elements.*

Finally, as a technique, poulet en soupière *is an excellent way to poach poultry. There are two variations,* Poulet aux écrevisses (118) *and* Pigeon en soupière (124). *Ed.*

In the deep saucepan, bring the chicken stock to a boil, lower the heat, add the trussed birds (which must be immersed in the stock), and simmer them for 10 to 12 minutes.

Remove the birds to a cutting board and carve them on each side as follows: Cut off the breast meat, together with the wing, all in one piece; cut off the wing tips if you wish. Remove the skin. Now cut off the second joint and leg in one piece, and remove the skin.

If you are using frozen snow peas, simply allow them to defrost. If you are using fresh ones, simmer them in the stock in which the birds have cooked. Start testing shortly after they are put into the simmering stock; drain them in the colander, reserving the stock, as soon as they are tender enough to eat but are still definitely crunchy. Turn them out into the bowl of ice water to stop their cooking, and drain again.

Rinse the live crayfish under cold running water. In the second saucepan, bring the salted water to a boil, add the crayfish, remove in 30 seconds, and drain.

Make the hot lobster sauce (*sauce homardière II*) now.

NOTE: *The recipe may be prepared ahead to this point. Moisten the pieces of chicken with a few spoonfuls of stock and cover them with aluminum foil. The sauce may be allowed to cool. Ed.*

Preheat the oven to 450°–475° F.

Divide the snow peas into four portions in the tureens, saving a few to put on top. Then, in each tureen, place a piece of breast meat and a second joint and leg of the Rock Cornish hens, mask with ¼ cup of the *sauce homardière,* and add 2 crayfish, 2 tablespoons of the reserved chicken stock, and the last of the snow peas.

Cover the tureens with the circles of aluminum foil and tie these in place with string, as you would do to cover a jelly jar. Bake the *poulet en soupière* in the preheated oven for 15 minutes.

Serve still covered with the foil so that the full aroma of the dish may be appreciated when the foil is removed at table. (*You will see when you discover the broth that has been achieved why this dish is served in tureens. Ed.*)

118

Poulet aux écrevisses
POACHED CHICKEN WITH CRAYFISH

NOTE: *This is a slightly simpler version of the preceding master recipe,* Poulet en soupière aux écrevisses. *The Notes in that recipe concerning the sauce and the live crayfish apply here also. Ed.*

To serve four:

One 2¼- to 2½-pound chicken
Salt and pepper
12 live crayfish

2 quarts of **chicken stock (5) (8)**
1 medium-size carrot, scraped and sliced
1 onion, peeled and sliced
Bouquet garni

Hot lobster sauce (49), made in advance
1 teaspoon of minced parsley
1 teaspoon of minced fresh tarragon

UTENSILS:

Oval enameled cast-iron casserole, with a lid
Perforated skimmer
To serve: Heated platter and/or 4 heated dinner plates

Make the lobster sauce (*sauce homardière II*) first.
It may be allowed to cool. Salt and pepper the inside
of the chicken, and truss it. Rinse the live crayfish
under cold running water.

In the casserole, bring to a boil together the stock
and the carrot, onion, and *bouquet garni*. Add the
chicken, lower the heat, and simmer it for 25 minutes.
While it cooks, cook the crayfish in the casserole with
it, a few at a time, according to how much room there
is for them, for 2 minutes each. Remove them with
the skimmer and keep them warm. Finish cooking
the chicken partially covered.

When it is done, remove the chicken to a carving
board, and carve the meat off the carcass in four
pieces—two breasts and wings, two second joints and
legs. Remove the skin. Arrange the chicken on the hot
platter, mask it with the hot lobster sauce, sprinkle
with the minced parsley and tarragon, and decorate
the platter with the red crayfish all around, claws
pointing up.

119

Gigot de poulette cuit à la vapeur de marjolaine
STUFFED CHICKEN DRUMSTICKS
WITH MARJORAM

To serve four or eight:

UTENSILS:

Heavy-bottomed saucepan for braising, with a lid
Large steamer or *couscoussière* (*see page 288*)
Saucepan for boiling vegetables
Small sharp poultry lacers, or soft kitchen string
Electric blender
Small saucepan for sauce
To serve: Heated deep oval platter and/or heated
    dinner plates

STUFFING:

2 tablespoons of olive oil
3 ounces of canned morels, in all
1 small onion, minced
2 fresh mushrooms, stems trimmed, rinsed, and
    cut in half
½ pound piece of veal sweetbread (*see page 299*)
A small (1½-ounce) piece of raw breast meat of chicken
½ teaspoon of salt
A pinch of pepper
2 tablespoons of port
5 tablespoons of veal stock (1) (4)

Drain the morels, cut each one in half lengthwise, and
set one-third of them aside for the vegetable *garniture*.

Heat the olive oil in the heavy-bottomed saucepan
and add the morels, onion, and fresh mushrooms. Over
low heat, cook the vegetables until they give off some
of their liquid, or for about 1 minute.

Add the piece of sweetbread, the piece of breast
meat of chicken, and the salt and pepper. Simmer all
together over low heat for 2 minutes, then add the
port and continue simmering until the liquid has re-

duced by more than half. Then add the 5 tablespoons of veal stock and cook gently, covered, for 30 minutes.

Let this braised mixture cool.

STOCK AND CHICKEN:

1 quart of veal stock (1) (4)
3 generous sprigs of fresh marjoram
8 chicken drumsticks
Salt and pepper
The braised mixture, above

While the stuffing ingredients are braising, bring the stock to a boil in the bottom of the steamer or *couscoussière*, turn off the heat, and add the marjoram and let it steep in the stock to perfume it.

Bone the drumsticks with a small knife (*see Note on page 219*).

Remove the morels, mushrooms, sweetbreads, and chicken-breast meat from their saucepan, and cut them all up into even, small dice (smaller than ¼ inch). Mix all together, adding 2 teaspoons of the braising liquid.

Lightly salt and pepper the cavities of the boned drumsticks. Spoon in the stuffing, pressing down on it in the cavity to pack it together. Close the drumsticks by pinning the skin with the poultry lacers or tying with kitchen string.

VEGETABLE GARNITURE:

A piece of celery root, cut into slim sticks
    2 inches long—enough to make about 24 sticks
1 large or 2 small carrots cut up in the same fashion—
    enough to make about 24 sticks
16 small, round spring or green onions, roots and tops
    trimmed off, and peeled if the outer layers are tough
Young green beans, cut in half or into 2-inch lengths
    unless they are very small—enough to make
    32 pieces
The morels, reserved from the stuffing, cut lengthwise
    into narrow strips
16 canned white asparagus stalks, cut to make tips 3
    inches long
1 truffle (*optional*), cut into fine *julienne* sticks

Prepare the vegetables.

NOTE: *The recipe is prepared ahead to this point. Ed.*

The next step is to steam the chicken (next paragraph). While it is cooking, boil the vegetables. In one saucepan, cook the vegetables in boiling salted water, putting them in in the following sequence: celery root and onions, to cook 15 minutes; five minutes later, carrots, to cook 10 minutes; five minutes later, green beans, to cook 5 minutes; three minutes later, the morels and asparagus tips, to heat through in 2 minutes—15 minutes' cooking time in all. Drain the vegetables with care and keep warm.

TO STEAM THE CHICKEN:

Prick the drumstick skins well with a two-pronged fork to keep them from bursting while they cook. Bring the marjoram-flavored stock to a simmer in the bottom of the steamer, put the drumsticks in the top section, and sprinkle a few fresh marjoram leaves over them. Steam over low heat, covered, for 30 minutes.

SAUCE:

   3 tablespoons of mushroom purée (136)
   1 tablespoon of water-cress purée (139) (*see Note*)
   1 tablespoon of fromage blanc (173)
   1 tablespoon of crème fraîche (172) (*optional*)
   1¾ cups of the hot veal stock over which the chicken has cooked

NOTE: *The water-cress purée is essential to this sauce. To preserve the fresh, green color, make the sauce at the last minute. Ed.*

Purée all the ingredients together in the electric blender, pour the sauce into a small saucepan, and keep warm.

TO SERVE:

With a small pointed knife, carefully slit the skin on the top side of each *gigot de poulette*. Spread the sauce—which will have a lovely pale-green color—in the center of the heated platter or heated dinner plates. Place the chicken in the middle, and spread the multicolored vegetable *garniture,* including the truffle *julienne,* all around it. Decorate each piece of chicken with leaves of fresh marjoram.

NOTE: *To bone the chicken drumsticks, with a cleaver first cut them off from the second joints; it will help later if you pull some of the second-joint skin down over the drumstick before cutting, so that there will be enough skin to skewer neatly over the stuffed cavity.*

With a small pointed knife, cut the chicken meat away from the knuckle at the large end of the drumstick until you get down, within about an inch, to the straight bone. Then stand the drumstick up and scrape downward all around the bone; the meat comes away very easily and turns inside out like a sweater sleeve. When you get to the bottom, scrape the skin away from the ankle knuckle from the inside, and pull the entire bone away. Turn the meat right side out, and it is ready to be stuffed. Ed.

120

Aiguillettes de caneton au poivre vert
BREAST OF DUCKLING WITH GREEN PEPPERCORNS

To serve four:

Two 5- to 5½-pound ducklings (*see Note*)
2 apples (*see Note*), peeled, quartered, and cored
2 fresh apricots, rinsed, halved and pitted, or
    4 canned unsweetened apricot halves
    (*see Note on page 256*)

SAUCE:

½ cup of dry white wine
2 tablespoons of armagnac or cognac
½ cup of **chicken stock (5) (8)**, or duck stock
    (*see Note*)
4 teaspoons of green peppercorns and a little of their
    juice (*see page 296*)
2 tablespoons of minced canned pimientos

LIAISON:

2 fresh mushrooms, stems trimmed, rinsed
1 cup of milk made with nonfat dry milk and water
4 teaspoons of **fromage blanc (173)**

UTENSILS:

Roasting pan (with a rack; *optional*)
Small baking dish
2 small heavy-bottomed saucepans
Electric blender
To serve: A heated platter and/or 4 heated dinner plates

NOTE: *The French ducks called for, Challans or Rouennais, are smaller, chunkier, and less fat than our ducks usually are. (The original recipe calls for 3¼-pound ducks which are roasted for only 15 to 20 minutes.) For this recipe, you use only the breast meat. Have the butcher cut off all the lower ends of the ducks for you, including the legs, and have him cut off the wings as well, leaving only the rib cages with their breast meat. Use the remainder of the ducks, without the fat, for something else (the meat, boned, in a pâté, for instance, and the bones for a duck stock; see page 39).*

The apples called for are pommes reinettes, *russet apples, which you will not find unless they are grown locally. Use small, crisp apples with a good, winy flavor; we used Greenings. Ed.*

Preheat the oven to 500° F.

Put the ducks in the roasting pan, on a rack if you wish, and prick the skins well all over. Arrange the apples in the baking dish and add a little water. Put both ducks and apples in the oven, the apples on the lowest rack of the oven, and roast for 20 minutes. Then, place an apricot half on each apple, lower the oven heat to 400° F., and continue cooking ducks and fruit for another 20 minutes. The duck breast meat should be cooked through but still a little rosy, and the apples tender but still holding their shapes.

Meanwhile, in one saucepan, simmer together the white wine and armagnac or cognac until all the alcohol is evaporated and the liquid is reduced to a couple of tablespoons. Then add a few drops of the juice from the can of green peppercorns diluted with a little water (the juice is very strong), and add the stock. Simmer over low heat for 10 or 15 minutes.

In the other saucepan, cook the mushrooms in the milk over low heat for 10 minutes. In the electric blender, purée together the mushrooms with half their cooking liquid and the *fromage blanc*. Stir this *liaison* into the reduced stock, and add the green peppercorns and the pimientos. Taste for seasoning and keep the sauce warm.

Remove the ducks to a carving board, let them cool a little, and remove all the skin. Carve off the four breasts, each in one piece, and cut these lengthwise into thin strips or *aiguillettes*. Arrange them on the heated platter or plates, mask them with the sauce, and add the *garniture* of baked apples and apricots.

121

Aiguillettes de caneton aux figues fraîches
BREAST OF DUCKLING WITH FRESH FIGS

To serve four:

Two 5- to 5½-pound ducklings (*see Note on page 220*)
12 thin-skinned figs, washed and unpeeled
⅝ cup of red wine
1 teaspoon of honey

SAUCE:
The reduced red wine, above
⅓ cup of reduced veal stock (1) (4)
⅓ cup of milk made with nonfat dry milk and water
1 tablespoon of mushroom purée (136)
2 teaspoons of fromage blanc (173)
2 teaspoons of crème fraîche (172)
Salt and pepper

UTENSILS:
Roasting pan (with a rack, *optional*)
Heavy-bottomed saucepan, with a lid
Whisk
To serve: A heated platter and/or 4 heated dinner plates

Have the ducks prepared for roasting as in the preceding recipe. Preheat the oven to 500° F. Put the ducks in the roasting pan, on a rack if you wish, and prick the skins well all over. Roast them for 20 minutes, then lower the heat to 400° F. and roast another 20 minutes. The breast meat should be cooked through but still a little rosy.

Meanwhile, put the figs in the saucepan; they should fit quite close together in one layer. Dissolve the honey in the wine, add this to the saucepan, bring to a simmer, and poach the figs, covered, for 2 minutes. Remove the figs to a heated plate, and continue simmering the wine until it is reduced by one quarter, or to less than ½ cup. With a small knife, section the tops of the figs with two or three crosscuts so they will open like flowers, and cover to keep them warm.

With the whisk, mix into the reduced wine the veal stock, milk, mushroom purée, *fromage blanc,* and *crème fraîche.* Taste for seasoning and keep the sauce warm.

Remove the ducks to a carving board, let them cool a little, and remove the skin. Carve off the four breasts, each in one piece, and cut these lengthwise into thin strips or *aiguillettes.* Arrange them on the heated platter or plates, mask them with the sauce, and add the *garniture* of figs.

122
Pigeon à la crème d'ail
GRILLED SQUAB WITH GARLIC CREAM SAUCE

To serve four:

4 squab
Salt and pepper

VEGETABLE GARNITURE:

12 or 16 small, round green or spring onions, peeled
1 medium-size carrot, scraped and cut into *julienne* sticks ¼ inch thick and 1½ inches long
1 medium-size stalk of celery, cut in the same way
Scant ¼ pound of young green beans, snapped, strung, and cut in half crosswise
¼ pound of stemmed spinach leaves
1 teaspoon of butter
1½ teaspoons of granulated sugar dissolved in ¼ cup of water

Garlic cream sauce (45)

UTENSILS:

2 saucepans
Colander
Charcoal grill (*see page 5*)
To serve: 4 heated dinner plates

NOTE: These squab are prepared for grilling in the old way called *à la crapaudine*. If your poultry man is not familiar with this, here is how it is done: After cleaning, with a long knife the bird is split in half down the middle of the back from the *inside*. All the bone of the spine is then cut away, and the bird is well flattened with the side of a cleaver. Then the wing tips are tucked into two small incisions made in the sides of the bird, to hold the wings flat and in place. (The same thing is also done with larger birds for grilling.)

Prepare the garlic cream sauce (*sauce crème d'ail*) and keep it warm.

In one saucepan, cook the vegetables in boiling salted water, putting them in in the following sequence: onions, to cook 15 minutes; five minutes later, carrot and celery, to cook 10 minutes; 6 minutes later, green beans and spinach, to cook 4 minutes—15 minutes' cooking time in all. Drain the vegetables, saving the cooking water; return some of it to the saucepan and keep the spinach warm in it.

In the other saucepan, heat the butter, add the drained vegetables, and sauté them briefly. Then add the sweetened water, stir all gently together, and leave over low heat until the liquid is evaporated and the vegetables are lightly glazed. Taste for seasoning.

The coals in the grill must be very hot; the squab are to cook quickly, about 5 minutes on each side. Start them skin side up. When they are done, remove their skins or not, as you wish, and salt and pepper the birds. Carve off the legs. Carve off the breasts, each in one piece, slice these thinly, horizontally (unless they are very small), and arrange the slices back on the ribs of the birds.

While the squab are cooking, drain the spinach well, divide it into four portions, and shape them into round "pancakes." Transfer these to one side of the heated plates and spoon the glazed vegetables over them. On the other sides of the plates, reconstitute the birds *en crapaudine* as they looked before carving, and pour the hot garlic cream sauce in a ribbon around them.

NOTE: The *sauce à la crème d'ail* may be replaced by apple and lemon sauce (47) —*sauce à la pomme*.

123

Pintadeau grillé au citron vert
GRILLED GUINEA HEN WITH LIME

To serve four:

   1 guinea hen weighing about 2 pounds (*see Note*)
   1 lime
   1 orange

MARINADE:

   1 large or 2 medium-size onions, peeled and thinly sliced
   ⅜ cup of **chicken stock (5) (8)**
   3 tablespoons of lime juice
   1½ tablespoons of orange juice
   Salt and pepper

SAUCE AND GARNITURE:

   Marinade, above
   ¼ cup of vinegar
   1½ teaspoons of granulated sugar
   1 teaspoon of **glace de viande (3)**
   1 teaspoon of **crème fraîche (172)**

   Rind of ½ lime, above
   Rind of ¼ orange, above
   Another lime, peeled and sliced

UTENSILS:

   Deep oval dish to marinate the bird
   2 saucepans, one with a lid
   Electric blender
   Charcoal grill (*see page 5*)
   To serve: 4 heated dinner plates

NOTE: *Have the guinea hen prepared* en crapaudine, *as described on page 224. The recipe may also be used for a broiler chicken weighing between 2 and 2½ pounds. Ed.*

Peel off the skins of ½ of the lime and of ¼ of the orange in thin strips and set aside. Squeeze the lime and orange, and measure the juices for the marinade. Put the prepared bird in the oval dish to marinate in the refrigerator for 12 hours with all the ingredients of the marinade.

Cut the lime and orange peels lengthwise into *julienne* strips as fine as pine needles, boil these in plain water for 10 minutes, drain, and set aside.

Remove the bird from the marinade. In one saucepan, simmer the marinade over low heat, covered, until the onions are soft. In the other saucepan, dissolve the sugar in the vinegar, and simmer for 5 minutes. In the electric blender, combine the cooked marinade, *glace de viande, crème fraîche,* and sweetened vinegar. Purée the sauce, taste for seasoning, and reheat when it is needed.

NOTE: *The recipe may be prepared ahead to this point. Ed.*

Peel the second lime completely, so that all of the white inner skin is cut away, and cut out the section from between the membranes; or, you may instead cut the lime into very thin slices. Set aside. Prick the skin of the bird well all over to allow the fat to drain out during cooking.

The coals in the grill must be very hot; the bird is to cook quickly, 10 minutes on each side. Start it skin side up, turn it around once before you turn it over, and turn it around once again when you cook the second side. The purpose is to sear it with crisscross brown marks on both sides.

To serve, first quarter the bird. Spoon the hot sauce onto the heated plates, place the carved pieces on top, sprinkle with the cooked lime and orange peels, and decorate with the sections or slices of lime.

124

Pigeon en soupière
POACHED SQUAB IN TUREENS
WITH VEGETABLES

To serve two:

1 squab pigeon (*see Note*), trussed
Chicken stock (5) (8) to cover the bird

VEGETABLE GARNITURE:

4 pieces of carrot, cut into olive shapes
4-inch piece of celery, cut into slim *julienne* sticks
    2 inches long
About a dozen leaves from a heart of Bibb or
    Boston lettuce
6 young green beans, cut in half crosswise
2 tablespoons of fresh young green peas
1 small cooked or canned artichoke bottom,
    cut into ½-inch dice

8 small fresh or canned button mushrooms
1 small fresh or canned *cèpe*, cut into ¼-inch dice
4 slices of truffle, cut into thin *julienne* sticks, or
    2 canned morels, drained and cut into thin
    julienne strips

SAUCE:

¼ cup of chicken stock (5) (8)
Salt and pepper
1 tablespoon of **truffle sauce** (19) (*optional*)

UTENSILS:

Deep saucepan for bird
Saucepan for vegetables
Colander
To bake and serve: 4 deep individual soup tureens
    (*see color picture 12*), 4 circles of aluminum foil,
    kitchen string

NOTE: *To serve two, you need a bird that weighs at
least 1 pound. The recipe calls for a young pigeon,
but another small game bird, or a Rock Cornish hen,*

which averages about 1¼ pounds, may also be used. The recipe is easily doubled to serve four. Ed.

The bird may be roasted, but it is simpler, and better *minceur* practice, to poach it. In the saucepan, bring the chicken stock to a boil, lower the heat, add the trussed bird (which must be immersed in the stock), and simmer it from 7 minutes for a squab to 10 or 12 minutes for a Rock Cornish hen.

Remove the bird to a cutting board and carve it on each side as follows: Cut off the breast meat all in one piece and slice it. *(Discard the wings or not, depending on the size of the bird. Ed.)* Then cut off the second joint and leg in one piece. *(For a lean squab or game bird, you do not have to remove the skin; remove all the skin of a Rock Cornish hen. Ed.)*

In one saucepan, cook the vegetables in boiling salted water, putting them in in the following sequence: carrot and celery, to cook 10 minutes; five minutes later, lettuce, green beans, and peas, to cook 5 minutes; three minutes later, the diced artichoke bottom, to heat through in 2 minutes—10 minutes' cooking time in all. All the vegetables should still be a little crisp. Drain them in the colander.

NOTE: *The recipe may be prepared ahead to this point. Cover bird and vegetables to keep them moist. Ed.*

Preheat the oven to 450°–475° F.

Put half the cooked vegetable *garniture,* in equal portions, in the two tureens, and add the button mushrooms, *cèpes,* and truffle or morels, all three of which —not having been cooked previously—will give the maximum of their flavor to the dish. Then add the slices of breast meat and a second joint and leg to each tureen, followed by the remainder of the cooked vegetables. Finally, divide the truffle sauce (*sauce périgueux*) and the chicken stock (seasoned, if needed, with salt and pepper) between the tureens.

Cover the tureens with the circles of aluminum foil and tie these in place with string. Bake the *pigeon en soupière* in the preheated oven for 10 minutes for a small bird, 15 minutes for a Rock Cornish hen.

Serve still covered with the foil so that the full aroma of the dish may be appreciated when the foil is removed at table.

125

Baron de lapereau à la vapeur d'hysope
STEAMED RABBIT WITH FRESH HERBS

To serve four:

The baron (hindquarters) of a young rabbit weighing 1 to 1¼ pounds (*see Note*)
5 branches of hyssop from your own herb garden, or branches of fresh tarragon and thyme
2 or 3 cups of **chicken stock (5) (8)**
Salt and pepper

SAUCE:

1 cup of hot stock, above
1 teaspoon of **glace de viande (3)**
1 tablespoon of **fromage blanc (173)**
1 tablespoon of **water-cress purée (138)**

UTENSILS:

Two-piece steamer or *couscoussière* (*see page 288*)
Electric blender
Small saucepan
To serve: Heated deep oval baking dish and a heated sauceboat

NOTE: *For steaming, you need a young rabbit, or* lapereau. *The baron of a rabbit, or hare, is the whole hindquarters of the animal—the loin (saddle) with the legs attached. However, to fit the rabbit into a steamer, and for carving, we found it more convenient to have the baron cut into three pieces—two legs and the loin. If you buy fresh rabbit (Italian butchers are the most likely to carry it), have the butcher prepare it for you.*

If you buy packaged frozen rabbit, which can be very good, the legs and loin will already be cut apart. Ed.

In the bottom of the steamer, simmer the stock and hyssop, or the tarragon and thyme, together gently for 10 minutes. Then put the rabbit in the top of the steamer, add a few leaves of the herb you are using, cover, and steam for 20 minutes.

Remove the rabbit, spoon a little hot stock over it, and keep it warm. In the electric blender, combine 1 cup of the hot stock, the *glace de viande, fromage blanc,* water-cress purée, and the herbs from the top of the steamer, and blend. Taste this sauce for seasoning, reheat, and keep it warm.

Salt and pepper the rabbit meat as you slice it. Carve off the loin in one piece and cut this into long thin slices; arrange these together, overlapping, at one end of the heated oval dish. Slice the meat off the legs and arrange at the other end. Serve the sauce from the heated sauceboat.

NOTE: *We found that, for lack of experience, we were slow to get the rabbit carved and that the slices tended to dry out and get cold while the carving was still in progress. The sensible thing to do appears to be to spoon a little of the hot herb-perfumed stock over the slices, as well as adding the salt and pepper, as you go along. Ed.*

126

Gâteau de lapin aux herbes et aux mirabelles
POTTED RABBIT WITH HERBS AND
FRESH PLUMS

To serve four as a first course:

The baron (hindquarters) of a rabbit, weighing about 1 pound (*see Note and page 229*)
½ pound of small, ripe fresh plums (*see Note*)
1 tablespoon of *eau de vie de mirabelle* (*see Note*), or brandy

1 tablespoon of minced parsley
1 tablespoon of minced fresh chervil
2 teaspoons of minced fresh tarragon
1 tablespoon of minced shallot
½ cup of dry white wine
Salt and pepper

1 tablespoon (1 envelope) of gelatin
2 cups of chicken stock (5)
2 tablespoons of minced parsley
1 teaspoon of minced tarragon
½ tablespoon of minced shallot

Cooked diced fresh tomatoes (130), chilled (*optional*)

UTENSILS:

Deep oval dish to marinate the rabbit
Bowls
Saucepan
Fine-mesh strainer
Oval earthenware *terrine,* with a lid (1½-quart capacity)
Baking pan for *bain marie*
To serve: A smaller *terrine,* with a lid, a large serving
    spoon, and a sauceboat (*optional*)

NOTE: *This recipe uses only the meatiest parts of the
rabbit, the legs and loin (for which another French expression is* arrière train de lapin), *cut into 6 pieces;
have the butcher do this for you.*

*The plums originally called for are 20 small, whole,
golden* mirabelles. *We used ½ pound of ripe green-
gage plums, unpeeled, pitted, and cut into eighths.*

Eau de vie de mirabelle *is one of the many fruit-
based distilled white spirits made in France and is
available here, but brandy will serve the purpose. Ed.*

Two days in advance, put the pieces of rabbit in the
oval dish to marinate in the refrigerator for 24 hours
with all the ingredients of the marinade.

The next day, marinate the plums in a bowl with
the *mirabelle* or brandy. Soak the gelatin in a little
water until it is soft.

Remove the rabbit from its dish and wipe it off. In the saucepan, simmer the marinade briefly to evaporate the alcohol in the wine, then strain it, discard the herbs and shallot, and return the liquid to the saucepan. Add the chicken stock and the soaked gelatin, stir until the gelatin is completely dissolved, and add the fresh parsley, tarragon, and shallot.

Preheat the oven to 350° F.

Arrange the pieces of rabbit and the plums in the larger *terrine*, and pour the stock-gelatin mixture over them; they should be well covered with the liquid. Cover the *terrine* and bake it in a pan of hot water (*bain marie*) in the preheated oven for 2½ hours. Remove it from the oven and let it cool.

Remove the pieces of rabbit and bone them. (*You will get chunks of meat, but also bits and pieces; we suggest mincing the latter evenly and placing them in the bottom of the final terrine when it is assembled. Ed.*) Transfer the rabbit meat and then the plums and cooking juices to the smaller *terrine* (all the ingredients will have cooked down), cover, and refrigerate for 24 hours.

Using a large serving spoon, serve the potted rabbit from the *terrine*, and pass the diced tomatoes separately in the sauceboat.

NOTE: *This recipe has been changed in that the rabbit is boned after cooking; in the original version it is boned raw, before cooking. We found one Italian butcher who knew how to do this, but he did not want to spend the time. A friend reported that he knew how to do it, but the consensus was that most people do not know the anatomy of a rabbit well enough to bone one efficiently. Boning after cooking is still a little awkward, but less difficult. Otherwise, the recipe is unchanged. Ed.*

127

Râble de lièvre aux betteraves
ROAST SADDLE OF HARE WITH BEETS

To serve two or three:

The loin of a hare, weighing a little under 1 pound,
ready for roasting (*see Note*)

MARINADE:

1 cup of red wine
1 carrot, scraped and cut into ½-inch dice
½ onion, peeled and cut into ½-inch dice
Bouquet garni
4 juniper berries
2 cloves
Salt and pepper

1 teaspoon of olive oil

½ pound of young beets, washed and unpeeled
1 tablespoon of red-wine vinegar
2 tablespoons of the sauce, below
Salt and pepper

SAUCE:

1 shallot, peeled and finely minced
1 tablespoon of red-wine vinegar
The strained marinade, above
1 tablespoon of mushroom purée (136)
½ teaspoon of Dijon mustard
1 teaspoon of nonfat dry milk
¼ cup of veal stock (1) (4)
4 tablespoons of hot water (*optional*)

UTENSILS:

Flameproof oval baking dish
Saucepan for beets
Electric blender
Small saucepan for sauce
Nonstick skillet
To serve: Long, narrow carving knife and 4 heated
dinner plates

NOTE: There may still be a fine, thin skin on the loin, or *râble; it should be removed.*

A day in advance, put the loin of hare in the baking dish to marinate in the refrigerator with all the ingredients of the marinade. Boil the beets, unpeeled, drain, cool, and store in the refrigerator.

The next day, remove the loin from its dish, wipe it off with a cloth, and strain the marinade into a bowl. Peel and slice the beets.

Preheat the oven to 475°–500° F.

Heat the teaspoon of olive oil in the baking dish, put in the loin, and, over brisk heat, let it brown on all sides, turning it several times. Then roast it, top side up, in the preheated oven for 12 minutes. Remove the loin and keep it warm; it will continue to poach in its own heat (*see page 12*).

Discard all the fat from the baking dish, put in the minced shallot, and cook it gently for 1 minute. Now stir in the tablespoon of vinegar and let it boil, at the same time scrapping up all the brown glaze in the bottom of the dish. Then add the strained marinade, and boil it until it is reduced to one quarter of its original volume, or to little more than ¼ cup. (The alcohol in the wine will be entirely evaporated.)

In the electric blender, purée together the mushroom purée, mustard, nonfat dry milk, veal stock, and the reduced marinade. Dilute with a little hot water if needed, taste this sauce for seasoning, and keep it warm in the small saucepan.

Heat the nonstick skillet, add the sliced beets, and "sauté" them until they are heated through, adding also the tablespoon of vinegar, which will give them a perfect flavor and a brilliant ruby color. Add 2 tablespoons of the hot sauce, season with salt and pepper, and keep warm.

To serve, with a long narrow knife, carve the loin lengthwise into long, thin slices or *aiguillettes*. Salt and pepper each one very lightly, and arrange them, overlapping in compact fan formation, on the heated plates. Arrange the beets on the plates, and mask the meat with the sauce.

Les légumes
VEGETABLES

128

Oignons Tante Louise
BAKED STUFFED ONIONS

To serve four:

8 onions of uniform size, 2 to 2½ inches in diameter, peeled, and the *top* ends sliced off

STUFFING:
1 teaspoon of olive oil
½ pound of zucchini
2 ounces of fresh or canned *cèpes* (*see Note*)
Salt and pepper
1 egg
½ cup of **chicken stock (5) (8)**
1 cup of **fresh tomato purée sauce (41)**

UTENSILS:
Heavy-bottomed enameled or stainless saucepan, with a lid
Electric blender
Bowl
Round baking dish
To serve: 4 heated plates

NOTE: *This is a simple, home recipe. Cèpes will give it a particular excellence; any good mushroom will serve. Ed.*

Unless the zucchini are very small, scrape them with a vegetable peeler. Chop them coarsely, and in the heavy-bottomed saucepan heat them in the olive oil until they give off some of their liquid. Then add the *cèpes*, whole. Season lightly with salt and pepper, and cook the vegetables, covered, over medium heat for 15 minutes, stirring occasionally with a wooden spoon.

Meanwhile, put the peeled whole onions in a saucepan of boiling salted water, boil them for 15 or 20 minutes, drain, and cool them under cold running water. With a teaspoon or a grapefruit knife, hollow out the centers of the onions.

Preheat the oven to 425° F.

Remove the mushrooms from the first saucepan and chop them. Purée the zucchini in the electric blender (*or not, as you prefer. Ed.*).

In the bowl, lightly beat the egg with a fork, then add the zucchini purée and the chopped mushrooms, and mix well together. Lightly salt and pepper the insides of the onions, and fill them with the egg-and-vegetable mixture. Arrange the stuffed onions in the baking dish —they should fit into it fairly close together—and add the chicken stock. Bake in the preheated oven for 30 minutes.

Heat the tomato purée sauce. To serve, spoon the sauce onto the heated plates, and place 2 onions in the center of each one.

129

Marmelade d'oignons au vinaigre de Jerez
ONIONS SIMMERED WITH SHERRY VINEGAR

To serve four:

1½ pounds of onions
1 teaspoon of olive oil
1 teaspoon of honey, or to taste (*optional*)
1 teaspoon of salt, or to taste
⅛ teaspoon of pepper
3 tablespoons of sherry vinegar, or less to taste

Heavy-bottomed enameled or stainless saucepan,
with a lid
Wooden spoon

Peel the onions and cut them into thin slices. Heat the
olive oil in the saucepan, and add the onions, honey,
and salt and pepper. Cook, covered, for 35 minutes,
letting the onions color slightly and stirring as needed
with a wooden spoon. Then add the vinegar and cook
for another 35 minutes over low heat, still covered
and stirring occasionally. The onions should reduce
gently throughout the cooking, without sticking, to
achieve the desired "marmalade."

130

Tomates concassées (crues ou cuites)
DICED FRESH TOMATOES (Raw or Cooked)

To make about 1½ quarts of raw diced tomatoes, or
about 1 quart of cooked tomatoes:

3 pounds of firm, ripe tomatoes, peeled

1 teaspoon of olive oil
2 shallots, peeled and finely minced
2 cloves of garlic, unpeeled, crushed
A *bouquet garni*
Salt and pepper

UTENSILS:

Kettle of boiling water
Bowl of ice water
Enameled or stainless saucepan
Glass or stainless container for storage

NOTE: *It is convenient to have these tomatoes prepared in advance for use in a variety of recipes. However, you can, of course, make as small an amount as you need at any given moment. Do not overseason when you cut the quantity down. The full recipe for the cooked version is required for* **Tarte de tomates fraîches au thym** (61). *Ed.*

To peel the tomatoes, they must be plunged into boiling water for 15 seconds and then plunged into cold water so the tomato just under the skin will not begin to cook. (*An easy way to do this is to put the tomatoes in the kitchen sink, stem ends up. Pour boiling water over them, which goes quickly down the drain. Turn the tomatoes over, pour boiling water over them again, and transfer them to the bowl of ice water. Ed.*) They are now very easy to peel.

After peeling, cut the tomatoes in half crosswise, gently squeeze them in the palm of your hand to eliminate the seeds and excess juice, and chop them coarsely. Store, unseasoned and covered, in the refrigerator to use raw.

To use these tomatoes on salads, drain the amount you need, and season lightly with salt and pepper or with **sauce vinaigrette minceur** (29) (30). It is not necessary to season them when they are used as an ingredient for a seasoned sauce or other recipe.

OR, TO USE COOKED:

Heat the olive oil in the saucepan and in it gently cook the shallots. Add the tomatoes, garlic, and *bouquet garni*, and season with salt and pepper. Simmer, uncovered, for 30 minutes, or until most of the liquid has evaporated. Remove the garlic cloves and store the cooked tomatoes, covered, in the refrigerator.

131

Emincé de poireaux è la menthe sauvage
STEWED LEEKS WITH WILD MINT

To serve two:

A bunch of leeks (about 2½ pounds)
A dozen small mint leaves, wild or cultivated, chopped
3 tablespoons of chicken stock (5) (8), or
    3 tablespoons of dry white wine
¾ teaspoon of salt
A pinch of pepper

UTENSILS:

Colander
Heavy-bottomed stainless or nonstick saucepan,
    with a lid

Cut the white parts of the leeks only into thin slices; they should weigh about 1¼ pounds. Rinse the slices in plenty of water to remove all traces of sand, and drain. In the saucepan, heat the leeks and chopped mint together, stirring often, for 5 minutes so they will give off some of their liquid. Then add the stock or wine and season with salt and pepper. Cook the leeks, uncovered, over low heat for about 30 minutes, or until they are reduced to a moist "marmalade." Taste for seasoning and serve with a sprinkling of fresh mint leaves cut into fine strips with scissors.

132

Confit bayaldi
BAKED ZUCCHINI, EGGPLANT AND TOMATOES

To serve four:

½ pound of young zucchini
½-pound piece of eggplant
2 ripe tomatoes
4 mushrooms

1 or 2 small onions
2 teaspoons of olive oil
½ teaspoon of thyme flowers, or a pinch of dried thyme
1 clove of garlic, peeled and finely minced
Salt and pepper

UTENSILS:

4 pieces of aluminum foil
To bake and serve: 4 individual baked-egg dishes,
    inside diameter 6 inches

Wash the zucchini and eggplant and partially peel them with a vegetable scraper; that is, take off strips of skin ¼ to ⅜ inch wide, leaving between the peeled areas strips of the same width. (This is done for color.) Peel the tomatoes, blanching them first for 15 seconds in boiling water. Cut all three vegetables into slices less than ¼ inch thick. Trim the stems of the mushrooms, rinse, and slice the mushrooms thinly. Peel, halve, and thinly slice the onions.

Preheat the oven to 400° F.

Arrange the vegetables, alternating the colors, in the baking dishes. Place the half-slices of onion so that they shield the mushroom slices, which tend to dry out during the cooking. Mix together the olive oil, thyme, and minced garlic, and spoon a quarter of this mixture over each dish. Season with salt and pepper.

Cover the dishes with the aluminum foil and bake them in the preheated oven for 20 minutes. Then remove the foil, lower the heat to 300° F., and cook another 25 to 30 minutes, or until the mixture has reduced to a vegetable "marmalade."

NOTE: Confit bayaldi *may be cooked ahead and reheated. Ed.*

133

Confiture de légumes de Maman Guérard
GREEN PEAS AND CARROTS BRAISED WITH LETTUCE

To serve four:

1½ cups of fresh, shelled young green peas
1 teaspoon of olive oil
1 medium-size carrot, scraped and cut into ¼-inch dice
1 medium-size fresh *cèpe* or other fresh mushroom,
    stem trimmed, rinsed, and cut into ¼-inch dice
20 small, round green or spring onions, peeled
The leaves of 2 large hearts of tender green lettuce
½ cup of chicken stock (5) (8)
Salt and pepper

UTENSILS:

Saucepan
To cook and serve: Enameled cast-iron casserole,
    with a lid

In the saucepan boil the peas in salted water for 5 minutes, and drain. Heat the olive oil in the casserole, and in it cook the carrot, covered, for 3 minutes without letting it color. Add a little salt and pepper, the *cèpe* or mushroom, and the onions. Cook, covered, for 3 minutes.

Then add the peas, cover the vegetables with the lettuce leaves, moisten with the stock, and add salt and pepper again. Braise over very low heat, covered, for 1¼ hours; the level of the liquid in the casserole should remain constant throughout the cooking.

To serve, bring the casserole to the table, and remove the lid only at the last moment.

NOTE: This "marmalade" of vegetables is, in principle, the opposite of cooking them crisp-tender.

Gratin de pommes du pays de Caux
NORMANDY FRUIT AND
ARTICHOKE GRATINÉ

To serve four:

2 medium-size tart apples, peeled, cored, and cut into
½-inch dice
2 fresh apricots, halved, pitted, poached, and cut into
½-inch dice, or 4 canned unsweetened apricot halves
(*see page 256*), rinsed and cut into ½-inch dice
2 cooked artichoke bottoms, cut into ½-inch dice
1 teaspoon of olive oil

CUSTARD:

2 eggs
¾ cup of milk made with nonfat dry milk and water
1½ teaspoons of salt
A pinch of pepper
A little freshly grated nutmeg

UTENSILS:

Heavy-bottomed saucepan
Bowl
To bake and serve: 4 individual baked-egg dishes, inside
diameter 6 inches

In the saucepan, heat the olive oil, add the diced
apples, and cook them until they are still a little firm.
Add the diced apricots and artichoke bottoms, and
cook all together for a few more minutes.

Preheat the oven to 425° F.

In the bowl, beat the eggs lightly with a fork just
to break up the yolks and whites, add the milk, salt,
pepper, and nutmeg, and mix. Put the cooked fruit
and artichoke bottoms in the baking dishes and cover
them with the custard mixture. Bake in the preheated
oven for 15 minutes.

NOTE: This *gratin* resembles the old-fashioned *cla-
foutis* (a fruit and custard dessert) and may be served
with duck, game, and grilled beef.

Ratatouille niçoise
BAKED ZUCCHINI, EGGPLANT AND TOMATOES NIÇOISE

To serve three or four:

3 medium-size onions
1 small green pepper
2 cloves of garlic
¼ pound of zucchini
¼-pound piece of eggplant
¾ pound of tomatoes
3 tablespoons of olive oil
Sprig of thyme
½ bay leaf
Salt and pepper

UTENSILS:
Skillet
Earthenware or Pyrex baking dish

Peel the onions and cut them into thin slices. Wash the green pepper, quarter it, and remove the seeds. Cut the quarters crosswise into strips ½ inch wide. Peel and crush the garlic. Wash the zucchini and partially peel them with a vegetable scraper; that is, take off strips of skin ¼ to ⅜ inch wide, leaving between the peeled areas strips of the same width. Cut the zucchini in half lengthwise and then into slices ¼ inch thick. Wash the eggplant, cut it into slices ¼ inch thick, and cut the slices into strips ½ inch wide. Peel the tomatoes, blanching them first for 15 seconds in boiling water. Cut them in half, gently press out the seeds and excess juice, and cut each half into 4 wedges.

Heat a little of the olive oil in the skillet, and in it sauté the onions, green pepper, and garlic until they are lightly colored. Remove them from the skillet and discard the garlic. Add a little more oil to the pan, sauté the eggplant and remove it, and then sauté the zucchini in a little more oil and remove it. Finally, heat the tomatoes in the skillet.

Preheat the oven to 400° F.

Combine all the ingredients, season to taste with salt and pepper, put the mixture in the baking dish, and add the thyme and bay leaf. Bake the *ratatouille*, uncovered, in the preheated oven for 30 minutes. After 15 minutes, if the juices in the dish are reducing too fast, cover it with aluminum foil.

Serve hot or chilled.

136

Purée mousse de champignons
MUSHROOM PURÉE

To serve four, but see also the Note below:

- 1 scant pound of fresh mushrooms
    (¾ pound after trimming)
- 1 tablespoon of lemon juice
- 3 cups of water
- 1 cup of nonfat dry milk
- 1½ teaspoons of salt
- A pinch of pepper
- A touch of freshly grated nutmeg

UTENSILS:

- Colander
- Bowl
- Saucepan
- Electric blender

Trim the gritty root ends of the mushroom stems. Do this on a slant, the way you would sharpen a pencil with a penknife. There should remain about ¾ pound. Rinse the mushrooms in plenty of cold water, wiping them clean with your hands. Drain them in the colander and roll them quickly in the lemon juice in the bowl to keep them from darkening. Cut them in half.

In the saucepan, heat the water, and add the mushrooms, salt, pepper, and nutmeg. Cover over low heat, uncovered, for 10 minutes, then stir in the nonfat dry milk, and simmer another 5 minutes, or until the mushrooms are tender.

Drain the mushrooms, reserving the cooking liquid. Purée them very finely in the electric blender. Thin the purée with ¼ to ½ cup of the cooking liquid, and taste for seasoning. Reheat, and keep warm over hot water.

NOTE: *Purée mousse de champignons* is served as a vegetable. It is also used in small quantities as a vegetable *liaison* to bind certain mixtures and sauces in a great number of my recipes. (*It is convenient to have on hand and may be stored in a screw-top jar in the refrigerator. The recipe yields about 1⅔ cups. Ed.*)

137

Purée mousse de carottes
CARROT PURÉE

To serve four:

1¼ pounds of carrots, scraped and cut in pieces
2 quarts of water
1½ tablespoons of coarse salt
Salt and pepper
2 teaspoons of butter (*optional*)

UTENSILS:

Saucepan
Electric blender
Little saucepan (butter warmer)

In the saucepan, boil the carrots in the salted water for 20 minutes, and drain. Purée them in the electric blender. Reheat, taste for seasoning, and keep warm over hot water. To serve, you may add a *beurre noisette:* In the little saucepan, heat the butter over high heat until it foams. When the foam subsides and the butter has taken on a fine golden color, it is ready to serve.

Purée mousse de cresson I
WATER-CRESS PURÉE

To make ¾ cup:

4 bunches of water cress
1½ quarts of water
1 tablespoon of coarse salt

UTENSILS:
Colander
Enameled or stainless saucepan
Electric blender

Cut off all of the stem ends of the bunches of water cress. Remove any coarse stems left among the leaves, and pick over the stems to rescue the leaves that have been cut off with them. Rinse the leaves under cold running water. Bring the salted water to a boil in the saucepan, add the water-cress leaves, and boil for 9 minutes. Take out a cupful of the hot water and reserve it, then drain the water cress and transfer it to the electric blender. Purée the water cress, adding just enough of the hot water to blend smoothly and give the purée a good consistency. The purée may be simmered to reduce it if it becomes too liquid.

Store in a screw-top jar in the refrigerator to use in small quantities in many of the recipes in this book.

NOTE: *The original instructions call for the water cress to be boiled only 3 minutes and to be plunged immediately into a bowl of ice water to stop its cooking. We found that the large, handsome water cress we had needed much longer cooking and that the stems had to be ruthlessly elminated. Clearly, our water cress was quite different from that used by the author, and small, tender varieties in this country may also require less than the 9 minutes' cooking we specify. Ed.*

139

Purée mousse de cresson II
WATER-CRESS PURÉE

To serve four:

8 to 10 bunches of water cress
3 quarts of water
2 level tablespoons of coarse salt

Lemon juice
1 teaspoon of crème fraîche (172)

Trim and rinse the water cress as described in the previous recipe. The leaves should weigh about 1 pound. Boil them for 9 minutes in the salted water, and purée in the electric blender. Just before serving, reheat the purée, reducing it if necessary, then add a little lemon juice to taste and the *crème fraîche*.

NOTE: *Serve immediately; the brilliant green of the water cress fades quickly after the addition of the lemon and cream. Ed.*

140

Mousse d'épinards aux poires
SPINACH PURÉE WITH PEARS

To serve four:

About 1¼ pounds of fresh spinach, or
    two 10-ounce packages of frozen chopped spinach
1 fine ripe pear
Salt and pepper

UTENSILS:
2 saucepans
Large enameled or stainless kettle
Colander or strainer
Electric blender

Remove the stems of the spinach and rinse it well. The leaves should weigh about 1 pound. Quarter, peel, and core the pear, and poach it in plain boiling water until the pieces are tender but not falling apart; depending on the ripeness of the pear, this may take up to 15 minutes.

In the kettle, cook the spinach in plenty of well-salted boiling water (1½ tablespoons of salt per quart of water) for 3 minutes. Drain the spinach in the colander, rinse under cold running water, and press down on it with a large spoon to squeeze out some of the water.

(To cook frozen chopped spinach, defrost, and follow the package directions for salting and cooking; do not overcook. Drain in the strainer but do not rinse, and squeeze out some of the water. Ed.)

Purée the spinach and pear together in the electric blender, reheat the purée in a saucepan, simmering gently if there is too much liquid, and taste for seasoning. Keep it warm over hot water. It is best to make this purée not too long before serving so that it will keep its fresh green color.

141
Purée mousse de haricots verts
GREEN-BEAN PURÉE

To serve four to six:

1½ pounds of young green beans
Boiling water
Coarse salt
1 teaspoon of butter

UTENSILS:

Large enameled or stainless kettle
Colander
Electric blender
Saucepan

Snap and string the beans as needed, rinse them under cold running water, and cut them into 1-inch lengths. Boil them, uncovered, in the large kettle of boiling water salted with 1½ tablespoons of coarse salt per quart for 10 minutes. *(For a smooth purée, the beans need to be cooked longer than to the usual crisp-tender texture. Ed.)* Drain them in the colander and cool them under cold running water for 15 seconds.

In the electric blender, purée the beans, a few at a time, adding a little of the cooking liquid if needed to allow the blades to turn and to give the purée a good consistency. Reheat the purée in the saucepan with the butter, taste for seasoning, and keep it warm over hot water.

142

Purée mousse de chou-fleur
CAULIFLOWER PURÉE

To serve four:

A 1½- to 2-pound cauliflower
1 quart or more of milk made with nonfat dry milk
   and water
Salt
A little freshly grated nutmeg
Pepper

UTENSILS:

Heavy-bottomed enameled or stainless saucepan
Perforated skimmer
Electric blender

Remove the leaves of the cauliflower, cut it apart from the stem end, removing the core and most of the large inside stems and leaving virtually only the broken-up "caulif)owerets." Rinse well in plenty of water.

In the saucepan, simmer the cauliflower in the milk, uncovered and over moderate to low heat, adding also salt and the nutmeg, for 15 to 20 minutes. *(Watch that the milk does not scorch, and skim it occasionally. Ed.)*

With the skimmer, transfer the cauliflower to the electric blender, and purée it, adding a little of the cooking liquid if necessary to give the purée a good consistency. Reheat, taste for seasoning, and keep warm over hot water.

143

Purée mousse de céleri au persil
CELERY-ROOT PURÉE WITH PARSLEY

To serve four:

1½ to 2 pounds of celery root (celeriac), peeled and cut into 1-inch cubes
1 quart or more of milk made with nonfat dry milk and water
Salt
A bunch of parsley (about ¼ pound), stemmed and rinsed
Pepper

UTENSILS:

Heavy-bottomed enameled or stainless saucepan
Colander
Perforated skimmer
Electric blender

Blanch the celery root in boiling salted water for 2 minutes, and drain. Return it to the saucepan, add the milk, and simmer it, uncovered and over moderate to low heat, for 20 minutes. Then add the parsley and cook another 10 minutes. *(Throughout, watch that the milk does not scorch, and skim it occasionally. Ed.)* The total cooking time should be about 30 minutes, or until the celery root is tender.

With the skimmer, transfer the celery root and parsley to the electric blender, and purée them with enough of the cooking liquid to give the purée a good consistency. Reheat, taste for seasoning, and keep warm over hot water.

144

Purée mousse de poireaux
LEEK PURÉE

To serve four:
  2 bunches of leeks (about 5 pounds)
  ⅜ cup of **chicken stock** (5) (8)
  1¼ teaspoons of salt
  A pinch of pepper
  2 teaspoons of butter (*optional*)

UTENSILS:
  Colander
  Heavy-bottomed stainless or nonstick saucepan,
     with a lid
  Electric blender
  Strainer
  Little saucepan (butter warmer) (*optional*)

Cut the white parts of the leeks only into thin slices; they should weigh about 2½ pounds. Rinse the slices in plenty of water to remove all traces of sand, and drain. In the saucepan, heat the leeks, stirring often, for 5 minutes so they will give off some of their liquid. Then add the stock and season with salt and pepper. Cook the leeks, uncovered, over low heat for about 30 minutes, or until they are reduced to a moist "marmalade."

Purée the cooked leeks in the electric blender. If the blender will not purée all the filaments, put the purée through the strainer. Reheat, taste for seasoning, and keep warm over hot water. To serve, you may add a *beurre noisette:* In the little saucepan, heat the butter over high heat until it foams. When the foam subsides and the butter has taken on a fine golden color, it is ready to serve.

Purée mousse d'artichauts
ARTICHOKE PURÉE

To serve four:

4 large artichokes, or 3½ to 4 pounds in all
2 or 3 tablespoons of coarse salt
Juice of 1 lemon
1 teaspoon of **crème fraîche (172)**
Hot water
Salt and pepper

UTENSILS:

Enameled or stainless kettle, with a lid
Electric blender

Wash the artichokes, cut off the stems, and cook the artichokes, covered, in boiling salted water acidulated with the lemon juice. Put them in cold water to cool.

Remove all the leaves and scoop out the chokes. Cut the artichoke bottoms into pieces, and purée them in the electric blender with the *crème fraîche* and a little hot water to thin the purée to a good consistency. Reheat, add salt and pepper to taste, and keep warm over hot water.

NOTE: In my opinion, it is best for this recipe to cook the artichoke bottoms still encased in their leaves to preserve all their depth of flavor.

146

Purée mousse d'oignons
ONION PURÉE

To make about ⅔ cup:

1¼ pounds of onions
2 cups of **chicken stock** (5) (8)
1½ teaspoons of salt
A pinch of pepper

UTENSILS:

Heavy-bottomed saucepan
Electric blender

Peel the onions and quarter them. Cook them in the chicken stock, seasoned with the salt and pepper, covered, over medium heat for 25 minutes, or until they are tender.

Drain them well, reserving the stock, and purée them in the electric blender. Return the pureé to the saucepan, simmer it until it has reduced by one half, and keep it warm over hot water.

The reserved stock may be used for other purposes, including a good soup.

DESSERTS

147

Sauce coulis de fraises, framboises ou cassis
STRAWBERRY, RASPBERRY OR
BLACK-CURRANT PURÉE SAUCE

To serve four or five:

½ pound of strawberries, or raspberries, or
    black currants (*see Note*)
¼ cup of water
3 tablespoons of raspberry jelly
Lemon juice, sparingly to taste

UTENSILS:
Electric blender
Fine-mesh strainer
Bowl
Small ladle

NOTE: *Black currants, or cassis, are only found in the wild in this country as far as we know. Their intense perfumed flavor is altogether extraordinary. Ed.*

Dissolve the raspberry jelly in the water. Purée the berries and dissolved jelly together in the electric blender. Strain the sauce, bearing down on it in the strainer with the ladle to push through all the fruit. Stir in the lemon juice, and store in a covered container in the refrigerator.

148

Sauce coulis d'abricots
APRICOT PURÉE SAUCE

To serve four or five:

  12 ripe fresh apricots, rinsed, halved, and pitted, or
      one 16-ounce can unsweetened apricot halves,
      drained (*see Note*)
  ¼ cup of water
  1 vanilla bean
  2 tablespoons of apricot jam

UTENSILS:
  Heavy-bottomed saucepan
  Electric blender

NOTE: *Apricots packed in concentrated unsweetened
fruit juice are available in health-food stores and in
supermarkets with dietetic-food departments. Ed.*

In the saucepan, simmer together all the ingredients
for 10 or 15 minutes, or until the mixture is reduced
by about one third, to make a moderately thick "marmalade."

Remove the vanilla bean, purée the apricots in the
electric blender, and store the sauce, covered, in the
refrigerator.

Pomme en surprise
APPLES STUFFED WITH FRESH FRUIT

To serve four:

4 apples, preferably green- or yellow-skinned
(*see the Note on page 263*)
An assortment of fresh fruits in season (strawberries, melon, peach, figs, mango, orange, cherries, etc.)
Lemon juice

Raspberry purée sauce (147)
8 small mint leaves

UTENSILS:

2 bowls
Small melon-ball cutter
To serve: 4 chilled shallow dessert bowls, fruit knives and forks, and dessert spoons

Wash the apples, slice off the stem ends, and reserve these caps in one bowl with the lemon juice. With the melon-ball cutter, scoop out the meat of the apples, discarding the cores. Add the apple balls to the bowl with the lemon juice, and squeeze a little lemon into the apple shells to keep them from darkening. Chill.

Over the second bowl to catch their juice, peel and/or cut the other fruits into even, small dice to make a modest quantity of *macédoine*. Chill.

Stuff the apple shells with the apple balls, drained, and the *macédoine*, spoon in some of the raspberry purée sauce, and put on the caps. Set the apples in the chilled dessert bowls, pour a ribbon of raspberry sauce around them, and decorate the caps with the mint leaves.

150

Melon en surprise
MELONS STUFFED WITH FRESH FRUITS

If you find ripe melons small enough to serve one person, they may be stuffed with fresh fruit like the apples in the preceding recipe. Cut off the caps, remove the seeds and filaments, and scoop out the melon with a small spoon or a melon-ball cutter. Be sure to include diced orange and grapefruit sections as well as other fruits and berries, and chill all the fruits together in their own juices. Spoon **raspberry purée sauce** (147) only inside the melons.

Or, for a more subtle *melon en surprise,* stuff the shells with **Melon ice** (159).

151

Fruits au vin de graves rouge
FRESH FRUIT IN RED WINE

To serve four:

> An assortment of fresh fruit: pear, peach, grapes, orange, cherries, strawberries, raspberries, melon, currants, etc., in season and ripe
> 1¼ cups of red bordeaux wine, preferably a Graves
> ⅜ cup of water
> 2 tablespoons of granulated sugar
> 1 vanilla bean, split lengthwise
> 8 small fresh mint leaves

UTENSILS:
> Small saucepan
> Bowl
> *To serve:* 4 chilled, large stemmed glasses
> (*verres ballons*) or glass dessert bowls

In the saucepan, simmer the red wine until it is reduced by half, so that virtually all the alcohol is evaporated. Add the water, sugar, and the split vanilla bean, and bring the mixture back to a boil. Let it cool, and then refrigerate.

Over a bowl to catch their juices, peel the larger fruits, core or pit them, and cut them into half-moon slices or sections. Leave the berries and grapes whole; pit cherries or not as you prefer. In the refrigerator, marinate the whole combination in the fruit juices for at least 1 hour.

To serve, spoon the fruit into the chilled glasses, pour the sweetened wine over them, and decorate with the vanilla bean, cut into quarters, and the mint leaves.

152

Orange aux zestes
ORANGES WITH CANDIED RINDS

To serve four:

    4 large navel oranges
    1 cup of water
    ½ cup of granulated sugar
    4 kiwis (*optional; see Note on page 262*)

SAUCE:
    ⅜ cup of **fruit purée sauce** (147)

UTENSILS:
    Small stainless saucepan
    Bowl
    To serve: 4 chilled plates

NOTE: *The original recipe is made with blood oranges, which you will rarely find; they are exceptionally delicious, but so are good navel oranges. More important, if you can find good oranges whose skins have not been treated to give them their bright commercial color, use those; the candied rinds will be better. Ed.*

Peel off the skins of one of the oranges in very thin strips, and cut the strips into a *julienne* of long thin sticks as fine as pine needles. In the small saucepan, bring the water and sugar to a boil together, add the orange skins, and simmer over very low heat for ½ hour. You will get "candied" orange rind coated with syrup. Drain and chill.

Meanwhile, peel all the oranges completely, cutting off all the white inner skin. Over a bowl to catch the juice, cut out the sections of the oranges between the membranes. Peel the kiwis and cut them crosswise into thin slices.

To serve, arrange the orange sections in pinwheels on the chilled plates, with the kiwi slices in a ring around them. Sprinkle a few candied rinds over the oranges, and spoon over the reserved orange juice. Mask sparingly with the fruit purée sauce you have chosen to use.

NOTE: *If you have the time, cut up the rinds of all four oranges and candy them. They can be kept in a screw-top jar in the refrigerator and used for other desserts. The oranges may be served simply with a little freshly grated rind instead of the candied. Ed.*

153

Fraise à la Chantilly
STRAWBERRIES WITH WHIPPED CREAM

To serve four:

1 quart of strawberries
1 tablespoon of kirsch

CRÈME CHANTILLY:

6 tablespoons of heavy cream
6 drops of vanilla extract
2 egg whites
2 tablespoons of granulated sugar

4 fresh mint leaves

Bowls
Whisk or egg beater
Wooden or rubber spatula
To serve: 4 chilled glass dessert bowls or
   stemmed *coupes*

Hull the strawberries, and marinate them with the kirsch in the refrigerator. Whip the cream, add the vanilla extract, and refrigerate.

Shortly before serving, beat together the egg whites and sugar until the whites are thick and glossy but not really stiff. With the spatula, gently fold the whipped cream into the beaten whites.

Serve the marinated strawberries in the chilled bowls topped with the *"crème Chantilly"* in turn topped with one perfect large berry and a mint leaf.

154

Fruits frais à la gelée d'amande
FRESH FRUIT WITH ALMOND JELLY

To serve four:

ALMOND JELLY:
   1½ teaspoons of gelatin
   ½ cup of milk made with water and nonfat dry milk
   A scant ½ teaspoon of almond extract

Eight or 9 kinds of fruits and berries, ripe and in season, chosen also to make a pretty combination of colors (*see color pictures 14 and 16*); leave berries, grapes, and cherries whole; peel fruits and cut them into thin half-moon slices; cut orange sections out from between the membranes. Only 2 or 3 pieces of each fruit are used for each serving.
4 tiny sprigs of mint

UTENSILS:

Small saucepan
Shallow round mold 7 inches in diameter
Small flexible spatula
Small round cooky cutter
Bowl
To serve: 4 chilled plates

NOTE: *Almond jelly seems rather bland when you first taste it, but it is the perfect foil for fresh fruit, as good as cream and more subtle.*

The jelly should not be very stiff and is a little precarious to get out of the mold. Ideal for the purpose is an artist's flexible palette knife with the blade bent at an angle just below the handle, or a small kitchen spatula constructed the same way.

Kiwis are a tropical fruit which you will find, newly popular, in fancy-food stores and Oriental fruit and vegetable markets. They are approximately egg-shaped and have a thin, prickly-fuzzy brown skin. In color picture 14, the slices of kiwi are the pale-green ones with a pattern of the dark seeds a little reminiscent of fig seeds. Ed.

Soak the gelatin in a spoonful of cold water until it is soft. Bring the milk to a boil, remove from the heat, and immediately add the softened gelatin and the almond extract. Stir until the gelatin has dissolved completely. Pour into the mold; the mixture should be ⅜ inch deep. Refrigerate.

Prepare the fruits over the bowl to collect their juices, and let them all marinate together in the refrigerator. (*Fruits that darken, such as pears, peaches, and apples, may be cut up at the last moment. Ed.*)

With a knife or the spatula or cooky cutter, cut the almond jelly into lozenges, squares, or circles as you prefer. Lift them out with the spatula, arrange them in the centers of the chilled plates, and decorate with tiny sprigs of mint. Place the fruit decoratively around the almond jelly, and spoon the fruit juice over the sliced fruits only. Serve immediately while everything is still chilled.

Compote de pommes à l'abricot
APPLE AND APRICOT COMPOTE

To serve two:

    4 small apples (*see Note*), peeled, quartered, and cored
    4 fresh apricots, rinsed, halved, and pitted, or
        8 canned unsweetened apricot halves
        (*see Note on page 256*)
    4 teaspoons of granulated sugar

UTENSILS:
    Heavy-bottomed saucepan, with a lid
    Electric blender
    To serve: Small serving bowl and 2 chilled dessert bowls

NOTE: *The apples called for are* pommes reinettes, *russet apples, which you will not find unless they are grown locally. Use crisp apples with a good, winy flavor. Greenings and Golden Delicious are possible choices. Ed.*

In the saucepan cook together, covered, the apples, 4 of the apricot halves, and the sugar, plus a spoonful of water, for 15 minutes. Meanwhile, cut the remaining 4 apricot halves into ¼-inch dice. Purée the cooked fruit in the electric blender, add the diced apricots, and pour the compote into the serving bowl. Chill before serving.

156

Pomme à la neige
SNOW APPLES

To serve four:

  4 apples, washed (*see Note*)
  1½ teaspoons of gelatin
  1 lemon
  5 teaspoons of granulated sugar
  2 egg whites

  Apricot purée sauce (148)
  8 small mint leaves

UTENSILS:

  Baking dish
  Small saucepan
  Small strainer
  Electric blender
  2 bowls
  Large egg whisk (balloon whisk), or an egg beater
  Rubber spatula
  To serve: 4 chilled plates

NOTE: *As in other recipes, the apple called for is the
flavorful, unobtainable* pomme reinette. *Because appearance is important for this recipe, we used the
preferred American baking apple, the Rome Beauty,
the skin of which will hold up perfectly to make a
pretty presentation. They should weigh 6 or 7 ounces
each, or less than ½ pound.*

*So the skin will not burst during baking, and to
make a neat cap for the final presentation: At the stem
end and about ½ inch down, cut into the apple in a
straight line all the way around, cutting into the meat
to a depth of about ½ inch. This cap is sliced off later,
after baking. Ed.*

Preheat the oven to 400° F.
  Pour a film of water into the baking dish to keep
the apples from sticking to it, add the apples, and
bake them in the preheated oven for 30 minutes.

Meanwhile, soak the gelatin in a little water, and heat it, stirring, over hot water until it is completely dissolved. Peel off the skin of the lemon in very thin strips, cut the strips into a *julienne* of long thin sticks as fine as pine needles, and cut these crosswise into tiny dice. In the small saucepan, blanch these in boiling water for 15 minutes, and drain them in the small strainer. Squeeze the lemon and strain the juice.

Remove the baked apples from the oven, let them cool, and slice off the caps. With a spoon, scoop out the meat of the apples, discarding the cores; purée in the electric blender together with the gelatin and lemon juice. Pour the purée into a bowl and stir in the diced lemon peel.

In another bowl, beat together the egg whites and the sugar until the whites are stiff but not dry. With the rubber spatula, gently fold the beaten whites into the apple-lemon purée. Spoon this mixture into the apple shells, put on the caps, and chill in the refrigerator for 1 hour.

To serve, set the apples on the chilled plates, surround them with a ribbon of the apricot sauce, and decorate the caps with the mint leaves.

157
Tarte fine aux pommes chaude
HOT APPLE TARTS

To serve four:

PASTRY (PÂTE BRISÉE):
   ⅞ cup (4½ ounces) of all-purpose flour, measured unsifted
   6 tablespoons (3 ounces) of cold butter (*see Note*), cut into small pieces
   1 tablespoon of water
   A pinch of salt

   2 or 3 medium-size apples of a crisp, tart variety
   ⅓ cup of **apricot purée sauce** (148), warmed

UTENSILS:

Flour sifter
Bowl
Floured pastry board or marble slab
Rolling pin
Saucer a little under 5 inches in diameter
Large spatula
Baking sheet
To serve: 4 heated plates

NOTE: *We owe to Julia Child the information that, made with American flour,* pâte brisée *will be more tender if you substitute a little cold vegetable shortening—about 1½ tablespoons—for part of the butter. Ed.*

Sift the flour. Put the butter in the electric blender and add the flour, salt, and water. Blend briefly, until the mixture is mealy; you will need to stop the blender at least once to push down the flour with a rubber spatula. Turn the mixture out onto a piece of waxed paper, gather it together in one mass, and press this dough together firmly into a ball.

Put the ball of dough on the floured pastry board and knead it quickly with the heel of your hand until you have a homogeneous dough; do not let it get sticky. Gather it together in a smooth round ball, flatten this somewhat, and refrigerate it in a plastic bag for at least 30 minutes or for several hours.

To roll out the dough: Lightly flour the board again. Divide the dough into 4 equal pieces, roll them into balls with your hands, flour them lightly, then, with the rolling pin, roll them out into very thin circles. Using the saucer as guide, trim the pieces of pastry into perfect circles. With the spatula, transfer them to the baking sheet.

NOTE: *The recipe may be prepared ahead to this point; simply refrigerate the pastry, covered. Ed.*

Preheat the oven to 425° F.

Peel and core the apples and cut them into thin half-moon slices. Arrange the slices pinwheel-style on the pastry, covering it completely with almost no edges showing. Bake the tarts in the preheated oven for 20 minutes. Remove them from the oven and mask them with the warm apricot purée sauce. With the spatula, transfer the tarts to the heated plates and serve immediately.

158

Banane en papillote
BANANAS BAKED IN FOIL

To serve four:

4 small ripe bananas, peeled
¼ cup of water
2 tablespoons of apricot jam
½ cup of **apricot purée sauce (148)**
Scant ¼ teaspoon of almond extract
2 vanilla beans, split lengthwise
Tiny sprigs of fresh mint (*optional*)

UTENSILS:

Small saucepan
Small whisk
4 pieces of aluminum foil, 12 inches by 8 inches
Baking sheet
To serve: 4 heated plates

Preheat the oven to 425° F.

Bring the water to a boil in the saucepan and stir in the apricot jam. Remove from the heat, add the apricot sauce and the almond extract, and mix well with the whisk.

Fold the sheets of foil in two lengthwise, and at the ends of the fold turn up and pinch the corners to make a sort of boat to hold the bananas and sauce. Put a banana in each foil boat, pour 3 tablespoons of apricot sauce over each one, and add the split vanilla beans. Close the foil by folding over the edges and pinching them together securely. Place on the baking sheet.

Bake the bananas in the preheated oven for 15 minutes (*20 minutes if the bananas are not small. Ed.*) Serve on the heated plates in the unopened foil; or, open the foil first and decorate the bananas with tiny sprigs of fresh mint.

NOTE: The same recipe may be used to make apples *en papillote.*

Concerning Sherbets, Ices, and Granités

The following recipes do not contain the amounts of gelatin, sugar, or egg whites which are used in most sherbet formulas to give them body. Their substance and texture depend primarily on proper freezing. Therefore, we do not recommend that they be "still-frozen" in refrigerator trays.

Instead, we recommend the type of small electric home ice-cream freezer that is used inside the refrigerator freezer. When the sherbet, ice, or granité mixture is made in advance, put it in the ice-cream freezer and put the freezer in the refrigerator (*not in the freezer compartment*). *Then, follow the directions in your instruction booklet for the timing of the freezing. Put the ice-cream freezer in the refrigerator freezer compartment—with the temperature at the coldest setting—starting it in time to have the ice ready when you want to serve it, including time to "ripen" it.*

How long the ice or sherbet will take to ripen—that is, freeze to a final good consistency—and how long it will hold in the refrigerator freezer after that, before freezing to a block of ice, depend on what it is made of. The more substance in the mixture originally, the longer it will hold.

First, the mixture should be removed from the ice-cream freezer when it is still softer than required for serving and be transferred to a plastic container with a lid. The covered container should go back into the refrigerator freezer, with the temperature setting of the refrigerator back to normal unless you are running short of time before serving. Our experience was that all these ices required this ripening period, but for varying lengths of time; the texture is improved if you stir the ice well several times while it ripens. **Strawberry or raspberry ice (160)** *held up well to about 2 hours,* **Melon ice (159)** *somewhat longer, and* **Pineapple ice (161)** *held well even longer—what we had left over was still of a good consistency the following day. Ed.*

159

Sorbet melon
MELON ICE

To make 1 quart:

½ cup of water
¼ cup of granulated sugar, or to taste
Enough ripe, sweet melons to make 3½ cups of purée,
    plus 3 or 4 small melon balls per serving
Lemon or lime juice to taste
1 unhulled strawberry or whole raspberry and
    1 small mint leaf per serving

UTENSILS:

Bowls
Melon-ball cutter
Electric blender
Electric ice-cream freezer (*see page 268*)
To serve: Chilled stemmed parfait glasses (*flutes*)

In a bowl, dissolve the sugar in the water. Refrigerate.
    Choose the best ripe melons, large or small, that you can find. Cut them in half and remove the seeds and filaments in the centers. Scoop out the number of melon balls you need for decoration with the cutter, and put them in the refrigerator.

With a spoon, scoop out the melons and purée the pulp in the electric blender; do this in batches, and measure until you have the 3½ cups. (Strain the purée if you wish.)

Add the dissolved sugar to the melon purée, add lemon or lime juice to taste, and put the mixture in the ice-cream freezer.

Start the ice-cream freezer in time to have the ice ready when you want to serve it (*see page 268*). To serve, spoon the ice into the chilled glasses, smoothing each portion into a neat dome. Decorate with the strawberries or raspberries and the leaves of mint.

160

Sorbet fraise ou framboise
STRAWBERRY OR RASPBERRY ICE

To make 1 quart:

1 cup of water
¼ cup of granulated sugar
Enough ripe, sweet berries to make 3 cups of purée,
     plus 1 perfect berry to decorate each serving
Lemon juice to taste
1 small mint leaf per serving

UTENSILS:

Small saucepan
Bowls
Electric blender
Fine-mesh strainer
Electric ice-cream freezer (*see page 268*)
To serve: Chilled stemmed parfait glasses (*flutes*)

Bring to a boil together in the saucepan the water and sugar, boil for 5 minutes, let cool, and refrigerate.

Choose the best ripe berries that you can find. Hull them, except for the ones you will use to decorate each serving; put these in the refrigerator.

In the electric blender, purée enough berries to make 3 cups of purée, and strain raspberry purée through a fine-mesh strainer. Add the sugar syrup, add lemon juice to taste, and put the mixture in the ice-cream freezer.

Start the ice-cream freezer in time to have the ice ready when you want to serve it (*see page 268*). To serve, spoon the ice into the chilled glasses, smoothing each portion into a neat dome. Decorate with a berry and a leaf of mint.

161

Ananas glacé aux fraises des bois
PINEAPPLE STUFFED WITH PINEAPPLE ICE AND WILD STRAWBERRIES

To serve eight:

1 ripe pineapple, weighing about 4 pounds
½ pound of wild strawberries (*see page 277*), or the same weight in ripe strawberries, sliced
1 tablespoon of kirsch
2 or 3 tablespoons of granulated sugar, to taste
1 cup of **raspberry purée sauce** (147)

UTENSILS:

Long narrow knife
Bowls
Electric blender
Electric ice-cream freezer (*see page 268*)
Flat plate chilled in the refrigerator freezer
Broad spatula
To serve: Chilled platter, folded white napkin, serving platter, chilled sauceboat, 4 chilled sherbet glasses

Cut a slice off the bottom of the pineapple so that it will stand up straight, then cut off another slice at the top, with the frond attached, which will be the "lid."

With the knife, cut into the pineapple between the shell and the meat, and from both ends carve out all the meat in a cylinder, keeping the shell whole. *(Afterward, with a grapefruit knife, you can get more of the pineapple out of the shell. Ed.)* Cut the cylinder in half lengthwise, and remove the hard core. Then cut enough of the pineapple into ¼-inch dice to make a generous ½ cup. Combine these in a bowl with the strawberries and the kirsch, and let them marinate together in the refrigerator. Also refrigerate the pineapple shell and lid.

Cut the remaining pineapple into chunks, and add the 2 or 3 tablespoons of sugar. In the electric blender, purée these, adding the pieces only a few at a time at first. Put the mixture in the ice-cream freezer.

NOTE: *The recipe is prepared ahead to this point. Ed.*

Start the ice-cream freezer in time to have the pineapple ice ready when you want to serve it (*see page 268*).

To serve: Put the pineapple shell on the chilled plate. Spoon enough of the pineapple ice into it to make a good layer at the bottom and to line part of the sides. Put in the diced pineapple and strawberries and fill the shell with the remainder of the pineapple ice. Arrange the folded napkin on the serving platter, slip the broad spatula under the pineapple, transfer it to the platter, and top with the pineapple-frond lid. Bring to the table immediately, serve into the chilled sherbet glasses, and top with the raspberry sauce from the sauceboat.

162

Blancs à la neige au coulis de cassis
FLOATING ISLAND WITH
BLACK-CURRANT SAUCE

To serve four:

  2 quarts of water
  ¾ teaspoon of salt

5 egg whites
3 tablespoons of granulated sugar
1 cup of **black-currant purée sauce** (147)
  (*see Note on page 255*)
Thin slices of chilled fruit and tiny fresh mint leaves
  (*optional*)

UTENSILS:

Broad shallow saucepan, or skillet, 10½ inches or more
  in diameter
Large bowl for beating eggs
Large egg whisk (balloon whisk)
Perforated skimmer
Wide metal spatula
To serve: 4 chilled dessert plates

In the saucepan or skillet, heat the salted water.

Meanwhile, beat the egg whites: Put them in the large bowl and with the egg whisk beat them slowly at first to break them up. When they start to turn white, beat faster. Add the sugar and speed up the beating. Beat until, when you lift up the whisk, the whites form a steady peak on the end of it. (The correct beating motion is an over-and-under circle which gathers up the whites from all around the inside of the bowl.)

Use the perforated skimmer and the spatula to form the egg whites into "islands." With the spatula, scoop up one-quarter of the whites at a time onto the skimmer and smooth them gently into a dome.

The hot water must stay over very low heat and be barely trembling on the surface; be sure not to let it start to boil. Gently place the bottom of the skimmer on the surface of the water; the egg white will float off of its own accord. (*Important: Now rinse and dry the skimmer. Ed.*) Make three more egg-white domes, each one of which is to poach 12 to 15 minutes in all. When they are half done, turn each one over gently with the skimmer to cook them evenly. Remove them to a dry cloth spread out on a flat surface to drain and cool.

To serve, spread the *cassis* or other sauce in the centers of the chilled plates, and place the poached islands on the sauce. They may be decorated with two or three thin slices of some ripe, exotic fruit, such as mango or kiwi, with a final touch of mint leaves.

163

Paris-Brest au café
CREAM PUFFS WITH COFFEE WHIPPED CREAM

NOTE: *This recipe is for a small quantity so that you can make individual cream puffs, or* choux, *that are put on the baking sheet with a spoon. Or, you can make with this amount a small* Paris-Brest *ring* (couronne), *piping out the dough in a 3-inch circle with a pastry bag fitted with a plain ⅝-inch nozzle; the same amount of* pâte à chou *will then make a ring to serve six or more. The recipe may be multiplied (larger amounts of dough are much easier to handle in a pastry bag), and preshaped* choux *and* Paris-Brest *rings may be frozen before baking. Ed.* To make individual cream puffs for four:

PÂTE À CHOU:
　¼ cup of water
　2 tablespoons of butter
　A pinch of salt
　⅓ cup of sifted all-purpose flour, measure after sifting
　1 large egg, lightly beaten
　1 egg (or 1 egg white) for glazing (*optional*)
　Confectioners' sugar (*optional*)

　"*Crème Chantilly*" (*see page 260*)
　1 teaspoon of powdered instant "espresso" coffee

Small (1-quart) heavy-bottomed saucepan
Wooden spatula
Small bowl heated to lukewarm over hot water
Small whisk
Baking sheet
Pastry bag (*optional*)
Pastry brush
Serrated knife
To serve: 4 dessert plates

PÂTE À CHOU:

Preheat the oven to 425° F.

In the heavy-bottomed saucepan, bring to a boil together the water, butter, and salt. Off the heat, add the flour, all at once, and rapidly beat the mixture together with the wooden spatula. Over very low heat, continue beating for ½ to 1 minute to achieve a homogeneous paste with a satiny sheen.

With the spatula, transfer the paste to the warm bowl and, with the whisk, beat in half the beaten egg and, in a few seconds, when the first addition is completely incorporated, whisk in the other half. Stop whisking when the mixture—which appears to separate each time the egg is added—returns to a smoothly blended consistency.

With a spoon, drop the *pâte à chou* onto the ungreased baking sheet in four even portions, rather far apart as they will more than double in size. The *choux* do not have to be glazed, but their color will be better if you do this: Use part of a whole beaten egg diluted with a teaspoonful of water or a lightly beaten egg white diluted with water. With the pastry brush, paint the tops of the *choux* lightly with the egg mixture, taking care that it does not drip down the sides to the baking sheet or they will stick.

Bake the *choux* in the preheated 425° F. oven for 15 minutes, with the oven door slightly ajar (propped open about an inch with a kitchen spoon is the old system). Then lower the heat to 375° F. and bake them for another 15 minutes. Remove the *choux* from the oven and promptly make a slit—to let the steam escape—on the sides at the point where you will later cut off the tops. Let them cool completely.

NOTE: *The cream puffs are made in advance to this point. Later, if they lose their crispness, heat them in a slow oven (300° F.) for 3 to 4 minutes before filling.*

The "crème Chantilly" must be made shortly before serving. Stir the teaspoon of instant coffee into the 6 tablespoons of heavy cream before you whip it.

The dessert is assembled just before serving. Ed.

To serve, with the serrated knife cut off the tops of the *choux*. If necessary, scoop out any soft dough on the insides with a small spoon. Fill them with the whipped cream, and cover with the tops. You may decorate the *choux* with just a little sifted confectioners' sugar. Serve on individual plates. (A *Paris-Brest* ring would be presented on a platter first and then cut.)

164

Soufflé aux fraises des bois
INDIVIDUAL WILD-STRAWBERRY SOUFFLÉS

To serve four or five (see Note):

½ pound of wild strawberries (*see Note*)
¼ cup of granulated sugar
1 teaspoon of **raspberry purée sauce** (147), or a few fresh raspberries
1 teaspoon of kirsch
A squeeze of lemon juice
2 egg yolks, lightly beaten
Soft butter
6 egg whites
A pinch of salt

Electric blender
2 small bowls for yolks
2 large bowls
Small pastry brush
Large egg whisk (balloon whisk)
Small whisk
Rubber spatula
To bake and serve: 4 or 5 small soufflé molds, inside diameter 4 inches, 1¾ inches deep (1-cup capacity; see Note)

NOTE: *With luck, you can occasionally buy cultivated "wild" strawberries. You can also grow them yourself. We made the soufflés successfully with regular strawberries.*

We did find, however, that the soufflés were exceptionally fragile and discovered, by accident, that a little extra batter we had left over from filling four 4-inch soufflé molds and had baked in a 3-inch mold (½-cup capacity instead of 1-cup) made a small soufflé of better texture. At the end of a several-course dinner party, this recipe will produce a charming little minceur dessert for as many as eight people. The dimensions of the smaller molds, which are used in a number of recipes in this book, are 3-inch inside diameter, depth 1½ inches. Ed.

In the electric blender, purée together the wild strawberries, sugar, raspberry purée sauce, kirsch, and lemon juice. *(If you add whole raspberries instead of the puréed sauce, strain the whole mixture through a fine-mesh strainer. Ed.)* Pour the purée into one bowl, add the egg yolks, and mix well.

Preheat the oven to 425° F. With the pastry brush, very lightly butter the inside of the soufflé molds.

Beat the egg whites: Separate them into the other bowl, add the pinch of salt, and with the egg whisk beat them slowly at first to break them up. When they start to turn white, beat faster, and speed up the beating. Beat until, when you lift up the whisk, the whites form a soft peak on the end of it. Do not let them get too stiff. (You may also use an electric beater.)

Add **about one-quarter** of the whites to the strawberry **purée, and blend** them in smoothly with the small **whisk. Then add** the remaining whites and gently **fold them in with** the spatula.

Fill the soufflé molds: Spoon in the soufflé batter just to the top of each mold, and level it off with the side of a spatula or the back of a knife. With your thumb, go around the edge of the mold to separate the top of the soufflé batter from it, making a small trench ½ inch wide; this will help the soufflé to rise.

Lower the oven heat to 375° F. and bake the soufflés for 8 to 10 minutes. Serve immediately.

165

Soufflé aux poires
INDIVIDUAL PEAR SOUFFLÉS

To serve four or five (see Note on page 277):

3 very ripe pears, (about 1 pound in all)

SYRUP:

3 cups of water
¼ cup of granulated sugar
1 vanilla bean, split lengthwise

3 tablespoons of granulated sugar, or to taste
½ teaspoon of *eau de vie de poire* (*see Note*),or kirsch
2 egg yolks, lightly beaten
Soft butter
6 egg whites
A pinch of salt

UTENSILS:

Saucepan
The utensils in the preceding recipe
To bake and serve: See Note on page 277.

NOTE: Eau de vie de poire *is one of the many fruit-based distilled white spirits made in France, and also in Switzerland, and is readily available here, but kirsch will serve the purpose. Ed.*

Peel, quarter, and core the pears. In the saucepan, bring to a boil together the ingredients of the syrup—water, sugar, and vanilla bean. Cook the pears in this for 10 to 15 minutes, and drain.

In the electric blender, purée them with a little more sugar and the *eau de vie de poire* or kirsch. Pour the purée into a bowl, add the egg yolks, and mix well.

Preheat the oven to 425° F., and follow the instructions from this point in the preceding recipe to the end.

166

Le grand dessert
FRESH FRUIT WITH FRESH-FRUIT SHERBETS

This dessert—a lavish variation of Fruits frais à la gelée d'amande *(154)—has no recipe and did not originate as a* minceur *dessert. Rather it represents a point of view: the presentation of perfect produce in a perfect way to achieve an extravaganza of natural flavors with a minimum of artifice.*

Michel Guérard will, not too long after this writing, publish his book of cuisine gourmande—*his personal and major contribution to the* nouvelle cuisine *that is the well-known concern of contemporary French chefs.* Le grand dessert, *and the recipes for the* gourmands sherbets *shown in color picture 16 (made with sugar syrup), will be included in that book. Meanwhile, its stringently low-calorie,* minceur *version simply substitutes one or several of the sherbets and ices in the present book. Ed.*

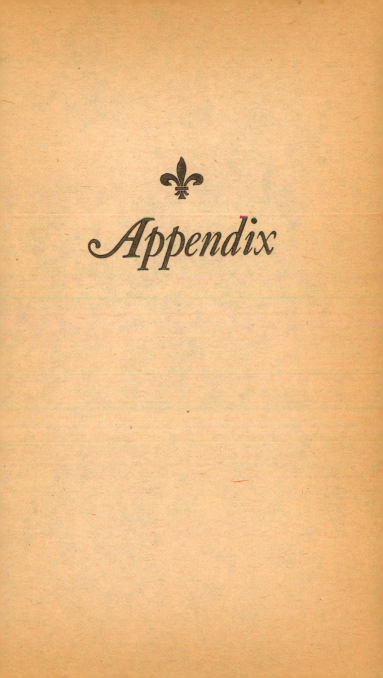

Appendix

Illustrated List of
Important Kitchen Tools

The utensils described here in no way comprise a complete list for the well-equipped kitchen. They are only the specific tools we found necessary for the special requirements of certain recipes in the book, plus a few that are generally indispensable. We simply suggest that, without these items, you will have needless logistical problems with some of the recipes. Ed.

ELECTRIC BLENDER: This instrument is crucial in *cuisine minceur.* It is the only one of all the miracle machines designed in such a way that it can purée the small quantities of ingredients used in the *liaisons* of some *minceur* sauces—and, at that, it needs at least ½ cup for the blades to reach the mixture; a little liquid sometimes has to be added.

An electric blender will also purée the raw ingredients of a forcemeat and easily makes vegetable purées. These mixtures do have to be blended in batches, raw ingredients must be cut up before blending, liquid sometimes needs to be added in order not to force the motor. Other machines are handier for such processes, but the blender is the only one that, with the proper precautions, will do everything *minceur* recipes require.

ENAMELED OR STAINLESS COOKWARE: In the lists of utensils, the expression "enameled or stainless" is used when certain foods (such as fish, acid vegetables) require such a saucepan, skillet, or kettle. We leave it to the reader's judgment precisely what cookware to use. We prefer enameled cast-iron and nonstick equipment for "stainless" purposes.

TEFLON AND OTHER NONSTICK PANS: Contrary to what you might expect, nonstick cookware is only occasionally mandatory in *cuisine minceur;* you can usually do without. When it is crucial, nonstick is specified in the lists of utensils. In practice, we did in fact use heavy-bottomed nonstick pans most of the time, including when "enameled or stainless" pans were required. We learned to love them. Note, however, that the weight and quality of the pan under a nonstick lining is as important as the lining itself. Thin pans that do not distribute heat evenly defeat the purpose. Specifically, aluminum and tin-lined copper will not do when "stainless" is listed as required.

WOODEN SPATULAS: Michel Guérard quite often specifies the use of wooden spatulas for stirring, folding beaten whites into soufflé mixtures, etc. If you use nonstick pans, they are a must; a nonstick pan of high quality can take the scraping of metal implements for a good while, but wood is still better in the long run. Wooden spatulas have more uses than wooden spoons and are handier as well.

KNIVES: This entry is gratuitous; everybody knows that good, sharp, carbon-steel knives are indispensable. Because this is a commonplace, knives are rarely mentioned in the lists of utensils. We suggest that two sizes are the most important, all other sizes are matters of preference: the paring knife (*couteau d'office*), no more than 8 inches long overall; and the "chef" knife, 12 to 14 inches long overall.

WHISKS: You need at least two, the crucial one being a small whisk (so specified in the lists of utensils), about 8 inches overall, for whisking sauces. A good size for a multipurpose whisk to do larger jobs is about 12 inches overall.

For beating egg whites, an electric hand beater is always acceptable. Requiring more muscle, but faster and better, is the balloon whisk, average size about 14 inches overall.

STRAINERS: "Fine-mesh" strainers are usually specified in the lists of utensils merely as a precaution; a coarse sieve is not often useful. The French conical *chinois* is necessary only in a fairly small size for its fine metallic mesh, almost as fine as cloth, to use for straining sauces that must be perfectly smooth. Standard

round strainers in a good variety of sizes are good enough for other purposes.

Bain marie: This old term has three applications. The classic *bain marie* is a very large oblong pan containing hot water into which a number of saucepans can be set to keep their contents warm. The pan is not usually set over direct heat, but rather in a warm place near or at the back of the stove. It is the ideal arrangement, always used in restaurant kitchens, but it can be awkward to set up in the average home kitchen. The second meaning of the term is simply a double boiler. And the third meaning is the pan of hot water placed in the oven in which molds, *terrines,* or other containers are set for baking.

Keeping things warm is a constant concern. One simply has to invent one's own *bain marie* systems as one goes along.

Perforated skimmer: A tool of many uses, often more efficient than the usual slotted spoon, and the only implement that works perfectly for making **Blancs à la neige** (162).

Storage containers: Anything with a lid—glass, ceramic, plastic—will do, of course, but we prefer screw-top preserving jars of all sizes to anything else because of the cup measures marked in the glass. This is most important for prepared ingredients such as stocks, vegetable purées, and basic sauces for which you really need to know how much you have on hand.

SCALE: Quantities for ingredients in this translation are not usually expressed by weight, since the use of a scale is not customary in most American kitchens. This is too bad; the European use of weights in recipes is more precise than our way and often more convenient. When we felt it was necessary, we did express certain small quantities in avdp. ounces and we feel a scale of some kind is important for *minceur* cooking. (This up-to-date little model happens to be a Terraillon.)

OVAL ENAMELED CAST-IRON CASSEROLE: This is the traditional *cocotte* which has innumerable uses. The two best sizes are one that will hold comfortably a medium-size whole chicken and a smaller one of 2- to 2½-quart capacity.

FISH POACHER: Used to poach fish in liquid to cover, it may also be used, with less liquid, as a fish steamer with the level of the liquid below the rack so that it does not touch the fish. The rack is not designed for this; it needs to be raised up off the bottom so that an adequate amount of liquid can be poured in. The simple home remedy is to put metal jar tops, such as preserving-jar tops, under the rack.

The most convenient fish poacher is the one illustrated, with a rack with handles for easy lifting. Manipulating a cooked fish out of a poacher without this type of rack is an unnecessary nuisance.

TERRINES: Two specific sizes are needed—1½-quart capacity and 1-cup capacity. The most available form for both is oval (with lids). The oblong *charcutier* mold (no lid) shown in color picture 4 is about double the required size and we did not find a 1½-quart version. This is too bad, as both the "Hure" de saumon (63) and the **Terrine de poissons** (64) are most attractively sliced from an oblong mold. But do not substitute an oblong metal pan of any sort! Use instead an oval *terrine*, which is not hard to find. Both sizes are made in earthenware and in white porcelain. Buy only the ovenproof.

STEAMERS: There are many different kinds, usually sold as vegetable steamers though they in fact have many other uses.

The collapsible steaming rack with three short legs and adjustable, folding, perforated "leaves" is best for short cooking times (up to 30 minutes), as not quite an inch of liquid can be poured under it without coming up to the level of the food to be steamed. It is used in ordinary saucepans from 6 to 8 inches in diameter. Imported from France, inexpensive, and easy to find.

The *couscoussière* referred to in the recipes looks a little different from the steamer illustrated here, but the principle is identical: The bottom section holds a considerable quantity of liquid for longer cooking times. The top section has a perforated bottom and holds the food well out of reach of the liquid below. We found this one, American-made, without difficulty in a department store.

a.

b.

SOUFFLÉ MOLDS: Only individual soufflé molds are used in the recipes in this book. Sometimes called ramekins, these round molds are easily available

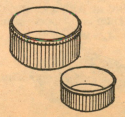

classics even though they seem always to be imported. The recipes require two very specific sizes: inside diameter 3½ inches, capacity ½ cup; inside diameter 4 inches, capacity 1 cup. The 1-cup size substitutes very well for the 1-cup oval *terrine* on page 288.

KUGELHOPF MOLD: Used only once, for the famous Carrot cake (58), this mold is set in a pan of hot water (*bain marie*) to bake the carrot cake. It is important to have, not only for the appearance of the unmolded cake, but primarily because the hot water reaches up in the center tube and cooks the cake from within as well as without. The recipe calls for a 1-pint mold. A plain ring mold could be substituted.

RIDGED CAST-IRON SKILLET: Though it is American-made, this marvelous skillet appears not to be well-known. Ours was bought in a particularly well-stocked department store. The raised ridges in the bottom have the same effect on a piece of meat as do the rods of a grill used over hot coals. It is the ideal indoor tool with which to sear a piece of meat or fish with the pattern of *quadrillage* described in a number of the recipes in this book. It also keeps a piece of meat, even hamburger, to be "panbroiled" up off the bottom of the pan, allowing a drainage of fat without scorching that is ideally *minceur*. This skillet is not mentioned in Michel Guérard's manuscript, but, lacking an outdoor grill and the space in which to use one, we used this skillet in the kitchen most successfully whenever the process of *quadrillage* was required.

SERVING BELLS OR CLOCHES: These are by no means a necessity, but it is interesting to know how dishes are presented by Michel Guérard at Les Prés d'Eugénie. As the color pictures, and most of the recipes, make clear, each individual serving is carefully presented on an ample dinner plate (piping hot) with a wide rim. Only rarely is a course presented first on a platter. As soon as a plate is arranged, it is covered with a large silver bell that serves two purposes: It keeps the food hot, but it also contains the aromas of the dish, which rise enticingly to greet each diner when the bells are removed at the table.

We did not acquire any silver bells or even a substitute for them, but we could well understand their usefulness when dealing with the problem of keeping things hot to the moment of serving.

BAKED-EGG DISHES: These should have an inside diameter at the top of about 6 inches. They are used not only for eggs but for individual servings of baked-vegetable recipes. They need to be not only ovenproof but also flameproof—that is, able to take direct heat on top of the stove. The best are those made of enameled cast iron.

SAUCE SPOON: In color picture 9, a spoon is shown which has come into use along with the large dinner plate and the practice of masking the center of the plate with sauce as part of the presentation of a dish. The spoon has an almost flat bowl and provides one with an approved, well-mannered way of retrieving every drop of sauce on one's plate.

Editor's Notes

Listed together here, for convenience and in alphabetical order, are general topics about which information was both provided in notes in Michel Guérard's manuscript and acquired through our own experiences in shopping for and testing recipes in this country. Ed.

ASPARAGUS: The European white asparagus with its distinctive flavor is always the original intent in the recipes. For those instances in which our own fresh green asparagus will do as well, it is suggested in the lists of ingredients. The French admire our green asparagus. It is not the lesser choice.

However, for some recipes the special flavor of white asparagus is needed. Imported canned white asparagus is usually magnificent, but remarkably expensive. We found the supermarket small "green-tipped white asparagus" to be an acceptable substitute at a modest price.

BOUQUET GARNI: A thoroughly French good-luck charm that lends flavor to the *minceur* stockpot as it does to all French cuisine. It consists of parsley stems, thyme, and a bay leaf, the last two in moderate amounts. One may also add a small piece of celery and other herbs—basil, tarragon, chervil—depending on the mood of the moment. Some recipes require special additions—peppercorns, a clove, juniper berries, fennel, garlic, extra parsley stems.

An all-fresh *bouquet garni* is merely tied together with string so that it may be removed when it has served its purpose. A *bouquet garni* made in part of dried herbs—this is one of their most satisfactory uses —or other ingredients that cannot be confined by a piece of string is tied up in cheesecloth.

Bay leaf is sometimes very strong, especially when it is fresh; half a leaf is often enough in a *bouquet garni* and for other uses as well.

CAVIAR: The price of real caviar being what it is, we investigated some of the substitutes. Most of them, irrespective of the well-known brand names on their labels, seemed to us uninteresting, over-salted, and not worth even the modest price. Exceptions were lumpfish caviars of *Danish* origin (sometimes black, sometimes red, the black being the more convincing). Rinsing some oversalty "caviar" helps, but nothing helps the inferior imitations. It is better to do without.

CRAYFISH: A well-known mail-order source for live crayfish is: Battistela's Sea Foods, Inc., 910 Touro Street, New Orleans, Louisiana 70116. You must buy a considerable quantity, the shipment comes by air, and the whole thing costs a bit of money. It's worth it, but you must plan ahead for the use of the crayfish in more than one recipe.

We found it more practical, in New York City, to go to a large fish market that is also a supplier for restaurants. In season, with three or four days' notice, the fish market was able to get crayfish in the wholesale market and was able to notify us within 24 hours whether and when we could expect them.

On the whole, we did without. And, we do not consider shrimp a good substitute.

CREAM: See Whipped cream

CRÈME FRAÎCHE: The wonderful, thick *crème fraîche* of France is heavy cream matured with natural ferments. This is now being done in this country, but the price of the American version is, so far, nothing less than horrendous. Of the several "recipes" we have tried for making it at home, the one below seems to us the best and it is certainly the easiest.

Crème fraîche is used in very small, therefore not particularly caloric, quantities in many *cuisine minceur* recipes. The purpose is never to "enrich" the dish or sauce, but to affect its texture. You will not be aware of it as cream in the final result. Sweet cream may be used instead, but it will usually not produce quite the desired effect.

167

Crème fraîche

To make 1 pint:

½ pint (1 cup) of sour cream
½ pint (1 cup) of heavy sweet cream

Put the sour cream into a bowl or wide-mouthed glass jar. With a fork, gradually stir in the sweet cream and stir until the mixture is smoothly blended. Cover and leave at room temperature for 8 to 12 hours. Stir again, and store in the refrigerator for 24 hours before using.

This simple formula makes a remarkably good facsimile of French *crème fraîche*. It should be allowed to "ripen" for about 36 hours, as indicated, for the two creams to blend. When they are first mixed together, the result is all right, but not exceptional. A day and a half later, it has in a subtle way become a new kind of cream altogether.

Fines herbes: See Herbs

French vegetables and lettuces: French vegetables are incomparable. Many of France's varieties are simply not raised for market in this country, but this does not mean that they cannot be grown here. For those who have a vegetable garden, it is no harder to grow a "French" vegetable than any other kind.

Seeds from Europe are imported, in limited quantity, for the retail market. One mail-order source is: Le Jardin du Gourmet, "Les Echalottes," West Danville, Vermont 05873. Green beans and the salad greens specifically mentioned in the salad recipes are listed in their catalog. For beans, the recommended varieties are *Fin de Villeneuve* and *Régalfin*. The lettuces *batavia rouge* and *trévise rouge* are listed, as are dozens and dozens of other vegetables and herbs.

See also Vegetable *garnitures*.

FROMAGE BLANC: Like *crème fraîche, fromage blanc* is used primarily to finish sauces. The one used by Michel Guérard in France is a very austere product indeed, with virtually 0% fat content.

We used American "diet" ricotta as a base in the recipe below for making our own *fromage blanc*. According to the labels of the brands we used, diet ricotta is made partly with whole milk, therefore the recipe is not quite as low in fat content as the French diet *fromage blanc*. But it is austere enough to do and has a good texture.

168
Fromage blanc

To make 1½ cups, or to make 1 pint:

Low-fat diet ricotta cheese
Low-fat yogurt
A very small pinch of salt

Put the ricotta in the electric blender. For a 15-ounce (1½-cup) jar of ricotta, add 4 level tablespoons of yogurt. For a 1-pint jar (2 cups), add 5 level tablespoons plus 1 teaspoon of yogurt. Add the pinch of salt.

Blend the mixture at high speed and taste several times. The objective is to purée the ricotta until there is no trace of graininess left in the texture. Keep blending until this happens. If you have trouble, the ricotta is not fresh enough; check the last sale date on the bottom of the jar when you buy it to be sure the date is a good month away. Store the *fromage blanc*, covered, in the refrigerator for 12 hours before using.

GREEN PEPPERCORNS: Preserved in water, green peppercorns have a subtle flavor and are mild enough to be eaten whole. But they do impose themselves on a dish and must be used with care. They have become very popular of recent years and are now easily found in specialty food stores. Dried green peppercorns may be ground from a pepper mill.

HERBS: *Cuisine minceur* relies a great deal on fresh herbs, which are, of course, always preferable to the dried.

The rule of thumb for dried herbs is to use one-half the amount specified for fresh herbs. It is not a rule to be trusted. For some herbs this may be too much, for others not enough. Judgment and caution are required.

The herbs you grow yourself are the best; for some, there is no other way. Fresh chervil, for instance, is rarely marketed and the dried has little flavor. Fresh chervil is used frequently in the recipes and we have added the alternative "or parsley" in preference to dried chervil or when only a fresh herb will do. Chopped chervil is used in *fines herbes*, which must always be fresh. Whole leaves (*pluches*) of chervil, which is a delicate and subtle herb, are eaten in soups and even in salads.

If you have your own herb garden, early in the season you will have the thyme flowers called for in some of the recipes.

A good out-of-season substitute for fresh tarragon is tarragon preserved in vinegar. The fresh is used in *fines herbes*.

Curly parsley (which most people use rather too often and too much to decorate platters) is a staple flavoring ingredient, but for flavoring Michel Guérard prefers the flat Italian variety. Both may be used minced, as a final *garniture*, both may be minced for *fines herbes*, and their stems are used in a *bouquet garni*.

The fourth herb in *fines herbes* is chive.

See also *Bouquet garni* and *Pistou*.

MILK: Throughout the book, milk is specified as made with nonfat dry milk and water. Instructions on packages of dry milk vary from brand to brand. For a brand that specifies that about 3.2 avdp. ounces will make 1 quart of milk, the following proportions are convenient to know; to make:

½ *cup*	½ cup of water 2 tablespoons plus 1½ teaspoons of nonfat dry milk
1 *cup*	1 cup of water ⅓ cup of nonfat dry milk, or 5 tablespoons
2 *cups*	2 cups of water ⅔ cup of nonfat dry milk, or 10 tablespoons
3 *cups*	2¾ cups of water 1 cup of nonfat dry milk
1 *quart*	3¾ cups of water 1⅓ cups of nonfat dry milk

When heated for any length of time, milk made with nonfat dry milk and water tends to stick to the bottom of the pan even more than regular milk. It must be watched carefully and the heat must be kept low. You will find in some recipes that the dry-milk powder is added toward the end of certain cooking processes; this is done to avoid the sticking problem.

MUSHROOMS: Fresh mushrooms, the equivalent of French *champignons de Paris* or *champignons de couche*, must be very fresh and white, particularly when they are puréed in the electric blender to finish a sauce or to make **mushroom purée** (136). In both instances, if the mushrooms are past their prime, the result will be disappointing. Stems, if they are white, usually do not need to be removed; they are trimmed with a small knife as one would sharpen a pencil.

Three kinds of wild mushrooms, *champignons des bois,* are called for: *morilles* (morels), *cèpes,* and *mousserons.* In France, these are available dried, which is practical and not excessively expensive. They can be used in small quantities without waste. We have been able to find only canned morels, and *cèpes,* usually in 7- or 8-ounce cans. They are good and very expensive. When using them, it is wise to plan in advance for their use in several dishes so none will go to waste. See recipes (26), (69), (111), (112), (113), (119), (124), and (128).

Tiny *mousserons* we have not found anywhere commercially. (Those who know precisely what they are doing when they pick mushrooms in the wild can find fresh *mousserons* quite easily.) Good substitutes are small canned Japanese *nameko* mushrooms. A 7-ounce can, once drained, contains only 3¼ ounces of *nameko,* but they are not expensive.

There are innumerable dried and canned Japanese and Chinese mushrooms on the market that could be investigated to serve as substitutes for morels and *cèpes.* But in order to tamper as little as possible with the recipes, we have in a few instances suggested only one other substitution, the Japanese dried *shiitake* mushroom. It is readily available in Oriental food stores.

After *shiitake* are soaked, the stems must be removed. *Shiitake* should *not* be used for recipes in which mushrooms are puréed in the blender or are finely diced or minced; they do not have the right texture for either treatment. But they are delicious in dishes where they may be used cut into *julienne* strips; when the *shiitake* are large, the strips should be cut again into shorter lengths.

PISTOU: As used in this book, *pistou* is another name for *basilique,* or basil, and is ground to a paste with a little olive oil to make a mixture itself called *pistou.* This is a flavoring, not a sauce like the similar Italian *pesto.* Only fresh basil can be used for it.

There are a number of varieties of basil, some stronger than others, so be cautious in the use of *pistou.*

Sorrel: You can buy it, but sometimes, depending on where you live, it will go by the name of sour grass or sour cress. You can grow it; any seed catalog with a good listing of vegetables will list sorrel.

Truffles: "Black gold," and priced accordingly. To preserve the volatile flavor of canned truffles until you make the next dish in which they will be used, replenish the liquid in the can with madeira so that the truffles are well covered, and wrap the can, airtight, with plastic wrap. Use them soon. It is unnecessary to peel truffles.

Presently, canned truffles for the retail market are processed in the manner called *de deuxième cuisson.* This means that the truffles are processed one time by heat, then weighed for their cooked weight, and packed and reprocessed in the final can. Without this double procedure, the precise gram weight required by French government regulations on the label of the can would not be accurate. Unfortunately, this is a punishing sequence of events for the truffle and its flavor.

Truffles processed only once for canning, *de première cuisson,* are considered far superior despite the uncertainty of the drained-weight content of each can. They are available only to commercial users in France, such as chefs and restaurants, and as far as we know are not available in retail outlets in this country either. But efforts have been made for the importation of truffles *de première cuisson* to be sold in normal retail fashion. If you want the best, watch for their appearance.

Veal sweetbreads: A whole veal sweetbread weighs about 1 pound and is made up of two lobes, one slightly larger than the other (the smaller one being considered superior). There is a connecting tube which must be removed. To prepare for cooking, rinse in cold water, then soak in cold water for 2 hours, changing the water occasionally, or put under cold running water for 2 hours.

Blanch the sweetbread: Put it in a saucepan of cold water, bring to a boil, and boil over high heat for 2 minutes. Rinse, carefully pull off the membrane that encloses the sweetbread, rinse again, and pat dry with a cloth.

If the sweetbread is to be sliced, to give it a better shape it is wrapped in a dry cloth and placed under a weight for an hour or so, which will also press out some of the water.

The sweetbread does not have to be blanched. In this case, before removing the membrane, give it an additional soaking for 1 hour in acidulated water (1 tablespoon of white vinegar or lemon juice to 1 quart of water). The juices of the unblanched sweetbread will add more flavor to the braising liquid though the resulting sauce may not be as delicate.

VEGETABLE GARNITURES: All Michel Guérard's vegetables are cooked crisp-tender when they are boiled (see green beans, page 26).

For vegetable *garnitures,* as many as six vegetables are cooked all in one saucepan of boiling salted water. Those that need the longest cooking go in first, and the rest are added successively according to their needs. The total cooking time does not exceed 15 minutes and specific instructions are given.

THE MOST FREQUENTLY USED VEGETABLES ARE:
Small round green or spring onions (*oignons grelots*)
Pieces of carrot, white turnip, and cucumber trimmed into olive shapes (or, trimmed to look like miniature vegetables—*mini-carottes, mini-navets, mini-con-combres*)
"Cauliflowerets"
Small leeks (for which we easily substituted large scallions when we could not find leeks)
Fresh asparagus tips
Fresh or canned button mushrooms, or larger fresh mushrooms, quartered

Put the vegetables into the saucepan of boiling salted water in the following sequence:

Onions, to cook 15 minutes.

Five minutes later, carrots, turnips, cauliflower, very small leeks or large scallions, to cook 10 minutes.

Five minutes later, asparagus, fresh mushrooms, to cook 5 minutes.

Three minutes later, cucumbers, canned mushrooms, to cook 2 minutes.

Which comes to 15 minutes' cooking time in all. However, obviously the quality of the produce available, the difference between the vegetables at different seasons, the way you cut them—all affect the actual timing. Test the vegetables with a wire cake tester, and, with a slotted spoon, remove those that show signs of overcooking before the rest are done.

Vegetable *garnitures* are cooked at the last minute to be ready just before serving. Keep them warm in their cooking liquid.

Index

ABOUT THE AUTHOR

Before the publication of this book, MICHEL GUÉRARD had already been the subject of articles in ten major magazines—a *New Yorker* profile, cover stories in *Time* International and *L'Express* in France, and stories in *Vogue, Gourmet, House & Garden, New York Magazine, Time, Newsweek,* and *Esquire*—plus *The New York Times.* His restaurant in the south of France earned two *Michelin* stars in its first year and the maximum, four stars, in 1976 in the new *Guide Gault-Millau.*

Michel Guérard was born in 1933 in Vétheuil, a small town north of Paris. He served his apprenticeship in nearby Mantes, where he was taught all the classic disciplines, including pastry-making. In 1955 he went to Paris to work at the Hôtel Crillon, where he was first pastry chef, then sauce chef. Later he worked with Jean Delaveyne of the Camélia in Bougival.

In 1965, weary of traditional cuisine, he opened his own restaurant in a small bistrot in the obscure Paris suburb of Asnières. This was soon to become the famous Pot-au-Feu to which all of Paris flocked, a rendezvous for gourmets from all over the world. It was here that Michel Guérard developed his own *cuisine gourmande* —his contribution to the *nouvelle cuisine* of France— helped in this through his friendship with many of the finest contemporary French chefs.

Since 1972 the Guérard restaurant has been located at Eugénie-les-Bains, in the Landes, just east of the Basque country, and is now called Les Prés d'Eugénie. In the quiet of this country spa he developed in a few short years the now famous *cuisine minceur.*

KITCHEN POWER!

☐	**MICHEL GUERARD'S CUISINE MINCEUR** —Michel Guerard	11107 •	$2.50
☐	**COOKING WITHOUT A GRAIN OF SALT**—Elma Bagg	2708 •	$1.95
☐	**ART OF FISH COOKERY**—Milo Milorandovich	2962 •	$1.25
☐	**THE ROMAGNOLIS' TABLE**—Romagnolis	2965 •	$1.95
☐	**BETTER HOMES & GARDENS COOKING FOR TWO**	6499 •	$1.25
☐	**BETTY CROCKER'S GOOD AND EASY COOKBOOK**	8667 •	$1.50
☐	**THE WORLD-FAMOUS RATNER'S MEATLESS COOKBOOK** —Judy Gethers	8809 •	$1.50
☐	**THE BETTER HOMES & GARDENS BARBECUE BOOK**	10157 •	$1.50
☐	**THE COMPLETE BOOK OF MEXICAN COOKING** —Elisabeth Ortiz	10168 •	$1.50
☐	**THE FRENCH CHEF COOKBOOK**—Julia Child	10348 •	$2.25
☐	**WHOLE EARTH COOKBOOK**—Cadwallader & Ohr	10467 •	$1.75
☐	**BLEND IT SPLENDID: THE NATURAL FOODS BLENDER BOOK** —Dworkins	10468 •	$1.50
☐	**BETTER HOMES & GARDENS CALORIE COUNTER'S COOKBOOK**	10532 •	$1.50
☐	**BETTY CROCKER'S DINNER FOR TWO**	10805 •	$1.50
☐	**BETTY CROCKER'S DINNER PARTIES**	11188 •	$1.50
☐	**THE SPANISH COOKBOOK**—Barbara Norman	11299 •	$1.50
☐	**CREPE COOKERY**—Mable Hoffman	11377 •	$1.95